OLD

DECCAN DAYS

OLD DECCAN DAYS

OR

HINDOO FAIRY LEGENDS

CURRENT IN SOUTHERN INDIA.

COLLECTED FROM ORAL TRADITION,

M. FRERE.

WITH AN INTRODUCTION AND NOTES,

SIR BARTLE FRERE.

GYAN

Published by

GYAN

Gyan Publishing House
5, Ansari Road
Daryaganj, New Delhi-110002
Phone: 011-47034999, 9811692060
E-mail: books@gyanbooks.com

Distribution Network
gyanbooks.com
India, USA, Canada, UK, Australia, France

ISBN : 978-81-212-9490-4 (PB)
First Published, 1869

2nd Impression 2023

Printed at: Gyan Press, Delhi.

OLD DECCAN DAYS
Author: M. FRERE

VICRAM MAHARAJAH.—p. 133.

OLD
DECCAN DAYS

OR

HINDOO FAIRY LEGENDS

CURRENT IN SOUTHERN INDIA.

COLLECTED FROM ORAL TRADITION,
BY M. FRERE.

WITH AN INTRODUCTION AND NOTES,
BY SIR BARTLE FRERE.

1870.

CONTENTS.

INTRODUCTION.

A FEW words seem necessary regarding the origin of these stories, in addition to what the Narrator says for herself in her Narrative, and what is stated in the Collector's "Apology."

With the exception of two or three, which will be recognized as substantially identical with stories of Pilpay or other well-known Hindoo fabulists, I never before heard any of these tales among the Mahrattas, in that part of the Deccan where the Narrator and her family have lived for the last two generations; and it is probable that most of the stories were brought from among the Lingaets of Southern India, the tribe, or rather sect, to which Anna de Souza tells us her family belonged before their conversion to Christianity.

The Lingaets form one of the most strongly marked divisions of the Hindoo races south of the river Kistna. They are generally a well-favored, well-to-do people, noticeable for their superior frugality, intelligence and industry, and for the way in which they combine and act together as a separate body apart from other Hindoos. They have many peculiarities of costume, of social ceremony and of religion, which strike even a casual observer; and though clearly not aboriginal, they seem to have much ground for their claim to belong to a more ancient race and an earlier wave of immigration than most of the Hindoo nations with which they are now intermingled.

The country they inhabit is tolerably familiar to most English readers on Indian subjects, for it is the theatre of many of the events described in the great Duke's earlier despatches, and in the writings of Munro, of Wilkes, and of Buchanan. The extraordinary beauty of some of the natural features of the coast scenery, and the abundance of the architectural and other remains of powerful and highly civilized Hindoo dynasties, have attracted the attention of tourists and antiquaries, though not to the extent their intrinsic merit deserves. Some knowledge of the land tenures and agriculture of the country is accessible to readers of Indian blue-books.

But of all that relates to the ancient history and politics of the former Hindoo sovereigns of these regions very little is known to the general reader, though from their power, and riches and long-sustained civilization, as proved by the monuments these rulers have left behind them there are few parts of India better worth the attention of the historian and antiquary.

Of the inner life of the people, past or present, of their social peculiarities and popular beliefs, even less is known or procurable in any published form. With the exception of a few graphic and characteristic notices of shrewd observers like Munro, little regarding them is to be found in the writings of any author likely to come in the way of ordinary readers.

But this is not from want of materials: a good deal has been published in India, though, with the common fate of Indian publications, the books containing the information are often rare in English collections, and difficult to meet with in England, except in a few public libraries. Of unpublished material there must be a vast amount, collected not only by the government servants, but by missionaries, and others residing in the country, who have peculiar opportunities for observation, and for collecting information not readily to be obtained by a stranger or an official. Collections of this kind are specially desirable as regards the popular non-Brahminical superstitions of the lower orders.

Few, even of those who have lived many years in India and made some inquiry regarding the external religion of its inhabitants, are aware how little the popular belief of the lower classes has in common with the Hindooism of the Brahmins, and how much it differs in different provinces, and in different races and classes in the same province.

In the immediate vicinity of Poona, where Brahminism

seems so orthodox and powerful, a very little observation will satisfy the inquirer that the favorite objects of popular worship do not always belong to the regular Hindoo Pantheon. No orthodox Hindoo deity is so popular in the Poona Deccan as the deified sage Vithoba and his earlier expounders, both sage and followers being purely local divinities. Wherever a few of the pastoral tribes are settled, there Byroba, the god of the herdsmen, or Kundoba, the deified hero of the shepherds, supersedes all other popular idols. Byroba the Terrible, and other remnants of Fetish or of Snake-worship, everywhere divide the homage of the lower castes with the recognized Hindoo divinities, while outside almost every village the circle of large stones sacred to Vetal, the demon-god of the outcast helot races, which reminds the traveler of the Druid circles of the northern nations, has for ages held, and still holds, its ground against all Brahminical innovations.

Some of these local or tribal divinities, when their worshipers are very numerous or powerful, have been adopted into the Hindoo Olympus as incarnations or manifestations of this or that orthodox divinity, and one or two have been provided with elaborate written legends connecting them with some known Puranic character or event; but, in general, the true history of the local deity, if it survives at all, is to be found only in popular tradition; and it thus becomes a matter of some ethnological and historical importance to secure all such fleeting remnants of ancient superstition before they are forgotten as civilization advances.

Some information of this kind is to be gleaned even from the present series of legends, though the object of the collector being simply amusement, and not antiquarian research, any light which is thrown on the popular superstitions of the country is only incidental.

Of the superhuman personages who appear in them, the "Rakshas" is the most prominent. This being has many features in common with the demoniacal Ogre of other lands. The giant bulk and terrible teeth of his usual form are the universal attributes of his congener. His habit of feasting on dead bodies will remind the reader of the Arabian Ghoul, while the simplicity and stupidity which qualify the supernatural powers of the Rakshas, and usually enable the quick-witted mortal to gain the victory over him, will recall many humorous passages in which giants figure in our own Norse and Teutonic legends.

The English reader must bear in mind that in India beings of this or of very similar nature are not mere traditions of the past, but that they form an important part of the existing practical belief of the lower orders. Grown men will sometimes refuse every inducement to pass at night near the supposed haunt of a Rakshas, and I have heard the cries of a belated traveler calling for help attributed to a Rakshas luring his prey.

Nor is darkness always an element in this superstition: I have known a bold and experienced tracker of game gravely assert that some figures which he had been for some time keenly scanning on the bare summit of a distant hill were beings of this order, and he was very indignant at the laugh which his observation provoked from his less-experienced European disciple. "If your telescope could see as far as my old eyes," the veteran said, "or if you knew the movements of all the animals of this hunting-ground as well as I do, you would see that those must be demons and nothing else. No men nor animals at this time of day would collect on an open space and move about in that way. Besides, that large rock close by them is a noted place for demons; every child in the village knows that."

I have heard another man of the same class, when asked why he looked so intently at a human footstep in the forest pathway, gravely observe that the footmark looked as if the foot which made it had been walking heel-foremost, and must therefore have been made by a Rakshas, "for they always walked so when in human form."

Another expressed particular dread of a human face, the eyes of which were placed at an exaggerated angle to each other, like those of a Chinese or Malay, "because that position of the eyes was the only way in which you could recognize a Rakshas in human shape."

In the more advanced and populous parts of the country the Rakshas seems giving way to the "Bhoot," which more nearly resembles the mere ghost of modern European superstition; but even in this diluted form such beings have an influence over Indian imaginations to which it is difficult in these days to find any parallel in Europe.

I found, quite lately, a traditionary order in existence at Government House, Dapoorie, near Poona, which directed the native sentry on guard "to present arms if a cat or dog, jackal or goat, entered or left the house or crossed near his beat" during certain hours of the night, "because it was the ghost" of a former governor, who was still remembered as one of the best and kindest of men.

How or when the custom originated I could not learn, but the order had been verbally handed on from one native sergeant of the guard to another for many years, without any doubts as to its propriety or authority, till it was accidentally overheard by an European officer of the governor's staff.

In the hills and deserts of Sind the belief in beings of this order, as might be expected in a wild and desolate country, is found strong and universal; there, however, the Rakshas has changed his name to that of our old friend the "Gin" of the Arabian Nights, and he has somewhat approximated in character to the Pwcca or Puck of our own country. The Gin of the Beelooch hills is wayward and often morose, but not necessarily malignant. His usual form is that of a dwarfish human being, with large eyes and covered with long hair, and apt to breathe with a heavy snoring kind of noise. From the circumstantial accounts I have heard of such "Gins" being seen seated on rocks at the side of lonely passes, I suspect that the great horned eagle-owl, which is not uncommon in the hill-country of Sind, has to answer for many well-vouched cases of Gin apparition.

The Gin does not, however, always retain his own shape; he frequently changes to the form of a camel, goat or other animal. If a Gin be accidentally met, it is recommended that the traveler should show no sign of fear, and, above all, keep a civil tongue in his head, for the demon has a special aversion to bad language. Every Beelooch has heard of instances in which such chance acquaintanceships with Gins have not only led to no mischief, but been the source of much benefit to the fortunate mortal who had the courage and prudence to turn them to account; for a Gin once attached to a man will work hard and faithfully for him, and sometimes show him the entrance to those great subterranean caverns under the hills, where there is perpetual spring, and trees laden with fruits of gold and precious stones; but the mortal once admitted to such a paradise is never allowed to leave it. There are few neighborhoods in the Beelooch hills which cannot show huge stones, apparently intended for building, which have been, "as all the country-side knows," moved by such agency, and the entrance to the magic cavern is never very far off, though the boldest Beelooch is seldom very willing to show or to seek for the exact spot.

Superstitions nearly identical were still current within the last forty years, when I was a boy, on the borders of Wales. In Cwm Pwcca (the Fairies' Glen), in the valley of the Clydach, between Abergavenny and Merthyr, the cave used to be shown into which a belated miner was decoyed by the Pwccas, and kept dancing for ten years; and a farm-house on the banks of the Usk, not far off, was, in the last generation, the abode of a farmer who had a friendly Pwcca in his service. The goblin was called Pwcca Trwyn, as I was assured from his occasionally being visible as a huge human nose. He would help the mortal by carrying loads and mending hedges, but usually worked only while the farmer slept at noon, and always expected as his guerdon a portion of the toast and ale which his friend had for dinner in the field. If none was left for him, he would cease to work; and he once roused the farmer from his noontide slumbers by thrashing him soundly with his own hedging-stake.

The Peris or Fairies of these stories have nothing distinctive about them. Like the fairies of other lands, they often fall in love with mortal men, and are visible to the pure eyes of childhood when hidden from the grosser vision of maturer years.

Next to the Rakshas, the Cobra, or deadly hooded snake, plays the most important part in these legends as a supernatural personage. This is one only of the many traces still extant of that serpent-worship formerly so general in Western India. I have no doubt that Mr. Ferguson, in his forthcoming work on Bhuddhist antiquities, will throw much light on this curious subject. I will, therefore, only now observe that this serpent-worship as it still exists is something more active than a mere popular superstition. The Cobra, unless disturbed, rarely goes far from home, and is supposed to watch jealously over a hidden treasure. He is always, in the estimation of the lower classes, invested with supernatural powers, and according to the treatment he receives he builds up or destroys the fortunes of the house to which he belongs. No native will willingly kill him if he can get rid of him in any other way; and the poorer classes always, after he is killed, give him all the honors of a regular cremation, assuring him, with many protestations, as the pile burns, "that they are guiltless of his blood; that they slew him by order of their master," or "that they had no other way to prevent his biting the children or the chickens."

A very interesting discussion on the subject of the Snake Race of Ancient India, between Mr. Bayley and Baboo Rajendralal Mitr, will be found in the *Proceedings of the Asiatic Society of Bengal*, for February, 1867.

THE COLLECTOR'S APOLOGY.

THE collection of these legends was commenced with the object of amusing a favorite young friend of mine. It was continued, as they appeared in themselves curious illustrations of Indian popular tradition, and in the hope that something might thus be done to rescue them from the danger of oral transmission.

Though varied in their imagery, the changes between the different legends are rung upon very few themes, as if purposely confined to what was most familiar to the people. The similarity between the incidents in some of these and in favorite European stories, particularly modern German ones, is curious; and the leading characteristics peculiar to all orthodox fairy tales are here preserved intact. Step-mothers are always cruel, and step-sisters, their willing instruments; giants and ogres always stupid; youngest daughters more clever than their elder sisters; and the Jackal (like his European cousin the Fox) usually overcomes every difficulty, and proves a bright moral example of the success of wit against brute force—the triumph of mind over matter.

It is remarkable that in the romances of a country where women are generally supposed by us to be regarded as mere slaves or intriguers, their influence (albeit most frequently put to proof behind the scenes) should be made to appear so great, and, as a rule, exerted wholly for good; and that, in a land where despotism has such a firm hold on the hearts of the people, the liberties of the subject should be so boldly asserted as by the old Milkwoman to the Rajah in "Little Surya Bai," or the old Malee* to the Rajah in "Truth's Tri-

* Gardener.

umph;" and few, probably would have expected to find the Hindoos owning such a romance as "Brave Seventee Bai;"* or to meet with such stories as "The Valiant Chattee Maker," and "The Blind Man, the Deaf Man and the Donkey," among a nation which, it has been constantly asserted, possesses no humor, no sense of the ridiculous, and cannot understand a joke.

In "The Narrator's Narrative" Anna Liberata de Souza's own story is related, as much as possible, in her own words of expressive but broken English. She did not, however, tell it in one continuous narrative: it is the sum of many conversations I had with her during the eighteen months that she was with us.

The legends themselves are altered as little as possible: half their charm, however, consisted in the Narrator's eager, flexible voice and graphic gestures.

I often asked her if there were no stories of elephants having done wonderful deeds (as from their strength and sagacity one would have imagined them to possess all the qualifications requisite to heroes of romance); but, strange to say, she knew of none in which elephants played any part whatsoever.

As regards the Oriental names, they have generally been written as Anna pronounced them. It was frequently not possible to give the true orthography, and the correctly spelt name does not always give a clue to the popular pronunciation. So with the interpretations and geography. Where it is possible to identify what is described, an attempt has been made to do so; but for other explanations Anna's is the sole authority: she was quite sure that "Seventee Bai" meant the "Daisy Lady," though no botanist would acknowledge the plant under that name; and she was satisfied that all gentlemen who have traveled know where "Agra Brum" is, though she had never been there, and no such province appears in any ordinary Gazeteer or description of the city of Akbar.

These few legends, told by one old woman to her grandchildren, can only be considered as representatives of a class.

* Was this narrative of feminine sagacity invented by some old woman, who felt aggrieved at the general contempt entertained for her sex?

"That world," to use her own words, "is gone;" and those who can tell us about it in this critical and unimaginative age are fast disappearing too before the onward march of civilization; yet there must be in the country many a rich gold mine unexplored. Will no one go to the diggings?

M. F.

THE NARRATOR'S NARRATIVE.

MY grandfather's family were of the Lingaet caste, and lived in Calicut; but they went and settled near Goa at the time the English were there. It was there my grandfather became a Christian. He and his wife, and all the family, became Christians at once, and when his father heard it he was very angry, and turned them all out of the house. There were very few Christians in those days. Now you see Christians everywhere, but then we were very proud to see one anywhere. My grandfather was Havildar* in the English army, and when the English fought against Tippo Sahib, my grandmother followed him all through the war. She was a very tall, fine, handsome woman, and very strong; wherever the regiment marched she went, on, on, on, on (great deal hard work that old woman done). Plenty stories my granny used to tell about Tippo and how Tippo was killed, and about Wellesley Sahib, and Monro Sahib, and Malcolm Sahib, and Elphinstone Sahib.† Plenty things had that old woman heard and seen. Ah, he was a good man, Elphinstone Sahib! My granny used often to tell us how he would go down and say to the soldiers, "Baba,‡ Baba, fight well. Win the battles, and each man shall have his cap full of money; and after the war is over I'll send every one of you to his own home." (And he did do it.) Then we children plenty proud, when we heard what Elphinstone Sahib had said. In those days the soldiers were not low-caste people like they are now. Many, very high-caste

* Sergeant of native troops.

† The Duke of Wellington, Sir Thomas Monro, Sir John Malcolm and Mr. Mountstuart Elphinstone.

‡ My children.

men, and come from very far, from Goa, and Calicut, and Malabar to join the English.

My father was a tent lascar,* and when the war was over my grandfather had won five medals for all the good he had done, and my father had three; and my father was given charge of the Kirkee stores.† My grandmother and mother, and all the family, were in those woods behind Poona at time of the battle at Kirkee.‡ I've often heard my father say how full the river was after the battle—baggage and bundles floating down, and men trying to swim across—and horses and all such a bustle. Many people got good things on that day. My father got a large chattee,§ and two good ponies that were in the river, and he took them home to camp; but when he got there the guard took them away. So all his trouble did him no good.

We were poor people, but living was cheap, and we had plenty comfort.

In those days house rent did not cost more than half a rupee‖ a month, and you could build a very comfortable house for a hundred rupees. Not such good houses as people now live in, but well enough for people like us. Then a whole family could live as comfortably on six or seven rupees a month as they can now on thirty. Grain, now a rupee a pound, was then two annas a pound. Common sugar, then one anna a pound, is now worth four annas a pound. Oil which then sold for six pice a bottle, now costs four annas. Four annas' worth of salt, chillies, tamarinds, onions and garlic, would then last a family a whole month; now the same money would not buy a week's supply. Such dungeree¶ as you now pay half rupee a yard for, you could then buy from twenty to forty yards of, for the rupee. You could not get such good calico then as now,

* Tent-pitcher. † The Field Arsenal at Kirkee (near Poona).

‡ The battle which decided the fate of the Deccan, and led to the downfall of Bajee Row Peishwa, and extinction of Mahratta rule. Fought 13th November, 1817. See Note A. § A Jar.

‖ The following shows the Narrator's calculation of currency:

1 Pie=1-4 of a cent.
3 Pie=1 Pice.
4 Pice=1 Anna.
16 Annas=1 Rupee=about 50 cents.

¶ A coarse cotton cloth.

but the dungeree did very well. Beef then was a pice a pound, and the vegetables cost a pie a day. For half a rupee you could fill the house with wood. Water also was much cheaper. You could then get a man to bring you two large skins full, morning and evening, for a pie; now he would not do it under half a rupee or more. If the children came crying for fruit, a pie would get them as many guavas as they liked in the bazaar. Now you'd have to pay that for each guava. This shows how much more money people need now than they did then.*

The English fixed the rupee to the value of sixteen annas, in those days there were some big annas, and some little ones, and you could sometimes get twenty-two annas for a rupee.

I had seven brothers and one sister. Things were very different in those days to what they are now. There were no schools then to send the children to; it was only the great people who could read and write. If a man was known to be able to write he was plenty proud, and hundreds and hundreds of people would come to him to write their letters. Now you find a pen and ink in every house! I don't know what good all this reading and writing does. My grandfather couldn't write, and my father couldn't write, and they did very well; but all's changed now.

My father used to be out all day at his work, and my mother often went to do coolie-work,† and she had to take my father his dinner (my mother did plenty work in the world); and when my granny was strong enough she used sometimes to go into the bazaar, if we wanted money, and grind rice for the shop-keepers, and they gave her half a rupee for her day's work, and used to let her have the bran and chaff besides. But afterward she got too old to do that, and besides there were so many of us children. So she used to stay at home and look after us while my mother was at work. Plenty bother 'tis to look after a lot of children. No sooner my granny's back turned than we all run out in the sun, and play with the dust and stones on the road.

Then my granny would call out to us, "Come here, children, out of the sun, and I'll tell you a story. Come in;

* See Note B.

† Such work as is done by the Coolie caste, chiefly fetching and carrying heavy loads.

you'll all get headaches." So she used to get us together (there were nine of us, and great little fidgets, like all children), into the house; and there she'd sit on the floor, and tell us one of the stories I tell you. But then she used to make them last much longer, the different people telling their own stories from the beginning as often as possible; so that by the time she'd got to the end, she had told the beginning over five or six times. And so she went on, talk, talk, talk, Mera Bap reh!* Such a long time she'd go on for, till all the children got quite tired and fell asleep. Now there are plenty schools to which to send the children, but there were no schools when I was a young girl; and the old women, who could do nothing else, used to tell them stories to keep them out of mischief.

We used sometimes to ask my grandmother, "Are those stories you tell us really true? Were there ever such people in the world?" She generally answered, "I don't know, but maybe there are somewhere." I don't believe there are any of those people living; I dare say, however, they did once live; but my granny believed more in those things than we do now. She was a Christian, she worshiped God and believed in our Saviour, but still she would always respect the Hindoo temples. If she saw a red stone, or an image of Gunputti† or any of the other Hindoo gods, she would kneel down and say her prayers there, for she used to say, "Maybe there's something in it."

About all things she would tell us pretty stories—about men, and animals, and trees, and flowers, and stars. There was nothing she did not know some tale about. On the bright cold-weather nights, when you can see more stars than at any other time of the year, we used to like to watch the sky, and she would show us the Hen and Chickens,‡ and the Key,§ and the Scorpion, and the Snake, and the Three Thieves climbing up to rob the Ranee's silver bedstead, with their mother (that twinkling star far away) watching for her sons' return. Pit-a-pat, pit-a-pat, you can see how her heart beats, for she is always frightened, thinking, "Perhaps they will be caught and hanged!"

* Oh, my Father!

† The Hindoo God of Wisdom.

‡ The Pleiades.

§ The Great Bear.

Then she would show us the Cross,* that reminds us of our Saviour's, and the great pathway of light† on which He went up to heaven. It is what you call the Milky Way. My granny usen't to call it that: she used to say that when our Lord returned up to heaven that was the way He went, and that ever since it has shone in memory of His ascension, so beautiful and bright.

She always said a star with a smoky tail (comet) meant war, and she never saw a falling star without saying, "There's a great man died;" but the fixed stars she used to think were all really good people, burning like bright lamps before God.

As to the moon, my granny used to say she's most useful to debtors who can't pay their debts. Thus: A man who borrows money he knows he cannot pay, takes the full moon for witness and surety. Then, if any man so silly as to lend him money and go and ask him for it, he can say, "The moon's my surety; go catch hold of the moon!" Now, you see, no man can do that; and what's more, when the moon's once full, it grows every night less and less, and at last goes out altogether.

All the Cobras in my grandmother's stories were seven-headed. This puzzled us children, and we would say to her, "Granny, are there any seven-headed Cobras now? For all the Cobras we see that the conjurors bring round have only one head each." To which she used to answer, "No, of course there are no seven-headed Cobras now. That world is gone, but you see each Cobra has a hood of skin; that is the remains of another head." Then we would say, "Although none of those old seven-headed Cobras are alive now, maybe there are some of their children living somewhere." But at this my granny used to get vexed, and say, "Nonsense! you are silly little chatter-boxes; get along with you!" And, though we often looked for the seven-headed Cobras, we never could find any of them.

My old granny lived till she was nearly a hundred; when she got very old she rather lost her memory, and often made mistakes in the stories she told us, telling a bit of one story

* The Southern Cross.

† The Milky Way. This is an ancient Christian legend.

and then joining on to it a bit of some other; for we children bothered her too much about them, and sometimes she used to get very tired of talking, and when we asked her for a story, would answer, "You must ask your mother about it; she can tell you."

Ah! those were happy days, and we had plenty ways to amuse ourselves. I was very fond of pets; I had a little dog that followed me everywhere, and played all sorts of pretty tricks, and I and my youngest brother used to take the little sparrows out of their nests on the roof of our house and tame them. These little birds got so fond of me they would always fly after me; as I was sweeping the floor one would perch on my head, and two or three on my shoulders, and the rest come fluttering after. But my poor father and mother used to shake their heads at me when they saw this, and say, "Ah, naughty girl, to take the little birds out of their nests: that stealing will bring you no good." All my family were very fond of music. You know that Rosie (my daughter) sings very nicely and plays upon the guitar, and my son-in-law plays on the pianoforte and the fiddle (we've got two fiddles in our house now), but Mera Bap reh! how well my grandfather sang! Sometimes of an evening he would drink a little toddy,* and be quite cheerful, and sing away; and all we children liked to hear him. I was very fond of singiug. I had a good voice when I was young, and my father used to be so fond of making me sing, and I often sang to him that Calicut song about the ships sailing on the sea† and the little wife watching for her husband to come back, and plenty more that I forget now; and my father and brothers would be so pleased at my singing, and laugh and say, "That girl can do anything." But now my voice is gone, and I didn't care to sing any more since my son died, and my heart been so sad.

In those days there were much fewer houses in Poona than there are now, and many more wandering gipsies, and such like. They were very troublesome, doing nothing but begging and stealing, but people gave them all they wanted, as it was believed that to incur their ill-will was very dangerous. It

* An intoxicating drink made from the juice of the palm tree.

† See N.te C.

was not safe even to speak harshly of them. I remember one day, when I was quite a little girl, running along by my mother's side, when she was on her way to the bazaar: we happened to pass the huts of some of these people, and I said to her "See, mother, what nasty, dirty people those are; they live in such ugly little houses, and they look as if they never combed their hair nor washed." When I said this, my mother turned round quite sharply and boxed my ears, saying, "Because God has given you a comfortable home and good parents, is that any reason for you to laugh at others who are poorer and less happy?" "I meant no harm," I said; and when we got home I told my father what my mother had done, and he said to her, "Why did you slap the child?" She answered, "If you want to know, ask your daughter why I punished her. You will then be able to judge whether I was right or not." So I told my father what I had said about the gipsies, and when I told him, instead of pitying me, he also boxed my ears very hard. So that was all I got for telling tales against my mother!

But they both did it, fearing if I spoke evil of the gipsies and were not instantly punished, some dreadful evil would befall me.

It was after my granny that I was named "Anna Liberata." She died after my father, and when I was eleven years old. Her eyes were quite bright, her hair black, and her teeth good to the last. If I'd been older then, I should have been able to remember more of her stories. Such a number as she used to tell! I'm afraid my sister would not be able to remember any of them. She has had much trouble; that puts those sort of things out of people's heads; besides, she is a goose. She is younger than I am, although you would think her so much older, for her hair turned gray when she was very young, while mine is quite black still. She is almost bald too, now, as she pulled out her hair because it was gray. I always said to her, "Don't do so; for you can't make yourself any younger, and it is better, when you are getting old, to look old. Then people will do whatever you ask them! But however old you may be, if you look young, they'll say to you, 'You are young enough and strong enough to do your own work yourself.'"

My mother used to tell us stories too; but not so many as my granny. A few years ago there might be found several old people who knew those sorts of stories; but now children go to school, and nobody thinks of remembering or telling them—they'll soon be all forgotten. It is true there are books with some stories something like these, but they always put them down wrong. Sometimes when I cannot remember a bit of a story, I ask some one about it; then they say, "There is a story of that name in my book. I don't know it, but I'll read." Then they read it to me, but it is all wrong, so that I get quite cross, and make them shut up the book. For in the books they cut the stories quite short, and leave out the prettiest part, and they jumble up the beginning of one story with the end of another—so that it is altogether wrong.

When I was young, old people used to be very fond of telling these stories; but instead of that, it seems to me that now the old people are fond of nothing but making money.

Then I was married. I was twelve years old then. Our native people have a very happy life till we marry. The girls live with their father and mother and brothers and sisters, and have got nothing to do but amuse themselves, and got father and mother to take care of them; but after they're married they go to live at their husband's house, and the husband's mother and sisters are often very unkind to them.

You English people can't understand that sort of thing. When an Englishman marries, he goes to a new house, and his wife is the mistress of it; but our native people are very different. If the father is dead, the mother and unmarried sisters live in the son's house, and rule it; his wife is nothing in the house. And the mother and sisters say to the son's wife, "This is not your house—you've not always lived in it; you cannot be mistress here." And if the wife complains to her husband, and he speaks about it, they say, "Very well, if you are such an unnatural son, you'd better turn your mother and sisters out of doors; but while we live here, we'll rule the house." So there is always plenty fighting. It's not unkind of the mother and sisters—it's custom.

My husband was a servant in Government House—that was when Lord Clare was governor here. When I was twenty years old, my husband died of a bad fever, and left me with two children—the boy and the girl, Rosie.

I had no money to keep them with, so I said, "I'll go to service," and my mother-in-law said, "How can you go with two children, and so young, and knowing nothing?" But I said, "I can learn, and I'll go;" and a kind lady took me into her service. When I went to my first place, I hardly knew a word of English (though I knew our Calicut language, and Portuguese, and Hindostani, and Mahratti well enough), and I could not hold a needle. I was so stupid, like a Coolie-woman;* but my mistress was very kind to me, and I soon learnt; she did not mind the trouble of teaching me. I often think, "Where find such good Christian people in these days?" To take a poor, stupid woman and her two children into the house—for I had them both with me, Rosie and the boy. I was a sharp girl in those days; I did my mistress' work and I looked after the children too. I never left them to any one else. If she wanted me for a long time, I used to bring the children into the room and set them down on the floor, so as to have them under my own eye whilst I did her work. My mistress was very fond of Rosie, and used to teach her to work and read. After some time my mistress went home, and since then I have been in eight places.

My brother-in-law was valet at that time to Napier Sahib, up in Sind. All the people and servants were very fond of that Sahib. My brother-in-law was with him for ten years; and he wanted me to go up there to get place as ayah, and said, "You quick, sharp girl, and know English very well; you easily get good place and make plenty money." But I such a foolish woman I would not go. I write and tell him, "No, I can't come, for Sind such a long way off, and I cannot leave the children." I plenty proud then. I give up all for the children. But now what good? I know your language. What use? To blow the fire? I only a miserable woman, fit to go to cook-room and cook the dinner. So go down in the world, a poor woman (not much good to have plenty in head and empty pocket!) but if I'd been a man I might now be a Fouzdar.†

* A low caste—hewers of wood and drawers of water. † Chief Constable.

I was at Kolapore* at the time of the mutiny, and we had to run away in the middle of the night; but I've told you before all about that. Then seven years ago my mother died (she was ninety when she died), and we came back to live at Poona, and my daughter was married, and I was so happy and pleased.

I gave a feast then to three hundred people, and we had music and dancing, and my son, he so proud he dancing from morning to night, and running here and there arranging everything; and on that day I said, "Throw the doors open, and any beggar, any poor person come here, give them what they like to eat, for whoever comes shall have enough, since there's no more work for me in the world." So, thinking I should be able to leave service, and give up work, I spent all the money I had left. That was not very much, for in sending my son to school I'd spent a great deal. He was such a beauty boy—tall, straight, handsome—and so clever. They used to say he looked more like my brother than my son, and he said to me, "Mammy, you've worked for us all your life; now I'm grown up, I'll get a clerk's place and work for you. You shall work no more, but live in my house." But last year he was drowned in the river. That was my great sad. Since then I couldn't lift up my head. I can't remember things now as I used to do, and all is muddled in my head, six and seven. It makes me sad sometimes to hear you laughing and talking so happy with your father and mother and all your family, when I think of my father, and mother, and brothers, and husband, and son, all dead and gone! No more happy home like that for me. What should I care to live for? I would come to England with you, for I know you would be good to me and bury me when I die, but I cannot go so far from Rosie. My one eye put out, my other eye left. I could not lose it too. If it were not for Rosie and her children I should like to travel about and see the world. There are four places I have always wished to see—Calcutta, Madras, England and Jerusalem (my poor mother always wished to see Jerusalem, too—that her great hope); but I shall not see them now. Many ladies wanted to take me to England with them, and if I had gone I should have saved plenty money, but now it is too late to think of

* Capital of the Kolapore State, in the Southern Mahratta country.

that. Besides, it would not be much use. What's the good of my saving money? Can I take it away with me when I die? My father and grandfather did not do so, and they had enough to live on till they died. I have enough for what I want, and I've plenty poor relations. They all come to me, asking for money, and I give it them. I thank our Saviour there are enough good Christians here to give me a slice of bread and cup of water when I can't work for it. I do not fear to come to want.

GOVERNMENT HOUSE,
PARELL, BOMBAY, 1866.

OLD DECCAN DAYS.

I.

PUNCHKIN.

ONCE upon a time there was a Rajah* who had seven beautiful daughters. They were all good girls; but the youngest, named Balna,† was more clever than the rest. The Rajah's wife died when they were quite little children, so these seven poor Princesses were left with no mother to take care of them.

The Rajah's daughters took it by turns to cook their father's dinner every day,‡ whilst he was absent deliberating with his ministers on the affairs of the nation.

About this time the Purdan § died, leaving a widow and one daughter; and every day, every day, when the seven Princesses were preparing their father's dinner, the Purdan's widow and daughter would come and beg for a little fire from the hearth. Then Balna used to say to her sisters, "Send that woman away;

* King. † The Little One. ‡ See Notes at the end.
§ Or, more correctly, *Prudhan*, Prime Minister.

send her away. Let her get the fire at her own house. What does she want with ours? If we allow her to come here, we shall suffer for it some day." But the other sisters would answer, "Be quiet, Balna; why must you always be quarreling with this poor woman? Let her take some fire if she likes." Then the Purdan's widow used to go to the hearth and take a few sticks from it; and, whilst no one was looking, she would quickly throw some mud into the midst of the dishes which were being prepared for the Rajah's dinner.

Now the Rajah was very fond of his daughters. Ever since their mother's death they had cooked his dinner with their own hands, in order to avoid the danger of his being poisoned by his enemies. So, when he found the mud mixed up with his dinner, he thought it must arise from their carelessness, as it appeared improbable that any one should have put mud there on purpose; but being very kind, he did not like to reprove them for it, although this spoiling of the currie was repeated many successive days.

At last, one day, he determined to hide and watch his daughters cooking, and see how it all happened; so he went into the next room, and watched them through a hole in the wall.

There he saw his seven daughters carefully washing the rice and preparing the currie, and as each dish was completed, they put it by the fire ready to be cooked. Next he noticed the Purdan's widow come to the door, and beg for a few sticks from the fire to cook her dinner with. Balna turned to her, angrily, and said, "Why don't you keep fuel in your own house, and not come here every day and take ours?

Sisters, don't give this woman any more; let her buy it for herself."

Then the eldest sister answered, "Balna, let the poor woman take the wood and the fire; she does us no harm." But Balna replied, "If you let her come here so often, maybe she will do us some harm, and make us sorry for it, some day."

The Rajah then saw the Purdan's widow go to the place where all his dinner was nicely prepared, and, as she took the wood, she threw a little mud into each of the dishes.

At this he was very angry, and sent to have the woman seized and brought before him. But when the widow came, she told him that she had played this trick because she wanted to gain an audience with him; and she spoke so cleverly, and pleased him so well with her cunning words, that instead of punishing her, the Rajah married her, and made her his Ranee, * and she and her daughter came to live in the palace.

The new Ranee hated the seven poor Princesses, and wanted to get them, if possible, out of the way, in order that her daughter might have all their riches and live in the palace as Princess in their place; and instead of being grateful to them for their kindness to her, she did all she could to make them miserable. She gave them nothing but bread to eat, and very little of that, and very little water to drink; so these seven poor little Princesses, who had been accustomed to have everything comfortable about them, and good food and good clothes all their lives long, were very miserable and unhappy; and they used to go out every day and sit by their dead mother's tomb and cry; and used to say,

* Queen.

"Oh mother, mother, cannot you see your poor children, how unhappy we are, and how we are starved by our cruel step-mother?"

One day, whilst they were sobbing and crying, lo and behold! a beautiful pomelo tree * grew up out of the grave, covered with fresh ripe pomeloes, and the children satisfied their hunger by eating some of the fruit; and every day after this, instead of trying to eat the nasty dinner their step-mother provided for them, they used to go out to their mother's grave and eat the pomeloes which grew there on the beautiful tree.

Then the Ranee said to her daughter, "I cannot tell how it is: every day those seven girls say they don't want any dinner, and won't eat any; and yet they never grow thin nor look ill; they look better than you do. I cannot tell how it is;" and she bade her watch the seven Princesses and see if any one gave them anything to eat.

So next day, when the Princesses went to their mother's grave, and were eating the beautiful pomeloes, the Purdan's daughter followed them and saw them gathering the fruit.

Then Balna said to her sisters, "Do you not see that girl watching us? Let us drive her away or hide the pomeloes, else she will go and tell her mother all about it, and that will be very bad for us."

But the other sisters said, "Oh no, do not be unkind, Balna. The girl would never be so cruel as to tell her mother. Let us rather invite her to come and have some of the fruit;" and calling her to them, they gave her one of the pomeloes.

No sooner had she eaten it, however, than the Pur-

* *Citrus decumana*—the Shaddock of the West Indies.

dan's daughter went home and said to her mother, "I do not wonder the seven Princesses will not eat the nasty dinner you prepare for them, for by their mother's grave there grows a beautiful pomelo tree, and they go there every day and eat the pomeloes. I ate one, and it was the nicest I have ever tasted."

The cruel Ranee was much vexed at hearing this, and all next day she stayed in her room, and told the Rajah that she had a very bad headache. The Rajah at hearing this was deeply grieved, and said to his wife, "What can I do for you?" She answered, "There is only one thing that will make my headache well. By your dead wife's tomb there grows a fine pomelo tree; you must bring that here, and boil it, root and branch, and put a little of the water in which it has been boiled on my forehead, and that will cure my headache." So the Rajah sent his servants, and had the beautiful pomelo tree pulled up by the roots, and did as the Ranee desired; and when some of the water in which it had been boiled was put on her forehead, she said her headache was gone and she felt quite well.

Next day, when the seven Princesses went as usual to the grave of their mother, the pomelo tree had disappeared. Then they all began to cry very bitterly.

Now there was by the Ranee's tomb a small tank,* and as they were crying they saw that the tank was filled with a rich cream-like substance, which quickly hardened into a thick white cake. At seeing this all the Princesses were very glad, and they ate some of the cake, and liked it; and next day the same thing happened, and so it went on for many days. Every morn-

* Reservoir for water.

ing the Princesses went to their mother's grave, and found the little tank filled with the nourishing cream-like cake. Then the cruel step-mother said to her daughter: "I cannot tell how it is: I have had the pomelo tree which used to grow by the Ranee's grave destroyed, and yet the Princesses grow no thinner nor look more sad, though they never eat the dinner I give them. I cannot tell how it is!"

And her daughter said, "I will watch."

Next day, while the Princesses were eating the cream cake, who should come by but their step-mother's daughter? Balna saw her first, and said, "See, sisters, there comes that girl again. Let us sit round the edge of the tank, and not allow her to see it; for if we give her some of our cake, she will go and tell her mother, and that will be very unfortunate for us."

The other sisters, however, thought Balna unnecessarily suspicious, and instead of following her advice, they gave the Purdan's daughter some of the cake, and she went home and told her mother all about it.

The Ranee, on hearing how well the Princesses fared, was exceedingly angry, and sent her servants to pull down the dead Ranee's tomb and fill the little tank with the ruins. And not content with this, she next day pretended to be very, very ill—in fact, at the point of death; and when the Rajah was much grieved, and asked her whether it was in his power to procure her any remedy, she said to him: "Only one thing can save my life, but I know you will not do it." He replied, "Yes, whatever it is, I will do it." She then said, "To save my life, you must kill the seven daughters of your first wife, and put some of their blood on my forehead and on the palms of my hands, and their death will be my life." At these words the Rajah was very sorrowful; but because he feared to break his word, he went out with a heavy heart to find his daughters.

He found them crying by the ruins of their mother's grave.

Then, feeling he could not kill them, the Rajah spoke kindly to them, and told them to come out into the jungle with him; and there he made a fire and cooked some rice, and gave it to them. But in the afternoon, it being very hot, the seven Princesses all fell asleep, and when he saw they were fast asleep, the Rajah, their father, stole away and left them (for he feared his wife), saying to himself: "It is better my poor daughters should die here than be killed by their step-mother."

He then shot a deer, and returning home, put some of the blood on the forehead and hands of the Ranee, and she thought then that he had really killed the Princesses, and said she felt quite well.

Meantime the seven Princesses awoke, and when they found themselves all alone in the thick jungle they were much frightened, and began to call out as loud as they could, in hopes of making their father hear; but he was by that time far away, and would not have been able to hear them, even had their voices been as loud as thunder.

It so happened that this very day the seven young sons of a neighboring Rajah chanced to be hunting in that same jungle, and as they were returning home after the day's sport was over, the youngest Prince said to his brothers: "Stop, I think I hear some one crying and calling out. Do you not hear voices? Let us go in the direction of the sound, and try and find out what it is."

So the seven Princes rode through the wood until they came to the place where the seven Princesses sat crying and wringing their hands. At the sight of them the young Princes were very much astonished, and still more so on learning their story; and they settled that each should take one of these poor forlorn ladies home with him and marry her.

So the first and eldest Prince took the eldest Princess home with him, and married her.

And the second took the second;

And the third took the third;

And the fourth took the fourth;

And the fifth took the fifth;

And the sixth took the sixth;

And the seventh, and handsomest of all, took the beautiful Balna.

And when they got to their own land, there was great rejoicing throughout the kingdom at the marriage of the seven young Princes to seven such beautiful Princesses.

About a year after this Balna had a little son, and his uncles and aunts were all so fond of the boy that it was as if he had seven fathers and seven mothers. None of the other Princes or Princesses had any children, so the son of the seventh Prince and Balna was acknowledged their heir by all the rest.

They had thus lived very happily for some time, when one fine day the seventh Prince (Balna's husband) said he would go out hunting, and away he went; and they waited long for him, but he never came back.

Then his six brothers said they would go and see what had become of him; and they went away, but they also did not return.

And the seven Princesses grieved very much, for they felt sure their kind husbands must have been killed.

One day, not long after this had happened, as Balna was rocking her baby's cradle, and whilst her sisters were working in the room below, there came to the palace door a man in a long black dress, who said that he was a Fakeer,* and came to beg. The servants said to him, "You cannot go into the palace—the Rajah's sons have all gone away; we think they must be dead, and their widows cannot be interrupted by your begging." But he said, "I am a holy man; you must let me in." Then the stupid servants let him walk through the palace, but they did not know that this man was no Fakeer, but a wicked Magician named Punchkin.

Punchkin Fakeer wandered through the palace, and saw many beautiful things there, till at last he reached the room where Balna sat singing beside her little boy's cradle. The Magician thought her more beautiful than all the other beautiful things he had seen, insomuch that he asked her to go home with him and to marry him. But she said, "My husband, I fear, is dead, but my little boy is still quite young; I will stay here and teach him to grow up a clever man, and when he is grown up he shall go out into the world, and try and learn tidings of his father. Heaven forbid that I should ever leave him or marry you." At these words the Magician was very angry, and turned her into a little black dog, and led her away, saying, "Since you will

* Holy beggar.

not come with me of your own free will, I will make you." So the poor Princess was dragged away, without any power of effecting an escape, or of letting her sisters know what had become of her. As Punchkin passed through the palace gate the servants said to him, "Where did you get that pretty little dog?" And he answered, "One of the Princesses gave it to me as a present." At hearing which they let him go without further questioning.

Soon after this the six elder Princesses heard the little baby, their nephew, begin to cry, and when they went up stairs they were much surprised to find him all alone, and Balna nowhere to be seen. Then they questioned the servants, and when they heard of the Fakeer and the little black dog, they guessed what had happened, and sent in every direction seeking them, but neither the Fakeer nor the dog were to be found. What could six poor women do? They had to give up all hopes of ever seeing their kind husbands, and their sister and her husband again, and they devoted themselves thenceforward to teaching and taking care of their little nephew.

Thus time went on, till Balna's son was fourteen years old. Then one day his aunts told him the history of the family; and no sooner did he hear it than he was seized with a great desire to go in search of his father and mother and uncles, and bring them home again if he could find them alive. His aunts, on learning his determination, were much alarmed and tried to dissuade him, saying, "We have lost our husbands, and our sister and her husband, and you are now our sole hope; if you go away, what shall we do?" But he replied, "I pray you not to be discouraged; I will return soon, and, if it is possible, bring my father and mother and uncles with me." So he sat out on his travels, but for some months he could learn nothing to help him in his search.

At last, after he had journeyed many hundreds of weary miles, and become almost hopeless of ever being able to hear anything further of his parents, he one day came to a country which seemed full of stones and rocks and trees, and there he saw a large palace with a high tower; hard by which was a Malee's* little house.

As he was looking about, the Malee's wife saw him, and ran out of the house and said, "My dear boy, who are you that dare venture to this dangerous place?" And he answered, "I am a Rajah's son, and I come in search of my father and my uncles, and my mother whom a wicked enchanter bewitched." Then the Malee's wife said, "This country and this palace belong to a great Enchanter; he is all-powerful, and if any one displeases him, he can turn them into stones and trees. All the rocks and trees you see here were living people once, and the Magician turned them to what they now are. Some time ago a Rajah's son came here, and shortly afterward came his six brothers, and they were all turned into stones and trees; and these are not the only unfortunate ones, for up in that tower lives a beautiful Princess, whom the Magician has kept prisoner there for twelve years, because she hates him and will not marry him."

Then the little Prince thought, "These must be my parents and my uncles. I have found what I seek at last." So he told his story to the Malee's wife, and begged her to help him to remain in that place a while,

* Gardener's.

and inquire further concerning the unhappy people she mentioned; and she promised to befriend him, and advised his disguising himself, lest the Magician should see him, and turn him likewise into stone. To this the Prince agreed. So the Malee's wife dressed him up in a saree,* and pretended that he was her daughter.

One day, not long after this, as the Magician was walking in his garden, he saw the little girl (as he thought) playing about, and asked her who she was. She told him she was the Malee's daughter, and the Magician said, "You are a pretty little girl, and to-morrow you shall take a present of flowers from me to the beautiful lady who lives in the tower."

The young Prince was much delighted at hearing this, and after some consultation with the Malee's wife, he settled that it would be more safe for him to retain his disguise, and trust to the chance of a favorable opportunity for establishing some communication with his mother, if it were indeed she.

Now it happened that at Balna's marriage her husband had given her a small gold ring, on which her name was engraved, and she put it on her little son's finger when he was a baby, and afterward, when he was older, his aunts had had it enlarged for him, so that he was still able to wear it. The Malee's wife advised him to fasten the well-known treasure to one of the bouquets he presented to his mother, and trust to her recognizing it. This was not to be done without difficulty, as such a strict watch was kept over the poor Princess (for fear of her ever establishing communication with her friends) that though the supposed Malee's daughter was permitted to take her flowers every day, the Magician or one

* A woman's dress.

of his slaves was always in the room at the time. At last one day, however, opportunity favored him, and when no one was looking the boy tied the ring to a nosegay and threw it at Balna's feet. The ring fell with a clang on the floor, and Balna, looking to see what made the strange sound, found the little ring tied to the flowers. On recognizing it, she at once believed the story her son told her of his long search, and begged him to advise her as to what she had better do; at the same time entreating him on no account to endanger his life by trying to rescue her. She told him that for twelve long years the Magician had kept her shut up in the tower because she refused to marry him, and she was so closely guarded that she saw no hope of release.

Now Balna's son was a bright, clever boy; so he said, "Do not fear, dear mother; the first thing to do is to discover how far the Magician's power extends, in order that we may be able to liberate my father and uncles, whom he has imprisoned in the form of rocks and trees. You have spoken to him angrily for twelve long years; do you now rather speak kindly. Tell him you have given up all hopes of again seeing the husband you have so long mourned, and say you are willing to marry him. Then endeavor to find out what his power consists in, and whether he is immortal or can be put to death."

Balna determined to take her son's advice; and the next day sent for Punchkin and spoke to him as had been suggested.

The Magician, greatly delighted, begged her to allow the wedding to take place as soon as possible.

But she told him that before she married him he

must allow her a little more time, in which she might make his acquaintance, and, that, after being enemies so long, their friendship could but strengthen by degrees. "And do tell me," she said, "are you quite immortal? Can death never touch you? And are you too great an enchanter ever to feel human suffering?"

"Why do you ask?" said he.

"Because," she replied, "if I am to be your wife, I would fain know all about you, in order, if any calamity threatens you, to overcome, or, if possible, to avert it."

"It is true," he said, "that I am not as others. Far, far away, hundreds of thousands of miles from this, there lies a desolate country covered with thick jungle. In the midst of the jungle grows a circle of palm trees, and in the centre of the circle stand six chattees full of water, piled one above another; below the sixth chattee is a small cage which contains a little green parrot: on the life of the parrot depends my life, and if the parrot is killed I must die. It is, however," he added, "impossible that the parrot should sustain any injury, both on account of the inaccessibility of the country, and because, by my appointment, many thousand evil genii surround the palm trees, and kill all who approach the place."

Balna told her son what Punchkin had said, but, at the same time, implored him to give up all idea of getting the parrot.

The prince, however, replied, "Mother, unless I can get hold of that parrot, you and my father and uncles cannot be liberated: be not afraid, I will shortly return. Do you, meantime, keep the Magician in good humor—still putting off your marriage with him on various pretexts; and before he finds out the cause of delay I will return." So saying, he went away.

Many, many weary miles did he travel, till at last he came to a thick jungle, and being very tired, sat down under a tree and fell asleep. He was awakened by a soft rustling sound, and looking about him, saw a large serpent which was making its way to an eagle's nest built in the tree under which he lay, and in the nest were two young eagles. The Prince, seeing the danger of the young birds, drew his sword and killed the serpent; at the same moment a rushing sound was heard in the air, and the two old eagles, who had been out hunting for food for their young ones, returned. They quickly saw the dead serpent and the young Prince standing over it; and the old mother eagle said to him, "Dear boy, for many years all our young have been devoured by that cruel serpent: you have now saved the lives of our children; whenever you are in need, therefore, send to us and we will help you; and as for these little eagles, take them, and let them be your servants."

At this the Prince was very glad, and the two eaglets crossed their wings, on which he mounted; and they carried him far, far away over the thick jungles, until he came to the place where grew the circle of palm trees, in the midst of which stood the six chattees full of water. It was the middle of the day. All round the trees were the genii fast asleep: nevertheless, there were such countless thousands of them that it would have been quite impossible for any one to walk through their ranks to the place. Down swooped the strong-winged eaglets—down jumped the prince: in an instant he had overthrown the six chattees full of water, and seized the little green parrot, which he rolled up in his cloak; while, as he mounted again into the air, all the genii below awoke, and, finding their treasure gone, set up a wild and melancholy howl.

Away, away flew the little eagles till they came to their home in the great tree; then the Prince said to the old eagles, "Take back your little ones; they have done me good service; if ever again I stand in need of help, I will not fail to come to you." He then continued his journey on foot till he arrived once more at the Magician's palace, where he sat down at the door and began playing with the parrot. The Magician saw him, and came to him quickly, and said, "My boy, where did you get that parrot? Give it to me, I pray you." But the Prince answered, "Oh no, I cannot give away my parrot; it is a great pet of mine; I have had it many years." Then the Magician said, "If it is an old favorite, I can understand your not caring to give it away; but come, what will you sell it for?" "Sir," replied the Prince, "I will not sell my parrot."

Then the Magician got frightened, and said, "Anything, anything; name what price you will, and it shall be yours." "Then," the Prince answered, "I will that you liberate the Rajah's seven sons who you turned into rocks and trees." "It is done as you desire," said the Magician, "only give me my parrot." (And with that, by a stroke of his wand, Balna's husband and his brothers resumed their natural shapes.) "Now give me my parrot," repeated Punchkin. "Not so fast, my master," rejoined the Prince; "I must first beg that you will restore to life all whom you have thus imprisoned."

The Magician immediately waved his wand again;

and whilst he cried in an imploring voice, "Give me my parrot!" the whole garden became suddenly alive: where rock and stones and trees had been before, stood Rajahs and Punts* and Sirdars,† and mighty men on prancing horses, and jeweled pages and troops of armed attendants.

"Give me my parrot!" cried Punchkin. Then the boy took hold of the parrot, and tore off one of his wings; and as he did so the Magician's right arm fell off.

Punchkin then stretched out his left arm, crying, "Give me my parrot!" The Prince pulled off the parrot's second wing, and the Magician's left arm tumbled off.

"Give me my parrot!" cried he, and fell on his knees. The Prince pulled off the parrot's right leg—the Magician's right leg fell off: the Prince pulled off the parrot's left leg—down fell the Magician's left.

Nothing remained of him save the limbless body and the head; but still he rolled his eyes, and cried, "Give me my parrot!" "Take your parrot, then," cried the boy, and with that he wrung the bird's neck and threw it at the Magician; and as he did so, Punchkin's head twisted round, and with a fearful groan he died!

Then they let Balna out of the tower; and she, her son and the seven Princes went to their own country, and lived very happily ever afterward. And as to the rest of the world, every one went to his own house.

* Principal ministers. † Nobles or chiefs.

II.

A FUNNY STORY.

ONCE upon a time there were a Rajah and Ranee who were much grieved because they had no children, and the little dog in the palace had also no little puppies. At last the Rajah and Ranee had some children, and it also happened that the pet dog in the palace had some little puppies; but, unfortunately, the Ranee's two children were two little puppies! and the dog's two little puppies were two pretty little girls! This vexed her majesty very much; and sometimes when the dog had gone away to its dinner, the Ranee used to put the two little puppies (her children) into the kennel, and carry away the dog's two little girls to the palace. Then the poor dog grew very unhappy, and said, "They never will leave my two little children alone. I must take them away into the jungle, or their lives will be worried out." So one night she took the little girls in her mouth and ran with them to the jungle, and there made them a home in a pretty cave in the rock, beside a clear stream; and every day she would go into the towns and carry away some nice currie and rice to give her little daughters; and if she found any pretty clothes or jewels that she could bring away in her mouth, she used to take them also for the children.

Now it happened some time after this, one day, when the dog had gone to fetch her daughters' dinner, two young Princes (a Rajah and his brother) came to hunt in the jungle, and they hunted all day and found nothing. It had been very hot, and they were thirsty; so they went to a tree which grew on a little piece of high ground, and sent their attendants to search all round for water; but no one could find any. At last one of the hunting dogs came to the foot of the tree quite muddy, and the Rajah said, "Look, the dog is muddy: he must have found water: follow him, and see where he goes." The attendants followed the dog, and saw him go to the stream at the mouth of the cave where the two children were; and the two children also saw them, and were very much frightened and ran inside the cave. Then the attendants returned to the two Princes, and said, "We have found clear, sparkling water flowing past a cave, and, what is more, within the cave are two of the most lovely young ladies that eye ever beheld, clothed in fine dresses and covered with jewels; but when they saw us they were frightened and ran away." On hearing this the Princes bade their servants lead them to the place; and when they saw the two young girls, they were quite charmed with them, and asked them to go to their kingdom and become their wives. The maidens were frightened; but at last the Rajah and his brother persuaded them, and they went, and the Rajah married the eldest sister, and his brother married the youngest.

When the dog returned, she was grieved to find her children gone, and for twelve long years the poor thing ran many, many miles to find them, but in vain. At last one day she came to the place where the two Princesses lived. Now it chanced that the eldest, the wife of the Rajah, was looking out of the window, and seeing the dog run down the street, she said, "That must be my dear long-lost mother." So she ran into the street as fast as possible, and took the tired dog in her arms, and brought her into her own room, and made her a nice comfortable bed on the floor, and bathed her feet, and was very kind to her. Then the dog said to her, "My daughter, you are good and kind, and it is a great joy to me to see you again; but I must not stay; I will first go and see your younger sister, and then return." The Ranee answered, "Do not do so, dear mother; rest here to-day; to-morrow I will send and let my sister know, and she, too, will come and see you." But the poor, silly dog would not stay, but ran to the house of her second daughter. Now the second daughter was looking out of the window when the unfortunate creature came to the door, and seeing the dog she said to herself, "That must be my mother. What will my husband think if he learns that this wretched, ugly, miserable-looking dog is my mother?" So she ordered her servants to go and throw stones at it, and drive it away, and they did so; and one large stone hit the dog's head, and she ran back, very much hurt, to her eldest daughter's house. The Ranee saw her coming, and ran out into the street and brought her in in her arms, and did all she could to make her well, saying, "Ah, mother, mother! why did you ever leave my house?" But all her care was in vain: the poor dog died. Then the Ranee thought her husband might be vexed if he found a dead dog (an unclean animal) in the palace; so she put the body in a small room into which the Rajah hardly ever went, intending to have it reverently buried; and over it she placed a basket turned topsy-turvy.

It so happened, however, that when the Rajah came to visit his wife, as chance would have it, he went through this very room: and tripping over the upturned basket, called for a light to see what it was. Then, lo and behold! there lay the statue of a dog, life size, composed entirely of diamonds, emeralds, and other precious stones, set in gold! So he called out to his wife, and said, "Where did you get this beautiful dog?" And when the Ranee saw the golden dog, she was very much frightened, and, I'm sorry to say, instead of telling her husband the truth, she told a story, and said, "Oh, it is only a present my parents sent me."

Now see what trouble she got into for not telling the truth.

"*Only!*" said the Rajah; "why this is valuable enough to buy the whole of my kingdom. Your parents must be very rich people to be able to send you such presents as this. How is it you never told me of them? Where do they live?" (Now she had to tell another story to cover the first.) She said, "In the jungle." He replied, "I will go and see them; you must take me and show where they live." Then the Ranee thought, "What will the Rajah say when he finds I have been telling him such stories? He will order my head to be cut off." So she said, "You must first give me a palanquin, and I will go into the jungle and tell them you are coming;" but really she determined to kill herself, and so get out of her difficulties. Away she went; and when she had gone some distance in her palanquin, she saw a large white ants' nest, over which hung a cobra, with its mouth wide open; then the Ranee thought, "I will go to that cobra and put my finger in his mouth, that he may bite me, and so I shall die." So she ordered the palkee-bearers to wait, and said she would be back in a while, and got out, and ran to the ants' nest, and put her finger in the cobra's mouth. Now a large thorn had run, a short time before, into the cobra's throat, and hurt him very much; and the Ranee, by putting her finger into his mouth, pushed out this thorn; then the cobra, feeling much better, turned to her, and said, "My dear daughter, you have done me a great kindness; what return can I make you?" The Ranee told him all her story, and begged him to bite her, that she might die. But the cobra said, "You did certainly very wrong to tell the Rajah that story; nevertheless, you have been very kind to me. I will help you in your difficulty. Send your husband here. I will provide you with a father and mother of whom you need not be ashamed." So the Ranee returned joyfully to the palace, and invited her husband to come and see her parents.

When they reached the spot near where the cobra was, what a wonderful sight awaited them! There, in the place which had before been thick jungle, stood a splendid palace, twenty-four miles long and twenty-four miles broad, with gardens and trees and fountains all round; and the light shining from it was to be seen a hundred miles off. The walls were made of gold and precious stones, and the carpets cloth of gold. Hundreds of servants, in rich dresses, stood waiting in the long, lofty rooms; and in the last room of all, upon golden thrones, sat a magnificent old Rajah and Ranee, who introduced themselves to the young Rajah as his papa and mamma-in-law. The Rajah and Ranee stayed at the palace six months, and were entertained the whole of that time with feasting and music; and they left for their own home loaded with presents. Before they started, however, the Ranee went to her friend, the cobra, and said, "You have conjured up all these beautiful things to get me out of my difficulties, but my husband, the Rajah, has enjoyed his visit so much that he will certainly want to come here again. Then, if he returns and finds nothing at all, he will be very angry with me." The friendly cobra answered, "Do not fear. When you have gone twenty-four miles on your journey, look back, and see what you will see." So they started; and on looking back at the end of twenty-four miles, saw the whole of the splendid palace in flames, the fire reaching up to heaven. The Rajah returned to see it he could help anybody to escape, or invite them in their distress to his court; but he found that all was burnt down—not a stone nor a living creature remained!

Then he grieved much over the sad fate of his parents-in-law.

When the party returned home, the Rajah's brother said to him, "Where did you get these magnificent presents?" He replied, "They are gifts from my father and mother-in-law." At this news the Rajah's brother went home to his wife very discontented, and asked her why she had never told him of her parents, and taken him to see them, whereby he might have received rich gifts as well as his brother. His wife then went to her sister, and asked how she had managed to get all the things. But the Ranee said, "Go away, you wicked woman. I will not speak to you. You killed the poor dog, our mother."

But afterward she told her all about it.

The sister then said, "I shall go and see the cobra, and get presents too." The Ranee then answered,—"You can go if you like."

So the sister ordered her palanquin, and told her husband she was going to see her parents, and prepare them for a visit from him. When she reached the ants' nest, she saw the cobra there, and she went and put her finger in his mouth, and the cobra bit her, and she died.

III.

BRAVE SEVENTEE BAI.

SIU RAJAH,* who reigned long years ago in the country of Agrabrum, had an only son, to whom he was passionately attached. The Prince, whose name was Logedas, was young and handsome, and had married the beautiful Princess, Parbuttee Bai.

Now it came to pass that Siu Rajah's Wuzeer† had a daughter called Seventee Bai (the Daisy Lady), who was as fair as the morning, and beloved by all for her gentleness and goodness; and when Logedas Rajah saw her, he fell in love with her, and determined to marry her. But when Siu Rajah heard of this he was very angry, and sent for his son, and said: "Of all that is rich and costly in my kingdom I have withheld nothing from you, and in Parbuttee Bai you have a wife as fair as heart could wish; nevertheless, if you are desirous of having a second wife, I freely give you leave to do so; there are daughters of many neighboring kings who would be proud to become your Queen, but it is beneath your dignity to marry a Wuzeer's daughter; and, if you do, my love for you shall not prevent my expelling you from the kingdom." Logedas did not heed his father's threat, and he married Seventee Bai; which the Rajah learning, ordered him

* Or Singh Rajah, the Lion King. † Or Vizier.

immediately to quit the country; but yet, because he loved him much, he gave Logedas many elephants, camels, horses, palanquins and attendants, that he might not need help on the journey, and that his rank might be apparent to all.

So Logedas Rajah and his two young wives set forth on their travels. Before, however, they had gone very far, the Prince dismissed the whole of his retinue, except the elephant on which he himself rode, and the palanquin, carried by two men, in which his wives traveled. Thus, almost alone, he started through the jungle in search of a new home; but, being wholly ignorant of that part of the country, before they had gone very far they lost their way. The poor Princesses were reduced to a state of great misery; day after day they wandered on, living on roots or wild berries and the leaves of trees pounded down; and by night they were terrified by the cries of wild beasts in search of prey. Logedas Rajah became more melancholy and desponding every day; until, one night, maddened by the thought of his wives' sad condition, and unable longer to bear the sight of their distress, he got up, and casting aside his royal robes, twisted a coarse handkerchief about his head, after the manner of a fakeer's (holy beggar's) turban, and throwing a woolen cloak around him, ran away in disguise into the jungle.

A little while after he had gone, the Wuzeer's daughter awoke and found Parbuttee Bai crying bitterly. "Sister dear," said she, "what is the matter?" "Ah, sister," answered Parbuttee Bai, "I am crying because in my dreams I thought our husband had dressed himself like a fakeer and run away into the jungle; and I awoke, and found it was all true · he has gone, and left us here alone. It would have been better we had died than that such a misfortune should have befallen us."

"Do not cry," said Seventee Bai: "if we cry we are lost, for the palkee-bearers* will think we are only two weak women, and will run away, and leave us in the jungle, out of which we can never get by ourselves. Keep a cheerful mind, and all will be well; who knows but we may yet find our husband? Meanwhile, I will dress myself in his clothes, and take the name of Seventee Rajah, and you shall be my wife; and the palkee-bearers will think it is only I that have been lost; and it will not seem very wonderful to them that in such a place as this a wild beast should have devoured me."

Then Parbuttee Bai smiled and said, "Sister, you speak well; you have a brave heart. I will be your little wife."

So Seventee Bai dressed herself in her husband's clothes, and next day she mounted the elephant as he had done, and ordered the bearers to take up the palkee in which Parbuttee Bai was, and again attempt to find their way out of the jungle. The palkee-bearers wondered much to themselves what had become of Seventee Bai, and they said to one another, "How selfish and how fickle are the rich! See now our young Rajah, who married the Wuzeer's daughter and brought all this trouble on himself thereby (and in truth 'tis said she was a beautiful lady), he seemed to love her as his own soul; but now that she has been devoured by some cruel animal in this wild jungle, he appears scarcely to mourn her death."

After journeying for some days under the wise direc-

* *I. e.*, palanquin-bearers.

tion of the Wuzeer's daughter, the party found themselves getting out of the jungle, and at last they came to an open plain, in the middle of which was a large city. When the citizens saw the elephant coming they ran out to see who was on it, and returning, told their Rajah that a very handsome Rajah, richly dressed, was riding toward the city, and that he brought with him his wife—a most lovely Princess. Whereupon the Rajah of that country sent to Seventee Bai, and asked her who she was, and why she had come? Seventee Bai replied, "My name is Seventee Rajah. My father was angry with me, and drove me from his kingdom; and I and my wife have been wandering for many days in the jungle, where we lost our way."

The Rajah and all his court thought they had never seen so brave and royal-looking a Prince; and the Rajah said that if Seventee Rajah would take service under him, he would give him as much money as he liked. To whom the Wuzeer's daughter replied: "I am not accustomed to take service under anybody; but you are good to us in receiving us courteously and offering us your protection; therefore, give me whatever post you please, and I will be your faithful servant." So the Rajah gave Seventee Bai a salary of £24,000 a-year and a beautiful house, and treated her with the greatest confidence, consulting her in all matters of importance, and entrusting her with many state affairs; and from her gentleness and kindness, none felt envious at her good fortune, but she was beloved and honored by all; and thus these two Princesses lived for twelve years in that city. No one suspected that Seventee Bai was not the Rajah she pretended to be, and she most strictly forbade Parbuttee Bai's making a great friend of anybody, or admitting any one to her confidence; for, she said, "Who knows, then, but some day you may, unawares, reveal that I am only Seventee Bai; and, though I love you as my very sister, if that were told by you, I would kill you with my own hands."

Now the King's palace was on the side of the city nearest to the jungle, and one night the Ranee was awakened by loud and piercing shrieks coming from that direction; so she woke her husband, and said, "I am so frightened by that terrible noise that I cannot sleep. Send some one to see what is the matter." And the Rajah called all his attendants, and said, "Go down toward the jungle and see what that noise is about." But they were all afraid, for the night was very dark, and the noise very dreadful, and they said to him: "We are afraid to go. We dare not do so by ourselves. Send for this young Rajah who is such a favorite of yours, and tell him to go. He is brave. You pay him more than you do us all. What is the good of your paying him so much, unless he can be of use when he is wanted?" So they all went to Seventee Bai's house, and when she heard what was the matter, she jumped up, and said she would go down to the jungle and see what the noise was.

This noise had been made by a Rakshas,* who was standing under a gallows on which a thief had been hanged the day before. He had been trying to reach the corpse with his cruel claws; but it was just too high for him, and he was howling with rage and disappoint-

* Gigantic demoniacal ogres, who can at will assume any shape. Their chief terrestrial delight is said to be digging dead bodies out of their graves and devouring them.

ment. When, however, the Wuzeer's daughter reached the place, no Rakshas was to be seen; but in his stead a very old woman, in a wonderful glittering saree, sitting wringing her withered hands under the gallows tree, and above, the corpse, swaying about in the night wind. "Old woman," said Seventee Bai, "what is the matter?" "Alas!" said the Rakshas (for it was he), "my son hangs above on that gallows. He is dead, he is dead! and I am too bent with age to be able to reach the rope and cut his body down." "Poor old woman!" said Seventee Bai; "get upon my shoulders, and you will then be tall enough to reach your son." So the Rakshas mounted on Seventee Bai's shoulders, who held him steady by his glittering saree. Now, as she stood there, Seventee Bai began to think the old woman was a very long time cutting the rope round the dead man's neck; and just at that moment the moon shone out from behind a cloud, and Seventee Bai, looking up, saw that instead of a feeble old woman, she was supporting on her shoulders a Rakshas, who was tearing down portions of the flesh and devouring it. Horror-stricken, she sprang back, and with a shrill scream the Rakshas fled away, leaving in her hands the shining saree.

Seventee Bai did not choose to say anything about this adventure to the Ranee, not wishing to alarm her; so she merely returned to the palace, and said that the noise was made by an old woman whom she had found crying under the gallows. She then returned home, and gave the bright saree to Parbuttee Bai.

One fine day, some time after this, two of the Rajah's little daughters thought they would go and see Parbuttee Bai; and as it happened, Parbuttee Bai had on the Rakshas' saree, and was standing by the half-closed window shutters looking out, when the Prin cesses arrived at her house. The little Princesses were quite dazzled by the golden sarec, and running home said to their mother, "That young Rajah's wife has the most beautiful saree we ever saw. It shines like the sun, and dazzles one's cyes. We have no sarees half so beautiful, and although you are Ranee, you have none so rich as that. Why do you not get one too?"

When the Ranee heard about Parbuttee Bai's saree she was very eager to have one like it; and she said to the Rajah, "Your servant's wife is dressed more richly than your Ranee. I hear Parbuttee Bai has a saree more costly than any of mine. Now, therefore, I beg you to get me one like hers; for I cannot rest until I have one equally costly."

Then the Rajah sent for Seventee Bai, and said, "Tell me where your wife got her beautiful golden saree; for the Ranee desires to have one like it." Seventee Bai answered, "Noble master, that saree came from a very far country—even the country of the Rakshas. It is impossible to get one like it here; but if you give me lcave I will go and search for their country, and, if I succeed in finding it, bring you home sarees of the same kind." And the Rajah was very much pleased, and ordered Seventee Bai to go. So she returned to her house and bade good-bye to Parbuttee Bai, and warned her to be discreet and cautious; and then, mounting her horse, rode away in search of the Rakshas' country.

Seventee Bai traveled for many days through the jungle, going one hundred miles every day, and staying to rest every now and then at little villages on her road. At last one day, after having gone several hundred miles, she came to a fine city situated on the banks of a beautiful river, and on the city walls a proclamation was painted in large letters. Seventee Bai inquired of the people what it meant, who told her that it was to say the Rajah's daughter would marry any man who could tame a certain pony belonging to her father, which was very vicious.

"Has no one been able to manage it?" asked Seventee Bai. "No one," they said. "Many have tried, but failed miserably. The pony was born on the same day as the Princess. It is so fierce that no one can approach it; but when the Princess heard how wild it it was, she vowed she would marry no one who could not tame it. Every one who likes is free to try." Then Seventee Bai said, "Show me the pony tomorrow. I think I shall be able to tame it." They answered, "You can try if you like, but it is very dangerous, and you are but a youth." She replied, "God gives his strength to the weak. I do not fear." So she went to sleep, and early next morning they beat a drum all round the town to let every one know that another man was going to try and tame the Rajah's pony, and all the people flocked out of their houses to see the sight. The pony was in a field near the river, and Seventee Bai ran up to it, as it came running toward her intending to trample her to death, and seized it firmly by the mane, so that it could neither strike her with its fore legs nor kick her. The pony tried to shake her off, but Seventee Bai clung firmly on, and finally jumped on its back; and when the pony found that it was mastered, it became quite gentle and tame. Then Seventee Bai, to show how completely she had conquered, put spurs to the pony to make it jump the river, and the pony immediately sprang up in the air and right across the river (which was a jump of three miles), and this it did three times (for it was strong and agile, and had never been ridden before); and when all the people saw this they shouted for joy, and ran down to the river bank and brought Seventee Bai, riding in triumph on the pony, to see the Rajah. And the Rajah said, "Oh, best of men, and worthy of all honor, you have won my daughter." So he took Seventee Bai to the palace and paid her great honor, and gave her jewels and rich clothes, and horses and camels innumerable. The Princess also came to greet the winner of her hand. Then they said, "To-morrow shall be the wedding day." But Seventee Bai replied, "Great Rajah and beautiful Princess, I am going on an important errand of my own Rajah's; let me, I pray you, first accomplish the duty on which I am bound, and on my way home I will come through this city and claim my bride." At this they were both pleased, and the Rajah said, "It is well spoken. Do not let us hinder your keeping faith with your own Rajah. Go your way. We shall eagerly await your return, when you shall claim the Princess and all your possessions, and we will have such a gay wedding as was not since the world began." And they went out with her to the borders of their land, and showed her on her way.

So the Wuzeer's daughter traveled on in search of the Rakshas' country, until at last one day she came in sight of another fine large town. Here she rested in the house for travelers for some days. Now the Rajah of this country had a very beautiful daughter, who was his only child, and for her he had built a splendid bath.

It was like a little sea, and had high marble walls all around, with a hedge of spikes at the top of the walls, so high that at a distance it looked like a great castle. The young Princess was very fond of it, and she vowed she would only marry a man who could jump across her bath on horseback. This had happened some years before, but no one had been able to do it, which grieved the Rajah and Ranee very much; for they wished to see their daughter happily married. And they said to her, "We shall both be dead before you get a husband. What folly is this, to expect that any one should be able to jump over those high marble walls, with the spikes at the top!" The Princess only answered, "Then I will never marry. It matters not; I will never have a husband who has not jumped those walls."

So the Rajah caused it to be proclaimed throughout the land that he would give his daughter in marriage, and great riches, to whoever could jump, on horseback, over the Princess' bath.

All this Seventee Bai learnt as soon as she arrived in the town, and she said, "To-morrow I will try and jump over the Princess' bath." The country people said to her, "You speak foolishly: it is quite impossible." She replied, "Heaven, in which I trust, will help me." So next day she rose up, and saddled her horse, and led him in front of the palace, and there she sprang on his back, and going at full gallop, leapt over the marble walls, over the spikes high up in the air, and down on to the ground on the other side of the bath; and this she did three times, which, when the Rajah saw, he was filled with joy, and sent for Seventee Bai, and said, "Tell me your name, brave

Prince; for you are the only man in the world—you have won my daughter." Then the Wuzeer's daughter replied, "My name is Seventee Rajah. I come from a far country on a mission from my Rajah to the country of the Rakshas; let me therefore, I pray you, first do my appointed work, and if I live to return, I will come through this country and claim my bride." To which the Rajah consented, for he did not wish the Princess, his daughter, to undertake so long and tiresome a journey. It was therefore agreed that the Princess should await Seventee Bai's return at her father's court, and that Seventee Bai herself should immediately proceed on her journey.

From this place she went on for many, many days without adventure, and traversed a dense jungle, for her brave heart carried her through all difficulties. At last she arrived at another large city, beautifully situated by a lake, with blue hills rising behind it, and sheltering it from the cutting winds; little gardens filled with pomegranates, jasmine and other fragrant and lovely flowers reached down from the city to the water's edge.

Seventee Bai, tired with her long journey, rode up to one of the Malees' houses, where the hospitable inmates, seeing she was a stranger and weary, offered her food and shelter for the night, which she thankfully accepted.

As they all sat round the fire cooking their evening meal, Seventee Bai asked the Malee's wife about the place and the people, and what was going on in the town. "Much excitement," she replied, "has of late been caused by our Rajah's dream, which no one can interpret." "What did he dream?" asked Seventee

Bai. "Ever since he was ten years old," she replied, "he has dreamed of a fair tree growing in a large garden. The stem of the tree is made of silver, the leaves are pure gold, and the fruit is bunches of pearls. The Rajah has inquired of all his wise men and seers where such a tree is to be found; but they all replied, 'There is no such tree in the world;' wherefore he is dissatisfied and melancholy. Moreover, the Princess, his daughter, hearing of her father's dream, has determined to marry no man save the finder of this marvelous tree." "It is very odd," said Seventee Bai; and, their supper being over, she dragged her mattress outside the little house (as a man would have done), and, placing it in a sheltered nook near the lake, knelt down, as her custom was, to say her prayers before going to sleep.

As she knelt there, with her eyes fixed on the dark water, she saw, on a sudden, a glorious shining light coming slowly toward her, and discovered, in a minute or two more, that a very large cobra was crawling up the steps from the water's edge, having in his mouth an enormous diamond, the size and shape of an egg, that sparkled and shone like a little sun, or as if one of the stars had suddenly dropped out of heaven. The cobra laid the diamond down at the top of the steps, and crawled away in search of food. Presently returning when the night was far spent, he picked up the diamond again, and slid down the steps with it into the lake. Seventee Bai knew not what to make of this, but she resolved to return to the same place next night and watch for the cobra.

Again she saw him bring the diamond in his mouth, and take it away with him after his evening meal; and again, a third night, the same thing. Then Seventee Bai determined to kill the cobra, and if possible secure the diamond. So early next morning she went into the bazaar, and ordered a blacksmith to make her a very strong iron trap, which should catch hold of anything it was let down upon so firmly as to require the strength of twelve men to get out of it. The blacksmith did as he was ordered, and made a very strong trap; the lower part of it was like knives, and when it caught hold of anything it required the strength of twelve men to break through it and escape.

Seventee Bai had this trap hung up by a rope to a tree close to the lake, and all around she scattered flowers and sweet scents, such as cobras love; and at nightfall she herself got into the tree just above the trap, and waited for the cobra to come as he was wont.

About twelve o'clock the cobra came up the steps from the lake in search of food. He had the diamond in his mouth, and, attracted by the sweet scents and flowers, instead of going into the jungle, he proceeded toward the tree in which Seventee Bai was.

When Seventee Bai saw him, she untied the rope and let down the trap upon him; but for fear he might not be quite dead, she waited till morning before going to get the diamond.

As soon as the sun was up, she went to look at her prey. There he lay cold and dead, with the diamond, which shone like a mountain of light, in his mouth. Seventee Bai took it, and, tired by her night of watching, thought she would bathe in the lake before returning to the Malee's cottage. So she ran and knelt down by the brink, to dip her hands and face in the cool water; but no sooner did she touch its surface with the diamond, than it rolled back in a wall on either hand, and she saw a pathway leading down below the lake, on each side of which were beautiful houses and gardens full of flowers, red, and white, and blue. Seventee Bai resolved to see whither this might lead, so she walked down the path until she came opposite a large door. She opened it, and found herself in a more lovely garden than she had ever seen on earth; tall trees laden with rich fruit grew in it, and on the boughs were bright birds singing melodiously, while the ground was covered with flowers, among which flew many gaudy butterflies.

In the centre of the garden grew one tree more beautiful than all the rest: *the stem was of silver, the leaves were golden, and the fruit was clusters of pearls.* Swinging amid the branches sat a young girl, more fair than any earthly lady; she had a face like the angels which men only see in dreams; her eyes were like two stars, her golden hair fell in ripples to her feet; she was singing to herself. When she saw the stranger, she gave a little cry, and said, "Ah, my lord, why do you come here?" Seventee Bai answered, "May I not come to see you, beautiful lady?" Then the lady said, "Oh, sir, you are welcome; but if my father sees you here, he will kill you. I am the great Cobra's daughter, and he made this garden for me to play in, and here I have played these many, many years all alone, for he lets me see no one, not even of our own subjects. I never saw any one before you. Speak, beautiful Prince—tell me how you came here, and who you are?" Seventee Bai answered, "I am Seventee Rajah: have no fear—the stern Cobra is no more." Then the lady was joyful, when she heard that the Cobra who had tyrannized over her was dead, and she said her name was Hera Bai (the Diamond Lady), and that she was possessor of all the treasures under the lake; and she said to Seventee Bai, "Stay with me here; you shall be king of all this country, and I will be your wife." "That cannot be," answered Seventee Bai, "for I have been sent on a mission by my Rajah, and I must continue my journey until I have accomplished it; but if you love me as I love you, come rather with me to my own land, and you shall be my wife." Hera Bai shook her head. "Not so, dearest," she said, "for if I go with you, all the people will see how fair I am, and they will kill you, and sell me for a slave; and so I shall bring evil upon you, and not good. But take this flute, dear husband (and saying this, she gave Seventee Bai a little golden flute); whenever you wish to see me, or are in need of my aid, go into the jungle and play upon it, and before the sound ceases I will be there; but do not play it in the towns, nor yet amid a crowd." Then Seventee Bai put the flute in the folds of her dress, and she bade farewell to Hera Bai and went away.

When she came back to the Malee's cottage, the Malee's wife said to her, "We became alarmed about you, sir; for two days we have seen nothing of you; and we thought you must have gone away. Where have you been so long?" Seventee Bai answered, "I had business of my own in the bazaar" (for she did not choose to tell the Malee's wife that she had been under the lake); "now go and inquire what time your Rajah's Wuzeer can give a stranger audience, for I must see him before I leave this city." So the Malee's wife went; whilst she was gone, Seventee Bai went down again to the edge of the lake, and there reverently burnt the cobra's body, both for the sake of Hera Bai, and because the cobra is a sacred animal. Next day (the Malee's wife having brought a favorable answer from the palace) Seventee Bai went to see the Wuzeer. Now the Wuzeer wondered much why she came to see him, and he said, "Who are you, and what is your errand?" Whereupon she answered, "I am Seventee Rajah. I am going a long journey on my own Rajah's account, and happening to be passing through this city, I came to pay you a friendly visit." Then the Wuzeer became quite cordial, and talked with Seventee Bai about the country and the city, and the Rajah and his wonderful dream. And Seventee Bai said, "What do you suppose your Rajah would give to any one who could show him the tree of which he has so often dreamed?" The Wuzeer replied, "He would certainly give him his daughter in marriage and the half of his kingdom." "Very well," said Seventee Bai, "tell your master that, upon these conditions, if he likes to send for me, I will show him the tree; he may look at it for one night, but he cannot have it for his own."

The Wuzeer took the message to the Rajah, and next day the Wuzeer, the Sirdars, and all the great men of the court, went in state by the Rajah's order to the Malee's hut, to say that he was willing to grant all Seventee Rajah's demands, and would like to see the tree that very night. Seventee Bai thereupon promised the Wuzeer that if the Rajah would come with his court, he should see the reality of his dream. Then she went into the jungle and played on her little flute, and Hera Bai immediately appeared as she had seen her before, swinging in the silver tree; and when she heard what Seventee Bai wanted, she bade her bring the Rajah, who should see it without fail.

When the Rajah came, he and all his court were overcome with astonishment; for there, in the midst of the desolate jungle, was a beautiful palace; fountains played in every court, the rooms were richly decorated with thousands and thousands of shining jewels; a light as clear as day filled all the place, soft music was played around by unseen hands, sweet odors filled the air, and in the midst of the palace garden there grew *a silver tree, with golden leaves and fruit of pearls.*

The next morning all had disappeared; but the Rajah, enchanted with what he had seen, remained true to his promise, and agreed to give Seventee Bai the half of his kingdom and his daughter in marriage; for, said he to himself, "A man who can convert the jungle into a paradise in one night must surely be rich enough and clever enough to be my son-in-law." But Seventee Bai said, "I am now employed on an errand of my Rajah's; let me, I beg, first accomplish it, and on my homeward journey I will remain a while in this town, and will marry the Princess." So they gave him leave to go, and the Rajah and all the great men of his kingdom accompanied Seventee Bai to the borders of their land. Thence the Wuzeer's daughter went on journeying many days until she had left that country far behind; but as yet she had gained no clue as to the way to the Rakshas' land. In this difficulty she bethought her of Hera Bai, and played upon the little golden flute. Hera Bai immediately appeared, saying, "Husband, what can I do for you?" Seventee Bai answered, "Kind Hera, I have now been wandering in this jungle for many days, endeavoring in vain to discover the Rakshas' country, whither my Rajah has ordered me to go. Can you help me to get there?" She answered, "You cannot go there by yourself. For a six months' journey round their land there is placed a Rakshas' guard, and not a sparrow could find his way into the country without their knowledge and permission. No men are admitted there, and there are more Rakshas employed in keeping guard than there are trees on the face of the earth. They are invisible, but they would see you, and instantly tear you to pieces. Be, however, guided by me, and I will contrive a way by which you may gain what you seek. Take this ring (and so saying, she placed a glorious ring on Seventee Bai's finger); it was given me by my dearest friend, the Rajah of the Rakshas' daughter, and will render you invisible. Look at that mountain, whose blue head you can just see against the sky; you must climb to the top of that, for it stands on the borders of the Rakshas' territory. When there, turn the stone on the ring I have given you toward the palm of your hand, and you will instantly fall through the earth into the space below the mountain where the Rakshas' Rajah holds his court, and find yourself in his daughter's presence. Tell her you are my husband; she will love and help you for my sake." Hera Bai so saying disappeared, and Seventee Bai continued her journey until she reached the mountain top, where she turned the ring round as she had been bidden, and immediately found herself falling through the earth, down, down, down, deeper and deeper, until at last she arrived in a beautiful room, richly furnished, and hung round with cloth of gold. In every direction, as far as the eye could reach, were thousands and thousands of Rakshas, and in the centre of the room was a gold and ivory throne, on which sat the most beautiful Princess that it is possible to imagine. She was tall and of a commanding aspect; her black hair was bound by long strings of pearl; her dress was of fine spun gold, and round her waist was clasped a zone of restless, throbbing, light-giving diamonds; her neck and her arms were covered with a profusion of costly jewels; but brighter than all shone her bright eyes, which looked full of gentle majesty. She could see Seventee Bai, although her attendants could not, because of the magic ring; and as soon as she saw her she started and cried, "Who are you? How came you here?" Seventee Bai answered, "I am Seventee Rajah, the husband of the Lady Hera, and I have come here by the power of the magic ring you gave her." The Rakshas' Princess then said, "You are welcome: but you must know that your coming is attended with much danger; for, did the guard placed around me by my father know of your presence, they would instantly put you to death, and I should be powerless to save you. Tell me why did you come?" Seventee Bai answered, "I came to see you, beautiful lady; tell me your name, and how it is you are here all alone." She replied, "I am the Rakshas' Rajah's only daughter, and my name is Tara Bai (the Star Lady), and because my father loves me very much he has built this palace for me, and placed this great guard of Rakshas all round for many thousand miles, to prevent any one coming in or out without his permission.

"So great is the state they keep that I seldom see my father and mother; indeed, I have not seen them for several years. Nevertheless, I will go now in person to implore their protection for you; for though I never saw king nor prince before, I love you very much."

So saying, she arose to go to her father's court, bidding Seventee Bai await her return.

When the Rajah and Ranee of the Rakshas heard that their daughter was coming to see them, they were very much surprised, and said, "What can be the matter with our daughter? Can she be ill? or can our Tara Bai be unhappy in the beautiful house we have given her?" And they said to her, "Daughter, why do you come? what is the matter?" She answered, "Oh, my father! I come to tell you I should like to be married. Cannot you find some beautiful Prince to be my husband?" Then the Rajah laughed, and said, "You are but a child still, my daughter; nevertheless, if you wish for a husband, certainly, if any Prince comes here, and asks you in marriage, we will let you wed him." She said, "If some brave and beautiful Prince were to come here, and get through the great guard you have placed around the palace, would you indeed protect him for my sake, and not allow them to tear him in pieces?" The Rajah answered, "If such a one come, he shall be safe." Then Tara Bai was very joyful, and ran and fetched Seventee Bai, and said to her father and mother, "See here is Seventee Rajah, the young Prince of whom I spoke." And when the Rajah and Ranee saw Seventee Bai they were greatly astonished, and could not think how she had managed to reach their land, and they thought she must be very brave and wise to have done so. And because also Seventee Bai looked a very noble Prince, they were the more willing that she should marry Tara Bai, and said, "Seventee Rajah, we are willing you should be our son-in-law, for you look good and true, and you must be brave, to have come so long and dangerous a journey for your wife; now, therefore, you shall be married; the whole land is open to you, and all that we have is yours; only take good care of our dear daughter, and if ever she or you are unhappy, return here and you shall find a home with us." So the wedding took place amidst great rejoicings. The wedding festivities lasted twelve days, and to it came hundreds and hundreds of thousands of Rakshas from every country under heaven; from the north and the south and the east and the west, from the depths of the earth and the uttermost parts of the sea. Troop after troop they came flocking in, an ever-increasing crowd, from all parts of this wide world, to be present at the marriage of their master's daughter.

It would be impossible to count all the rich and costly presents that the Rakshas' Rajah and Ranee gave Tara Bai. There were jewels enough to fill the seas; diamonds and emeralds, rubies, sapphires and pearls; gold and silver, costly hangings, carved ebony and ivory, more than a man could count in a hundred years; for the Rajah gave his daughter a guard of 100,000,000,000,000 Rakshas, and each Rakshas carried a bundle of riches, and each bundle was as big as a house! and so they took leave of the Rakshas' Rajah and Ranee, and left the Rakshas' country.

When they got to the country of the Rajah who had dreamed about the silver tree, with leaves of gold and fruit of pearl (because the number of their retinue was so great that if they had come into a country they would have devoured all that was in it like a swarm of locusts), Seventee Bai and Tara Bai determined that Tara Bai should stay with the guard of Rakshas in the jungle, on the borders of the Rajah's dominions, and that Seventee Bai should go to the city, as she had promised, to marry the Rajah's daughter. And there they stayed a week, and the Rajah's daughter was married with great pomp and ceremony to Seventee Bai; and when they left the city the Rajah gave Seventee Bai and the bride, his daughter, horses and camels and elephants, and rich robes and jewels innumerable; and he and all his court accompanied them to the borders of the land.

Thence they went to the country where lived the Princess whose great marble bath Seventee Bai had jumped over; and there Seventee Bai was married to her, amid great rejoicings, and the wedding was one of surpassing splendor, and the wedding festivities lasted for three whole days.

And leaving that city, they traveled on until they reached the city where Seventee Bai had tamed the Rajah's wild pony, and there they spent two days in great honor and splendor, and Seventee Bai married that Princess also; so with her five wives—that is to say, Hera Bai the Rajah of the Cobras' daughter, Tara Bai the Rajah of the Rakshas' daughter, and the three other Princesses—and a great tribe of attendants and elephants and camels and horses, she returned to the city where she had left Parbuttee Bai.

Now when news was brought to Seventee Bai's master (the friendly Rajah), of the great cavalcade that was approaching his city, he became very much alarmed, taking Seventee Bai for some strange Rajah who had come to make war upon him. When Seventee Bai heard how alarmed he was, she sent a messenger to him, on a swift horse, to say, "Be not alarmed; it is only thy servant, Seventee Rajah, returning from the errand on which thou didst send him." Then the Rajah's heart was light, and he ordered a royal salute to be fired, and went out with all his court to meet Seventee Bai, and they all went together in a state procession into the city. And Seventee Bai said to the Rajah, "You sent your servant to the Rakshas' country to fetch a golden saree for the Ranee. Behold, I have done as you wish." And so saying, she gave to the Rajah five Rakshas' bundles of rich hangings and garments covered with jewels (that is to say, five housefuls of costly things; for each Rakshas carried as much in the bundle on his shoulders as a house would hold); and to the Wuzeer she gave two bundles.

After this, Seventee Bai discharged almost all her immense train of attendants (for fear they should create a famine in the land), sending them to their own houses with many valuable presents; and she took the three Princesses, her wives, to live with her and Parbuttee Bai; but Hera Bai and Tara Bai, on account of their high rank and their surpassing beauty, had a splendid palace of their own in the jungle, of which no one knew but Seventee Bai.

Now when she again saw Seventee Bai, the Rajah's little daughter said to her father, "Father, I do not think there is such a brave and beautiful Prince in all the world as this Seventee Rajah. I would rather have him for my husband than any one else." And the Rajah said, "Daughter, I am very willing you should marry him." So it was settled Seventee Bai should marry the little Princess; but she said to the Rajah, "I am willing to marry your daughter, but we must have a very grand wedding; give me time, therefore, to send into all the countries round, and invite all their Rajahs to be present at the ceremony." And to this the Rajah agreed.

Now, about this time, Seventee Bai one day found Parbuttee Bai crying, and said to her, "Little sister, why are you unhappy?" And Parbuttee Bai answered, "Oh sister, you have brought us out of all our difficulties, and won us honor and great riches, but yet I do not feel merry; for I cannot help thinking of our poor husband, who is now, maybe, wandering about a wretched beggar, and I long with my whole heart to see him again." Then Seventee Bai said, "Well, cheer up, do not cry; mind those women do not find out I am not Seventee Rajah. Keep a good heart, and I will try and find your husband for you." So Seventee Bai went into the jungle palace to see Hera Bai, and said to her, "I have a friend whom I have not seen since he became mad twelve years ago, and ran away into the jungle disguised as a Fakeer. I should like very much to find out if he is still alive. How can I learn?" Now Hera Bai was a very wise Princess, and she answered, "Your best plan will be to provide a great feast for the poor, and cause it to be proclaimed in all lands, far and near, that you are about to give it as a thank-offering for all the blessings God has bestowed on you. The poor will flock from all countries to come to it, and perhaps among the rest you may find your friend."

Seventee Bai did as Hera Bai had advised, causing two long tables to be spread in the jungle, whereat hundreds of poor from all parts of the world were daily entertained; and every day, for six months, Seventee Bai and Parbuttee Bai walked down the long rows of people, apparently to see how they were all getting on, but in reality to look for Logedas Rajah; but they found him not.

At last one day, as Seventee Bai was going her accustomed round, she saw a wretched wild-looking man, black as pitch, with tangled hair, a thin wrinkled face, and in his hand a wooden bowl, such as Fakeers carry about to collect broken meat and scraps of bread in, and touching Parbuttee Bai, she said to her, "See, Parbuttee, there is your husband." When Parbuttee Bai saw this pitiful sight (for it was, indeed, Logedas, but so changed and altered that even his wives hardly recognized him), she began to cry. Then Seventee Bai said, "Do not cry; go home quickly. I will take care of him." And when Parbuttee Bai was gone, she called one of the guard and said to him, "Catch hold of that man and put him in prison." Then Logedas Rajah said, "Why do you seize me? I have done no harm to any one." But Seventee Bai ordered the guard not to heed his remonstrances, but to take him to prison instantly, for she did not wish the people around to discover how interested she was in him. So the guard took Logedas Rajah away to lock him up. Poor Logedas Rajah said to them, "Why has this wicked Rajah had me taken prisoner? I have harmed no one. I have not fought, nor robbed; but for twelve years I have been a wretched beggar, living on the bread of charity." For he did not tell them he was a Rajah's son, for he knew they would only laugh at him. They replied. "You must not call our Rajah wicked: it is you that are wicked, and not he, and doubtless he will have your head cut off."

When they put him in prison he begged them again to say what was to be done to him. "Oh!" said they, "you will certainly be hanged to-morrow morning, or perhaps, if you like it better, beheaded, in front of the palace."

Now as soon as Seventee Bai got home, she sent for her head servants, and said to them, "Go at once to the prison, and order the guard to give you up the Fakeer I gave into their charge, and bring him here in a palanquin, but see that he does not escape." Then Seventee Bai ordered them to lock up Logedas in a distant part of the palace, and commanded that he should be washed, and dressed in new clothes, and given food, and that a barber should be sent for, to cut his hair and trim his beard. Then Logedas said to his keepers, "See how good the Rajah is to me! He will not surely hang me after this." "Oh, never fear," they answered; "when you are dressed up and made very smart, it will be a much finer sight to see you hanged than before." Thus they tried to frighten the poor man. After this Seventee Bai sent for all the greatest doctors in the kingdom, and said to them, "If a Rajah wanders about for twelve years in the jungle, until all trace of his princely beauty is lost, how long will it take you to restore him to his original likeness?" They answered, "With care and attention it may be done in six months." "Very well," said Seventee Bai, "there is a friend of mine now in my palace of whom this is the case. Take him and treat him well, and at the end of six months I shall expect to see him restored to his original health and strength."

So Logedas was placed under the doctors' care; but all this time he had no idea who Seventee Bai was, nor why he was thus treated. Every day Seventee Bai came to see him and talk to him. Then he said to his keepers, "See, good people, how kind this great Rajah is, coming to see me every day; he can intend for me nothing but good." To which they would answer, "Don't you be in a hurry; none can fathom the hearts of kings. Most probably, for all this delay, he will in the end have you taken and hanged." Thus they amused themselves by alarming him.

Then, some day, when Seventee Bai had been more than usually kind, Logedas Rajah would say again, "I do not fear the Rajah's intentions toward me. Did you not notice how very kind he was to day!" And to this his keepers would reply—

"Doubtless it is amusing for him, but hardly, we should think, for you. He will play with you probably for some time (as a cat does with a mouse); but in three months is the Rajah's birthday; most likely he is keeping you to kill you then." And so the time wore on.

Seventee Bai's birthday was fixed for the day also of her wedding with the Rajah's daughter. For this great event immense preparations were made all over the plain outside the city walls. Tents made of cloth of gold were pitched in a great square, twelve miles long and twelve miles broad, for the accommodation of the neighboring Rajahs, and in the centre was a larger tent than all the rest, covered with jewels and shining like a great golden temple, in which they were to assemble.

Then Seventee Bai said to Parbuttee Bai, "On my

birthday I will restore you to your husband." But Parbuttee Bai was vexed and said, "I cannot bear the thought of him; it is such a terrible thing to think of our once handsome husband as none other than that miserable Fakeer."

Seventee Bai smiled. "In truth," she said, "I think you will find him again altered, and for the better. You cannot think what a change rest and care have made in him; but he does not know who we are, and as you value my happiness, tell no one now that I am not the Rajah." "Indeed I will not, dearest sister," answered Parbuttee Bai. "I should in truth be loath to vex you, after all you have done for me; for owing to you here have we lived happily for twelve years like sisters, and I do not think as clever a woman as you was ever before born in this world."

Among other guests invited to the wedding were Siu Rajah and his wife, and the Wuzeer, Seventee Bai's father, and her mother. Seventee Bai arranged thrones for them all, made of gold and emeralds, and diamonds, and rubies, and ivory. And she ordered that in the seat of honor on her left-hand side should be placed the Wuzeer, her father, and next to him her mother, and next to them Siu Rajah and his wife, and after them all the other Rajahs and Ranees, according to their rank; and all the Rajahs and Ranees wondered much that the place of honor should have been given to the stranger Wuzeer. Then Seventee Bai took her most costly Rajah dress, and ordered that Logedas Rajah should be clothed in it, and escorted to the tent; and she took off the man's clothes which she had worn, and dressed herself in a saree. When she was dressed in it she looked a more lovely woman than she had before looked a handsome man. And she went to the tent leading Parbuttee Bai, while with her came Hera Bai and Tara Bai of more than mortal beauty, and the three other Princesses clothed in the most costly robes. Then before all the Rajahs and Ranees, Seventee Bai knelt down at Logedas Rajah's feet, and said to him, "I am your true wife. O husband, have you forgotten her whom you left in the jungle with Parbuttee Bai twelve years ago? See here she also is; and behold these rich jewels, these tents of gold, these hangings of priceless worth, these elephants, camels, horses, attendants and all this wealth. It is all yours, as I am yours; for I have collected all for you."

Then Logedas Rajah wept for joy, and Siu Rajah arose and kissed Seventee Bai, and said to her, "My noble daughter, you have rescued my son from misery, and done more wisely and well than woman ever did before. May all honor and blessing attend you henceforth and for ever."

And the assembled Rajahs and Ranees were surprised beyond measure, saying, "Did any one ever hear of a woman doing so much?" But more than any was the good Rajah astonished, whom Seventee Bai had served so well for twelve years, and whose daughter she was to have married that day, when he learnt that she was a woman! It was then agreed by all that Logedas Rajah should on that day be newly married to his two wives, Parbuttee Bai and Seventee Bai; and should also marry the six other beautiful Princesses—the Princess Hera Bai, the Princess Tara Bai, the Rajah's little daughter, and the three other Princesses; and that he should return with his father to his own kingdom. And the weddings took place amid great splendor and rejoicings unheard of; and of all the fine things that were seen and done on that day it is impossible to tell. And afterward Logedas Rajah and his eight wives, and his father and mother, and the Wuzeer and his wife, and all their attendants, returned to their own land, where they all lived very happily ever after. And so may all who read this story live happily too.

IV.

TRUTH'S TRIUMPH.

SEVERAL hundred years ago there was a certain Rajah who had twelve wives, but no children, and though he caused many prayers to be said, and presents made in temples far and near, never a son nor a daughter had he. Now this Rajah had a Wuzeer who was a very, very wise old man, and it came to pass that one day, when he was traveling in a distant part of his kingdom, accompanied by this Wuzeer and the rest of his court, he came upon a large garden, in walking round which he was particularly struck by a little tree which grew there. It was a bringal * tree, not above two feet in height. It had no leaves, but on it grew a hundred and one bringals. The Rajah stopped to count them, and then turning to the Wuzeer in great astonishment, said, "It is to me a most unaccountable thing, that this little tree should have no leaves, but a hundred and one bringals growing on it. You are a wise man—can you guess what this means?" The Wuzeer replied, "I can interpret this marvel to you, but if I do, you will most likely not believe me promise therefore that if I tell you, you will not cause me to be killed as having told (as you imagine) a lie."

* *Solanum molengena*—the egg-shaped fruit of which is a favorite vegetable all over India.

The Rajah promised, and the Wuzeer continued: "The meaning of this little bringal tree, with the hundred and one bringals growing on it, is this. Whoever marries the daughter of the Malee in charge of this garden will have a hundred and one chidren—a hundred sons and one daughter." The Rajah said, "Where is the maiden to be seen?" The Wuzeer answered, "When a number of great people like you and all your court come into a little village like this, the poor people, and especially the children, are frightened and run away and hide themselves; therefore, as long as you stay here as Rajah you cannot hope to see her. Your only means will be to send away your suite, and cause it be announced that you have left the place. Then, if you walk daily in this garden, you may some morning meet the pretty Guzra Bai,* of whom I speak."

Upon this advice the Rajah acted; and one day whilst walking in the garden he saw the Malee's young daughter, a girl of twelve years old, busy gathering flowers. He went forward to accost her, but she, seeing that he was not one of the villagers, but a stranger, was shy, and ran home to her father's house.

The Rajah followed, for he was very much struck with her grace and beauty; in fact, he fell in love with her as soon as he saw her, and thought he had never seen a king's daughter half so charming.

When he got to the Malee's house the door was shut; so he called out, "Let me in, good Malee; I am the Rajah, and I wish to marry your daughter." The Malee only laughed, and answered, "A pretty tale to tell a simple man, indeed! You a Rajah! why the

* Flower Girl.

Rajah is miles away. You had better go home, my good fellow, for there's no welcome for you here!" But the Rajah continued calling till the Malee opened the door; who then was indeed surprised, seeing it was truly no other than the Rajah, and he asked what he could do for him.

The Rajah said, "I wish to marry your beautiful daughter, Guzra Bai." "No, no," said the Malee, "this joke wont do. None of your Princes in disguise for me. You may think you are a great Rajah and I only a poor Malee, but I tell you that makes no difference at all to me. Though you were king of all the earth, I would not permit you to come here and amuse yourself chattering to my girl, only to fill her head with nonsense, and to break her heart."

"In truth, good man, you do me wrong," answered the Rajah, humbly: "I mean what I say; I wish to marry your daughter."

"Do not think," retorted the Malee, "that I'll make a fool of myself because I'm only a Malee, and believe what you've got to say, because you're a great Rajah. Rajah or no Rajah is all one to me. If you mean what you say, if you care for my daughter and wish to be married to her, come and be married; but I'll have none of your new-fangled forms and court ceremonies hard to be understood; let the girl be married by her father's hearth and under her father's roof, and let us invite to the wedding our old friends and acquaintance whom we've known all our lives, and before we ever thought of you."

The Rajah was not angry, but amused, and rather pleased than otherwise at the old man's frankness, and he consented to all that was desired.

The village beauty, Guzra Bai, was therefore married with as much pomp as they could muster, but in village fashion, to the great Rajah, who took her home with him, followed by the tears and blessings of her parents and playmates.

The twelve kings' daughters were by no means pleased at this addition to the number of the Ranees; and they agreed amongst themselves that it would be highly derogatory to their dignity to permit Guzra Bai to associate with them, and that the Rajah, their husband, had offered them an unpardonable insult in marrying a Malee's daughter, which was to be revenged upon her the very first opportunity.

Having made this league, they tormented poor Guzra Bai so much that to save her from their persecutions, the Rajah built her a little house of her own, where she lived very, very happily for a short time.

At last one day he had occasion to go and visit a distant part of his dominions, but fearing his high-born wives might ill-use Guzra Bai in his absence, at parting he gave her a little golden bell,* saying, "If while I am away you are in any trouble, or any one should be unkind to you, ring this little bell, and wherever I am I shall instantly hear it, and will return to your aid."

No sooner had the Rajah gone, than Guzra Bai thought she would try the power of the bell. So she rang it. The Rajah instantly appeared. "What do you want?" he said. "Oh, nothing," she replied. "I was foolish. I could hardly believe what you told me

* "It must have been a kind of telegraph to go so quick." my Narrator said.

could be true, and thought I would try." "Now you will believe, I hope," he said, and went away. A second time she rang the bell. Again the Rajah returned. "Oh, pardon me, husband," she said; "it was wrong of me not to trust you, but I hardly thought you could return again from so far." "Never mind," he said, "only do not try the experiment again." And again he went away. A third time she rang the golden bell. "Why do you ring again, Guzra Bai?" asked the Rajah sternly, as for a third time he returned. "I don't know, indeed; indeed I beg your pardon," she said; "but I know not why, I felt so frightened." "Have any of the Ranees been unkind to you?" he asked. "No, none," she answered; "in fact, I have seen none of them." "You are a silly child," said he, stroking her hair. "Affairs of the state call me away. You must try and keep a good heart till my return;" and for the fourth time he disappeared.

A little while after this, wonderful to relate, Guzra Bai had a hundred and one children!—a hundred boys and one girl. When the Ranees heard this, they said to each other, "Guzra Bai, the Malee's daughter, will rank higher than us; she will have great power and influence as mother to the heir to the Raj;* let us kill these children, and tell our husband that she is a sorceress; then will he love her no longer, and his old affection for us will return." So these twelve wicked Ranees all went over to Guzra Bai's house. When Guzra Bai saw them coming, she feared they meant to do her some harm, so she seized her little golden bell, and rang, and rang, and rang—but no Rajah came. She had called him back so often that he did not be-

* Kingdom.

lieve she really needed his help. And thus the poor woman was left to the mercy of her implacable enemies.

Now the nurse who had charge of the hundred and one babies was an old servant of the twelve Ranees, and moreover a very wicked woman, able and willing to do whatever her twelve wicked old mistresses ordered. So when they said to her, "Can you kill these children?" she answered, "Nothing is easier; I will throw them out upon the dust-heap behind the palace, where the rats and hawks and vultures will have left none of them remaining by to-morrow morning. "So be it," said the Ranees. Then the nurse took the hundred and one little innocent children—the hundred little boys and the one little girl—and threw them behind the palace on the dust-heap, close to some large rat-holes; and after that, she and the twelve Ranees placed a very large stone in each of the babies' cradles, and said to Guzra Bai, "Oh, you evil witch in disguise, do not hope any longer to impose by your arts on the Rajah's credulity. See, your children have all turned into stones. See these, your pretty babies!"—and with that they tumbled the hundred and one stones down in a great heap on the floor. Then Guzra Bai began to cry, for she knew it was not true; but what could one poor woman do against thirteen? At the Rajah's return the twelve Ranees accused Guzra Bai of being a witch, and the nurse testified that the hundred and one children she had charge of had turned into stones, and the Rajah believed them rather than Guzra Bai, and he ordered her to be imprisoned for life.

Meanwhile a Bandicote* had heard the pitiful cries

* A species of large rat.

of the children, and taking pity on them, dragged them all, one by one, into her hole, out of the way of kites and vultures. She then assembled all the Bandicotes from far and near, and told them what she had done, begging them to assist in finding food for the children. Then every day a hundred and one Bandicotes would come, each bringing a little bit of food in his mouth, and give it to one of the children; and so day by day they grew stronger and stronger, until they were able to run about, and then they used to play of a morning at the mouth of the Bandicote's hole, running in there to sleep every night. But one fine day who should come by but the wicked old nurse! Fortunately, all the boys were in the hole, and the little girl, who was playing outside, on seeing her ran in there too, but not before the nurse had seen her. She immediately went to the twelve Ranees and related this, saying, "I cannot help thinking some of the children may still be living in those rat-holes. You had better send and have them dug out and killed." "We dare not do that," answered they, "for fear of causing suspicion; but we will order some laborers to dig up that ground and make it into a field, and that will effectually smother any of the children who may still be alive." This plan was approved and forthwith carried into execution; but the good Bandicote, who happened that day to be out on a foraging expedition in the palace, heard all about it there, and immediately running home, took all the children from her hole to a large well some distance off, where she hid them in the hollows behind the steps leading down to the well, laying one child under each step.

Here they would have been quite safe, had not the

Dhobee* happened to go down to the well that day to wash some clothes, taking with him his little girl. While her father was drawing up water, the child amused herself running up and down the steps of the well. Now each time her weight pressed down a step it gave the child hidden underneath a little squeeze. All the hundred boys bore this without uttering a sound; but when the Dhobee's child trod on the step under which the little girl was hidden, she cried out, "How can you be so cruel to me, trampling on me in this way? Have pity on me, for I am a little girl as well as you."

When the child heard these words proceeding from the stone, she ran in great alarm to her father, saying, "Father, I don't know what's the matter, but something alive is certainly under those stones. I heard it speak; but whether it is a Rakshas or an angel or a human being I cannot tell." Then the Dhobee went to the twelve Ranees to tell them the wonderful news about the voice in the well; and they said to each other, "Maybe it's some of Guzra Bai's children; let us send and have this inquired into." So they sent some people to pull down the well and see if some evil spirits were not there.

Then laborers went to pull down the well. Now close to the well was a little temple dedicated to Gunputti, containing a small shrine and a little clay image of the god. When the children felt the well being pulled down they called out for help and protection to Gunputti, who took pity on them and changed them into trees growing by his temple—a hundred little mango trees all round in a circle (which were the hun-

* Washerman.

dred little boys), and a little rose bush in the middle, covered with red and white roses, which was the little girl.

The laborers pulled down the well, but they found nothing there but a poor old Bandicote, which they killed. Then, by order of the twelve wicked Ranees, the sacrilegiously destroyed the little temple. But they found no children there either. However, the Dhobee's mischievous little daughter had gone with her father to witness the work of destruction, and as they were looking on, she said, "Father, do look at all those funny little trees; I never remember noticing them here before." And being very inquisitive, she started off to have a nearer look at them. There in a circle grew the hundred little mango trees, and in the centre of all the little rose bush, bearing the red and white roses.

The girl rushed by the mango trees, who uttered no words, and running up to the rose bush, began gathering some of the flowers. At this the rose bush trembled very much, and sighed and said, "I am a little girl as well as you; how can you be so cruel? You are breaking all my ribs." Then the child ran back to her father and said, "Come and listen to what the rose bush says." And the father repeated the news to the twelve Ranees, who ordered that a great fire should be made, and the hundred and one little trees be burnt in it, root and branch, till not a stick remained.

The fire was made, and the hundred and one little trees were dug up and just going to be put into it, when Gunputti, taking pity on them, caused a tremendous storm to come on, which put out the fire and flooded the country and swept the hundred and one trees into the river, where they were carried down a long, long way by the torrent, until at last the children were landed, restored to their own shapes, on the river bank, in the midst of a wild jungle, very far from any human habitation.

Here these children lived for ten years, happy in their mutual love and affection. Generally every day fifty of the boys would go out to collect roots and berries for their food, leaving fifty at home to take care of their little sister: but sometimes they put her in some safe place, and all would go out together for the day; nor were they ever molested in their excursions by bear, panther, snake, scorpion, or other noxious creature. One day all the brothers put their little sister safely up in a fine shady tree, and went out together to hunt. After rambling on for some time, they came to the hut of a savage Rakshas, who in the disguise of an old woman had lived for many years in the jungle. The Rakshas, angry at this invasion of her domain, no sooner saw them than she changed them all into crows. Night came on, and their little sister was anxiously awaiting her brothers' return, when on a sudden she heard a loud whirring sound in the air, and round the tree flocked a hundred black crows, cawing and offering her berries and roots which they had dug up with their sharp bills. Then the little sister guessed too truly what must have happened—that some malignant spirit had metamorphosed her brothers into this hideous shape; and at the sad sight she began to cry.

Time wore on; every morning the crows flew away to collect food for her and for themselves, and every evening they returned to roost in the branches of the high tree where she sat the livelong day, crying as if her heart would break.

At last so many bitter tears had she shed that they made a little stream which flowed from the foot of the tree right down through the jungle.

Some months after this, one fine day, a young Rajah from a neighboring country happened to be hunting in this very jungle; but he had not been very successful. Toward the close of the day he found himself faint and weary, having missed his way and lost his comrades, with no companion save his dogs, who, being thirsty, ran hurriedly hither and thither in search of water. After some time, they saw in the distance what looked like a clear stream: the dogs rushed there and the tired prince, following them, flung himself down on the grass by the water's brink, thinking to sleep there for the night; and, with his hands under his head, stared up into the leafy branches of the tree above him. Great was his astonishment to see high up in the air an immense number of crows, and above them all a most lovely young girl, who was feeding them with berries and wild fruits. Quick as thought, he climbed the tree, and bringing her carefully and gently down, seated her on the grass beside him, saying, "Tell me, pretty lady, who you are, and how you come to be living in this dreary palace?" So she told him all her adventures, except that she did not say the hundred crows were her hundred brothers. Then the Rajah said, "Do not cry any more, fair Princess; you shall come home with me and be my Ranee, and my father and mother shall be yours." At this she smiled and dried her eyes, but quickly added, "You will let me take these crows with me, will you not? for I love them dearly, and I cannot go away unless they may come too." "To be sure," he answered. "You may bring all the animals in the jungle with you, if you like, so you will only come."

So he took her home to his father's house, and the old Rajah and Ranee wondered much at this jungle Lady, when they saw her rare beauty, her modest gentle ways and her queenly grace. Then the young Rajah told them how she was a persecuted Princess, and asked their leave to marry her; and because her loving goodness had won all hearts, they gave their consent as joyfully as if she had been daughter of the greatest of Rajahs, and brought with her a splendid dower; and they called her Draupadi Bai.*

Draupadi had some beautiful trees planted in front of her palace, in which the crows, her brothers, used to live, and she daily with her own hands boiled a quantity of rice, which she would scatter for them to eat as they flocked around her. Now some time after this, Draupadi Bai had a son, who was called Ramchundra. He was a very good boy, and his mother Draupadi Bai used to take him to school every morning, and go and fetch him home in the evening. But one day, when Ramchundra was about fourteen years old, it happened that Draupadi Bai did not go to fetch him home from school as she was wont; and on his return he found her sitting under the trees in front of her palace, stroking the glossy black crows that flocked around her, and weeping.

Then Ramchundra threw down his bundle of books, and said to his mother, putting his elbows on her knees, and looking up in her face, "Mammy, dear, tell me

* Doubtless after the beautiful Princess Draupadi, daughter of the Rajah of Panchala, and a famous character in the great Hindoo epic, the "Maha Bharata."

why you are now crying, and what it is that makes you so often sad." "Oh, nothing, nothing," she answered. "Yes, dear mother," said he, "do tell me. Can I help you? If I can, I will." Draupadi Bai shook her head. "Alas, no, my son," she said; "you are too young to help me; and as for my grief, I have never told it to any one. I cannot tell it to you now." But Ramchundra continued begging and praying her to tell him, until at last she did; relating to him all her own and his uncles' sad history; and lastly, how they had been changed by a Rakshas into the black crows he saw around him. Then the boy sprang up and said, "Which way did your brothers take when they met the Rakshas?" "How can I tell?" she asked. "Why," he answered, "I thought perhaps you might remember on which side they returned that first night to you, after being bewitched?" "Oh," she said, "they came toward the tree from that part of the jungle which lies in a straight line behind the palace." "Very well," cried Ramchundra, joyfully, "I also will go there, and find out this wicked old Rakshas, and learn by what means they may be disenchanted." "No, no, my son," she answered, "I cannot let you go: see, I have lost father and mother, and these my hundred brothers; and now, if you fall into the Rakshas' clutches as well as they, and are lost to me, what will life have worth living for?" To this he replied, "Do not fear for me, mother; I will be wary and discreet." And going to his father, he said, "Father, it is time I should see something of the world. I beg you to permit me to travel and see other lands." The Rajah answered, "You shall go. Tell me what attendants you would like to accompany you?" "Give me," said Ramchundra, "a horse to ride, and a groom to take care of it." The Rajah consented, and Ramchundra set off riding toward the jungle; but as soon as he got there, he sent his horse back by the groom with a message to his parents, and proceeded alone, on foot.

After wandering about for some time he came upon a small hut, in which lay an ugly old woman fast asleep. She had long claws instead of hands, and her hair hung down all around her in a thick black tangle. Ramchundra knew, by the whole appearance of the place, that he must have reached the Rakshas' abode of which he was in search; so, stealing softly in, he sat down and began shampooing her head. At last the Rakshas woke up. "You dear little boy," she said, "do not be afraid; I am only a poor old woman, and will not hurt you. Stay with me, and you shall be my servant." This she said not from any feeling of kindness or pity for Ramchundra, but merely because she thought he might be helpful to her. So the young Rajah remained in her service, determining to stay there till he should have learnt from her all that he wished to know.

Thus one day he said to her, "Good mother, what is the use of all those little jars of water you have arranged round your house?" She answered, "That water possesses certain magical attributes: if any of it is sprinkled on people enchanted by me, they instantly resume their former shape." "And what," he continued, "is the use of your wand?" "That," she replied, "has many supernatural powers: for instance, by simply uttering your wish and waving it in the air, you can conjure up a mountain, a river or a forest in a moment of time."

Another day Ramchundra said to her, "Your hair, good mother, is dreadfully tangled; pray let me comb it." "No," she said, "you must not touch my hair; it would be dangerous; for every hair has power to set the jungle on fire." "How is that?" he asked. She replied, "The least fragment of my hair thrown in the direction of the jungle would instantly set it in a blaze." Having learnt all this, one day when it was very hot, and the old Rakshas was drowsy, Ramchundra begged leave to shampoo her head, which speedily sent her to sleep; then, gently pulling out two or three of her hairs, he got up, and taking in one hand her wand, and in the other two jars of the magic water, he stealthily left the hut; but he had not gone far before she woke up, and instantly divining what he had done, pursued him with great rapidity. Ramchundra, looking back and perceiving that she was gaining upon him, waved the enchanted wand and created a great river, which suddenly rolled its tumultuous waves between them; but, quick as thought, the Rakshas swam the river.

Then he turned, and waving the wand again, caused a high mountain to rise between them; but the Rakshas climbed the mountain. Nearer she came, and yet nearer; each time he turned to use the wand and put obstacles in her way, the delay gave her a few minutes' advantage, so that he lost almost as much as he gained. Then, as a last resource, he scattered the hairs he had stolen to the winds, and instantly the jungle on the hill side, through which the Rakshas was coming, was set in a blaze; the fire rose higher and higher, the wicked old Rakshas was consumed by the flames, and Ramchundra pursued his journey in safety until he reached his father's palace. Draupadi Bai was overjoyed to see her son again, and he led her out into the garden, and scattered the magic water on the hundred black crows, which instantly recovered their human forms, and stood up one hundred fine, handsome young men.

Then were there rejoicings throughout the country, because the Ranee's brothers had been disenchanted; and the Rajah sent out into all neighboring lands to invite their Rajahs and Ranees to a great feast in honor of his brothers-in-law.

Among others who came to the feast was the Rajah Draupadi Bai's father, and the twelve wicked Ranees his wives.

When they were all assembled, Draupadi arose, and said to him, "Noble sir, we had looked to see your wife Guzra Bai with you. Pray you tell us wherefore she has not accompanied you." The Rajah was much surprised to learn that Draupadi Bai knew anything about Guzra Bai, and he said, "Speak not of her: she is a wicked woman; it is fit that she should end her days in prison." But Draupadi Bai and her husband, and her hundred brothers, rose and said, "We require, O Rajah, that you send home instantly and fetch hither that much injured lady, which, if you refuse to do, your wives shall be imprisoned, and you ignominiously expelled this kingdom."

The Rajah could not guess what the meaning of this was, and thought they merely wished to pick a quarrel with him: but not much caring whether Guzra Bai came or not, he sent for her as was desired. When she arrived, her daughter Draupadi Bai, and her hundred sons, with Draupadi Bai's husband and the young Ramchundra, went out to the gate to meet her, and conducted her into the palace with all honor. Then, standing around her, they turned to the Rajah her husband, and related to him the story of their lives; how that they were his children, and Guzra Bai their mother; how she had been cruelly calumniated by the twelve wicked Ranees, and they in constant peril of their lives; but having miraculously escaped many terrible dangers, still lived to pay him duteous service and to cheer and support his old age.

At this news the whole company was very much astonished. The Rajah, overjoyed, embraced his wife Guzra Bai, and it was agreed that she and their hundred sons should return with him to his own land, which accordingly was done. Ramchundra lived very happily with his father and mother to the day of their death, when he ascended the throne, and became a very popular Rajah; and the twelve wicked old Ranees, who had conspired against Guzra Bai and her children, were, by order of the Rajah, burnt to death. Thus truth triumphed in the end; but so unequally is human justice meted out that the old nurse, who worked their evil will, and was in fact the most guilty wretch of all, is said to have lived unpunished, to have died in the bosom of her family, and to have had as big a funeral pile as any virtuous Hindoo.

V.

RAMA AND LUXMAN; OR, THE LEARNED OWL.

"With a lengthened loud halloo,
Tuwhoo, tuwhit, tuwhit, tuwhoo."

ONCE upon a time there was a Rajah whose name was Chandra Rajah,* and he had a learned Wuzeer or Minister, named Butti. Their mutual love was so great that they were more like brothers than master and servant. Neither the Rajah nor the Wuzeer had any children, and both were equally anxious to have a son. At last, in one day and one hour, the wife of the Rajah and the wife of the Wuzeer had each a little baby boy. They named the Rajah's son Rama, and the son of the Wuzeer was called Luxman, and there were great rejoicings at the birth of both. The boys grew up and loved each other tenderly: they were never happy unless together; together they went to daily school, together bathed and played, and they would not eat except from off one plate. One day, when Rama Rajah was fifteen years old, his mother, the Rance, said to Chandra Rajah: "Husband, our son associates too much with low people; for instance, he is always at play with the Wuzeer's son, Luxman, which is not befitting his rank. I wish you would

* Moon-King.

endeavor to put an end to their friendship, and find him better playmates."

Chandra Rajah replied, "I cannot do it: Luxman's father is my very good friend and Wuzeer, as his father's father was to my father; let the sons be the same." This answer annoyed the Ranee, but she said no more to her husband; she sent, however, for all the wise people, and seers, and conjurors in the land, and inquired of them whether there existed no means of dissolving the children's affection for each other; they answered they knew of none. At last one old Nautch* woman came to the Ranee and said, "I can do this thing you wish, but for it you must give me a great reward." Then the Ranee gave the old woman an enormous bag full of gold mohurs,† and said, "This I give you now, and if you succeed in the undertaking I will give you as much again." So this wicked old woman disguised herself in a very rich dress, and went to a garden-house which Chandra Rajah had built for his son, and where Rama Rajah and Luxman, the young Wuzeer, used to spend the greater part of their playtime. Outside the house was a large well and a fine garden. When the old woman arrived, the two boys were playing cards together in the garden close to the well. She drew near, and began drawing water from it. Rama Rajah looking up, saw her, and said to Luxman, "Go, see who that richly-dressed woman is, and bring me word." The Wuzeer's son did as he was bidden, and asked the woman what she wanted. She answered, "Nothing, oh nothing," and nodding her head went away; then, returning to the Ranee,

* The caste to which conjurors belong.

† Gold pieces, worth about $7.50.

she said, "I have done as you wished; give me the promised reward," and the Ranee gave her the second bag of gold. On Luxman's return, the young Rajah said to him, "What did the woman want?" Luxman answered, "She told me she wanted nothing." "It is not true," replied the other, angrily; "I feel certain she must have told you something. Why should she come here for no purpose? It is some secret which you are concealing from me; I insist on knowing it." Luxman vainly protesting his innocence, they quarreled and then fought, and the young Rajah ran home very angry to his father. "What is the matter, my son?" said he. "Father," he answered, "I am angry with the Wuzeer's son. I hate that boy; kill him, and let his eyes be brought to me in proof of his death, or I will not eat my dinner." Chandra Rajah was very much grieved at this, but the young Rajah would eat no dinner, and at last his father said to the Wuzeer, "Take your son away and hide him, for the boys have had a quarrel." Then he went out and shot a deer, and showing its eyes to Rama, said to him, "See, my son, the good Wuzeer's son has by your order been deprived of life," and Rama Rajah was merry, and ate his dinner. But a while after he began to miss his kind playmate; there was nobody he cared for to tell him stories and amuse him. Then for four nights running he dreamed of a beautiful Glass Palace, in which dwelt a Princess white as marble, and he sent for all the wise people in the kingdom to interpret his dream, but none could do it; and, thinking upon this fair princess and his lost friend, he got more and more sad, and said to himself: "There is nobody to help me in this matter. Ah! if my Wuzeer's son were here now, how quickly would he interpret the dream! Oh, my friend, my friend, my dear lost friend!" and when Chandra Rajah, his father, came in, he said to him: "Show me the grave of Luxman, son of the Wuzeer, that I also may die there." His father replied, "What a foolish boy you are! You first begged that the Wuzeer's son might be killed, and now you want to die on his grave. What is all this about?" Rama Rajah replied, "Oh, why did you give the order for him to be put to death? In him I have lost my friend and all my joy in life; show me now his grave, for thereon, I swear, will I kill myself." When the Rajah saw that his son really grieved for the loss of Luxman, he said to him, "You have to thank me for not regarding your foolish wishes; your old playmate is living, therefore be friends again, for what you thought were his eyes were but the eyes of a deer." So the friendship of Rama and Luxman was resumed on its former footing. Then Rama said to Luxman, "Four nights ago I dreamed a strange dream. I thought that for miles and miles I wandered through a dense jungle, after which I came upon a grove of Cocoa-nut trees, passing through which I reached one compound entirely of Guava trees, then one of Soparee* trees, and lastly one of Copal trees: beyond this lay a garden of flowers, of which the Malee's wife gave me a bunch; round the garden ran a large river, and on the other side of this I saw a fair palace composed of transparent glass, and in the centre of it sat the most lovely Princess I ever saw, white as marble and covered with rich jewels; at the sight of her beauty I fainted—and so awoke. This has happened now four times, and as yet I have found no one capable of throwing

* *Areca catechu*—the betel-nut palm.

any light on the vision." Luxman answered, "I can tell you. There exists a Princess exactly like her you saw in your dreams, and, if you like, you can go and marry her." "How can I?" said Rama; "and what is your interpretation of the dream?" The Wuzeer's son replied, "Listen to me, and I will tell you. In a country very far away from this, in the centre of a great Rajah's kingdom, there dwells his daughter, a most fair Princess; she lives in a glass palace. Round this palace runs a large river, and round the river is a garden of flowers. Round the garden are four thick groves of trees—one of Copal trees, one of Soparee trees, one of Guava trees, and one of Cocoa-nut trees. The Princess is twenty-four years old, but she is not married, for she has determined only to marry whoever can jump this river and greet her in her crystal palace, and though many thousand kings have essayed to do so, they have all perished miserably in the attempt, having either been drowned in the river, or broken their necks by falling; thus all that you dreamed of is perfectly true." "Can we go to this country?" asked the young Rajah. "Oh, yes," his friend replied. "This is what you must do. Go tell your father you wish to see the world. Ask him for neither elephants nor attendants, but beg him to lend you for the journey his old war-horse."

Upon this Rama went to his father, and said, "Father, I pray you give me leave to go and travel with the Wuzeer's son. I desire to see the world." "What would you have for the journey, my son?" said Chandra Rajah; "will you have elephants and how many?—attendants, how many?" "Neither, father," he answered, "give me rather, I pray you, your old war-horse, that I may ride him during the journey."

"So be it, my son," he answered, and with that Rama Rajah and Luxman set forth on their travels. After going many, many thousands of miles, to their joy one day they come upon a dense grove of Cocoa-nut trees, and beyond that to a grove of Guava trees, then to one of Soparee trees, and lastly to one of Copal trees; after which they entered a beautiful garden, where the Malee's wife presented them with a large bunch of flowers. Then they knew that they had nearly reached the place where the fair Princess dwelt. Now it happened that, because many kings and great people had been drowned in trying to jump over the river that ran round the Glass Palace where the Princess lived, the Rajah, her father, had made a law that, in future, no aspirants to her hand were to attempt the jump, except at stated times and with his knowledge and permission, and that any Rajahs or Princes found wandering there, contrary to this law, were to be imprisoned. Of this the young Rajah and the Wuzeer's son knew nothing, and having reached the centre of the garden they found themselves on the banks of a large river, exactly opposite the wondrous Glass Palace, and were just debating what further steps to take, when they were seized by the Rajah's guard, and hurried off to prison.

"This is a hard fate," said Luxman. "Yes," sighed Rama Rajah; "a dismal end, in truth, to all our fine schemes. Would it be possible, think you, to escape?" "I think so," answered Luxman; "at all events, I will try." With that he turned to the sentry who was guarding them, and said, "We are shut in here and can't get out: here is money for you if you will only have the goodness to call out that the Malee's Cow has strayed away." The sentry thought this a very easy way of making a fortune; so he called out as he was bidden, and took the money. The result answered Luxman's anticipations. The Malee's wife, hearing the sentry calling out, thought to herself, "What, sentries round the guard-room again! then there must be prisoners; doubtless they are those two young Rajahs I met in the garden this morning; at least, I will endeavor to release them." So she asked two old beggars to accompany her, and taking with her offerings of flowers and sweetmeats, started as if to go to a little temple which was built within the quadrangle where the prisoners were kept. The sentries, thinking she was only going with two old friends to visit the temple, allowed her to pass without opposition. As soon as she got within the quadrangle she unfastened the prison door, and told the two young men (Rama Rajah and Luxman) to change clothes with the two old beggars, which they instantly did. Then, leaving the beggars in the cell, she conducted Rama and Luxman safely to her house. When they had reached it she said to them, "Young Princes, you must know that you did very wrong in going down to the river before having made a salaam to our Rajah, and gained his consent; and so strict is the law on the subject that had I not assisted your escape, you might have remained a long time in prison; though, as I felt certain you only erred through ignorance, I was the more willing to help you; but to-morrow morning early you must go and pay your respects at court."

Next day the guards brought their two prisoners to the Rajah, saying; "See, O King, here are two young Rajahs whom we caught last night wandering near the river contrary to your law and commandment." But when they came to look at the prisoners, lo and behold! they were only two old beggars whom everybody knew and had often seen at the palace gate.

Then the Rajah laughed and said, "You stupid fellows, you have been over vigilant for once; see here your fine young Rajahs. Don't you yet know the looks of these old beggars?" Whereupon the guards went away much ashamed of themselves.

Having learnt discretion from the advice of the Malee's wife, Rama and Luxman went betimes that morning to call at the Rajah's palace. The Rajah received them very graciously, but when he heard the object of the journey he shook his head, and said, "My pretty fellows, far be it from me to thwart your intentions, if you are really determined to strive to win my daughter, the Princess Bargaruttee;* but as a friend I would counsel you to desist from the attempt. You can find a hundred Princesses elsewhere willing to marry you; why, therefore, come here, where already a thousand Princes as fair as you have lost there lives? Cease to think of my daughter—she is a headstrong girl." But Rama Rajah still declared himself anxious to try and jump the dangerous river, whereupon the Rajah unwillingly consented to his attempting to do so, and caused it to be solemnly proclaimed around the town that another Prince was going to risk his life, begging all good men and true to pray for his success. Then Rama, having dressed gorgeously, and mounted his father's stout war-horse, put spurs to it and galloped to the river. Up, up in the air, like a bird, jumped the good war-horse, right across the river and into the very centre courtyard of the Glass Palace of the Princess

* A name of the Ganges.

Bargaruttee; and, as if ashamed of so poor an exploit, this feat he accomplished three times. At this the heart of the Rajah was glad, and he ran and patted the brave horse, and kissed Rama Rajah, and said, "Welcome, my son-in-law." The wedding took place amid great rejoicings, with feasts, illuminations and much giving of presents, and there Rama Rajah and his wife, the Ranee Bargaruttee, lived happily for some time. At last, one day Rama Rajah said to his father-in-law, "Sire, I have been very happy here, but I have a great desire to see my father and my mother, and my own land again." To which the Rajah replied, "My son, you are free to go; but I have no son but you, nor daughter but your wife: therefore, as it grieves me to lose sight of you, come back now and then to see me and rejoice my heart. My doors are ever open to you; you will be always welcome."

Rama Rajah promised to return occasionally; and then, being given many rich gifts by the old Rajah, and supplied with all things needful for the journey, he, with his beautiful wife Bargaruttee, his friend the young Wuzeer, and a great retinue, set out to return home. Before going, Rama Rajah and Luxman richly rewarded the kind Malee's wife, who had helped them so ably. On the first evening of their march the travelers reach the borders of the Cocoa-nut grove, on the outskirts of the jungle; here they determined to halt and rest for the night. Rama Rajah and the Ranee Bargaruttee went to their tent; but Luxman (whose tender love for them was so great that he usually watched all night through at their door), was sitting under a large tree close by, when two little owls flew over his head, and perching on one of the highest branches, began chattering to each other.* The Wuzeer's son, who was in many ways wiser than most men, could understand their language. To his surprise he heard the little lady owl say to her husband, "I wish you would tell me a story, my dear, it is such a long time since I have heard one." To which her husband, the other little owl, answered, "A story! what story can I tell you? Do you see these people encamped under our tree? Would you like to hear their story?" She assented; and he began: "See first this poor Wuzeer; he is a good and faithful man, and has done much for this young Rajah, but neither has that been to his advantage heretofore, nor will it be hereafter." At this Luxman listened more attentively, and taking out his writing tablets determined to note down all he heard. The little owl commenced with the story of the birth of Rama and Luxman, of their friendship, their quarrel, the young Rajah's dream, and their reconciliation, and then told of their subsequent adventures in search of the Princess Bargaruttee, down to that very day on which they were journeying home. "And what more has Fate in store for this poor Wuzeer?" asked the lady owl. "From this place," replied her husband, "he will journey on with the young Rajah and Ranee, until they get very near Chandra Rajah's dominions; there, as the whole cavalcade is about to pass under a large Banyan tree, this Wuzeer Luxman will notice some of the topmost branches swaying about in a dangerous manner; he will hurry the Rajah and Ranee away from it, and the tree (which would otherwise have inevitably killed them,) will fall to the ground with a tremendous crash;

* See Notes at the end.

but even his having thus saved the Rajah's life shall not avert his fate." (All this the Wuzeer noted down.) "And what next?" said the wife, "what next?" "Next," continued the wise little story-teller, "next, just as the Rajah Rama and the Ranee Bargaruttee and all their suite are passing under the palace doorway, the Wuzeer will notice that the arch is insecure, and by dragging them quickly through, prevent their being crushed in its fall." "And what will he do after that, dear husband?" she asked. "After that," he went on, "when the Rajah and Ranee are asleep, and the Wuzeer Luxman keeping guard over them, he will perceive a large cobra slowly crawling down the wall and drawing nearer and nearer to the Ranee. He will kill it with his sword, but a drop of the cobra's blood shall fall on the Ranee's white forehead. The Wuzeer will not dare to wipe the blood off her forehead with his hand, but shall instead cover his face with a cloth that he may lick it off with his tongue; but for this the Rajah will be angry with him, and his reproaches will turn this poor Wuzeer into stone."

"Will he always remain stone?" asked the lady owl. "Not for ever," answered the husband, "but for eight long years he will remain so." "And what then?" demanded she. "Then," answered the other, "when the young Rajah and Ranee have a baby, it shall come to pass that one day the child shall be playing on the floor, and to help itself along shall clasp hold of the stony figure, and at that baby's touch the Wuzeer will come to life again. But I have told you enough for one night; come, let's catch mice—tuwhit, tuwhoo, tuwhoo," and away flew the owls. Luxman had written down all he heard, and it made him heavy-hearted, but he thought, "Perhaps, after all, this may not be true." So he said nothing about it to any living soul. Next day they continued their journey, and as the owl had prophesied, so events fell out. For, as the whole party were passing under a large Banyan tree, the Wuzeer noticed that it looked unsafe. "The owl spake truly," he thought to himself, and, seizing the Rajah and Ranee, he hurried them from under it, just as a huge limb of the tree fell prone with a fearful crash.

A little while after, having reached Chandra Rajah's dominions, they were just going under the great arch of the palace court-yard, when the Wuzeer noticed some of the stones tottering. "The owl was a true prophet," thought he again, and catching hold of the hands of Rama Rajah and Bargaruttee Ranee, he pulled them rapidly through, just in time to save their lives. "Pardon me," he said to the Rajah, "that unbidden I dared thus to touch your hand and that of the Ranee, but I saw the danger imminent." So they reached home, where they were joyfully welcomed by Chandra Rajah, the Ranee, the Wuzeer (Luxman's father), and all the court.

A few nights afterward, when the Rajah and Ranee were asleep, and the young Wuzeer keeping guard over them as he was wont, he saw a large black cobra stealthily creeping down the wall just above the Ranee's head. "Alas!" he thought, "then such is my fate, and so it must be; nevertheless, I will do my duty," and, taking from the folds of his dress the history of his and the young Rajah's life, from their boyhood down to that very time (as he had written it from the owl's narrative), he laid it beside the sleeping Rama, and drawing his sword, killed the cobra. A few drops of the serpent's blood fell on the Ranee's forehead: the Wuzeer did not dare to touch it with his hand, but, that her sacred brow might not be defiled with the vile cobra's blood, he reverently covered his face and mouth with a cloth to lick the drops of blood away. At this moment the Rajah started up, and seeing him, said: "O Wuzeer, Wuzeer, is this well done of you? O Luxman, who have been to me as a brother, who have saved me from so many difficulties, why do you treat me thus, to kiss her holy forehead? If indeed you loved her (as who could help it?), could you not have told me when we first saw her in that Glass Palace, and I would have exiled myself that she might be your wife? O my brother, my brother, why did you mock me thus?" The Rajah had buried his face in his hands; he looked up, he turned to the Wuzeer, but from him came neither answer nor reply. He had become a senseless stone. Then Rama for the first time perceived the roll of paper which Luxman had laid beside him, and when he read in it of what Luxman had been to him from boyhood, and of the end, his bitter grief broke through all bounds; and, falling at the feet of the statue, he clasped its stony knees and wept aloud. When daylight dawned, Chandra Rajah and the Ranee found Rama still weeping and hugging the stone, asking its forgiveness with penitent cries and tears. Then they said to him, "What is this you have done?" When he told them, the Rajah his father was very angry, and said: "Was it not enough that you should have once before unjustly desired the death of this good man, but that now by your rash reproaches you should have turned him into stone? Go to; you do but continually what is evil."

Now eight long years rolled by without the Wuzeer returning to his original form, although every day Rama Rajah and Bargaruttee Ranee would watch beside him, kissing his cold hands, and adjuring him by all endearing names to forgive them and return to them again. When eight years had expired, Rama and Bargaruttee had a child; and from the time it was nine months old and first began to try and crawl about, the father and mother would sit and watch beside it, placing it near the Wuzeer's statue, in hopes that the baby would some day touch it as the owl had foretold.

But for three months they watched in vain. At last, one day when the child was a year old, and was trying to walk, it chanced to be close to the statue, and tottering on its unsteady feet, stretched out its tiny hands and caught hold of the foot of the statue. The Wuzeer instantly came back to life, and stooping down seized the little baby who had rescued him in his arms, and kissed it. It is impossible to describe the delight of Rama Rajah and his wife at regaining their long-lost friend. The old Rajah and Ranee rejoiced also, with the Wuzeer (Luxman Wuzeer's father), and his mother.

Then Chandra Rajah said to the Wuzeer: "Here is my boy happy with his wife and child, while your son has neither; go fetch him a wife, and we will have a right merry wedding."

So the Wuzeer of the Rajah fetched for his son a kind and beautiful wife, and Chandra Rajah and Rama Rajah caused the wedding of Luxman to be grander than that of any great Rajah before or since, even as if he had been a son of the royal house; and they all lived very happy ever after, as all good fathers, and mothers, and husbands, and wives, and children do.

VI.

LITTLE SURYA BAI.

A POOR Milkwoman was once going into the town with cans full of milk to sell. She took with her her little daughter (a baby of about a year old), having no one in whose charge to leave her at home. Being tired, she sat down by the road-side, placing the child and the cans full of milk beside her; when, on a sudden, two large eagles flew over-head; and one, swooping down, seized the child, and flew away with her out of the mother's sight.

Very far, far away the eagles carried the little baby, even beyond the borders of her native land, until they reached their home in a lofty tree. There the old eagles had built a great nest; it was made of iron and wood, and was as big as a little house; there was iron all round, and to get in and out you had to go through seven iron doors.

In this stronghold they placed the little baby, and because she was like a young eaglet they called her Surya Bai (the Sun Lady). The eagles both loved the child; and daily they flew into distant countries to bring her rich and precious things—clothes that had been made for princesses, precious jewels, wonderful playthings, all that was most costly and rare.

One day, when Surya Bai was twelve years old, the

old husband Eagle said to his wife, "Wife, our daughter has no diamond ring on her little finger, such as princesses wear; let us go and fetch her one." "Yes," said the other old Eagle; "but to fetch it we must go very far." "True," rejoined he, "such a ring is not to be got nearer than the Red Sea, and that is a twelvemonth's journey from here; nevertheless we will go." So the Eagles started off, leaving Surya Bai in the strong nest, with twelve months' provisions (that she might not be hungry whilst they were away), and a little dog and cat to take care of her.

Not long after they were gone, one day the naughty little cat stole some food from the store, for doing which Surya Bai punished her. The cat did not like being whipped, and she was still more annoyed at having been caught stealing; so, in revenge, she ran to the fireplace (they were obliged to keep a fire always burning in the Eagle's nest, as Surya Bai never went down from the tree, and would not otherwise have been able to cook her dinner), and put out the fire. When the little girl saw this she was much vexed, for the cat had eaten their last cooked provisions, and she did not know what they were to do for food. For three whole days Surya Bai puzzled over the difficulty, and for three whole days she and the dog and the cat had nothing to eat. At last she thought she would climb to the edge of the nest, and see if she could see any fire in the country below; and, if so, she would go down and ask the people who lighted it to give her a little with which to cook her dinner. So she climbed to the edge of the nest. Then, very far away on the horizon, she saw a thin curl of blue smoke. So she let herself down from the tree, and all day long she walked in the direction whence the smoke came. Toward evening she reached the place, and found it rose from a small hut in which sat an old woman warming her hands over a fire. Now, though Surya Bai did not know it, she had reached the Rakshas' country, and this old woman was none other than a wicked old Rakshas, who lived with her son in the little hut. The young Rakshas, however, had gone out for the day. When the old Rakshas saw Surya Bai, she was much astonished, for the girl was beautiful as the sun, and her rich dress was resplendent with jewels; and she said to herself, "How lovely this child is; what a dainty morsel she would be! Oh, if my son were only here we would kill her, and boil her, and eat her. I will try and detain her till his return." Then, turning to Surya Bai, she said, "Who are you, and what do you want?" Surya Bai answered, "I am the daughter of the great Eagles, but they have gone a far journey, to fetch me a diamond ring, and the fire has died out in the nest. Give me, I pray you, a little from your hearth." The Rakshas replied, "You shall certainly have some, only first pound this rice for me, for I am old, and have no daughter to help me." Then Surya Bai pounded the rice, but the young Rakshas had not returned by the time she had finished; so the old Rakshas said to her, "If you are kind, grind this corn for me, for it is hard work for my old hands." Then she ground the corn, but still the young Rahshas came not; and the old Rakshas said to her, "Sweep the house for me first, and then I will give you the fire." So Surya Bai swept the house; but still the young Rakshas did not come.

Then his mother said to Surya Bai, "Why should

you be in such a hurry to go home? fetch me some water from the well, and then you shall have the fire." And she fetched the water. When she had done so, Surya Bai said, "I have done all your bidding, now give me the fire, or I will go elsewhere and seek it."

The old Rakshas was grieved because her son had not returned home; but she saw she could detain Surya Bai no longer, so she said, "Take the fire and go in peace; take also some parched corn, and scatter it along the road as you go, so as to make a pretty little pathway from our house to yours,"—and so saying, she gave Surya Bai several handsful of parched corn. The girl took them, fearing no evil, and as she went she scattered the grains on the road. Then she climbed back into the nest and shut the seven iron doors, and lighted the fire, and cooked the food, and gave the dog and the cat some dinner, and took some herself, and went to sleep.

No sooner had Surya Bai left the Rakshas' hut, than the young Rakshas returned, and his mother said to him, "Alas, alas, my son, why did not you come sooner? Such a sweet little lamb has been here, and now we have lost her." Then she told him all about Surya Bai. "Which way did she go?" asked the young Rakshas; "only tell me that, and I'll have her before morning."

His mother told him how she had given Surya Bai the parched corn to scatter on the road; and when he heard that, he followed up the track, and ran, and ran, and ran, till he came to the foot of the tree.

There, looking up, he saw the nest high in the branches above them.

Quick as thought, up he climbed, and reached the

great outer door; and he shook it, and shook it, but he could not get in, for Surya Bai had bolted it. Then he said, "Let me in, my child, let me in; I'm the great Eagle, and I have come from very far, and brought you many beautiful jewels; and here is a splendid diamond ring to fit your little finger." But Surya Bai did not hear him—she was fast asleep.

He next tried to force open the door again, but it was too strong for him. In his efforts, however, he had broken off one of his finger nails (now the nail of a Rakshas is most poisonous), which he left sticking in the crack of the door when he went away.

Next morning Surya Bai opened all the doors, in order to look down on the world below; but when she came to the seventh door a sharp thing, which was sticking in it, ran into her hand, and immediately she fell down dead.

At that same moment the two poor old Eagles returned from their long twelvemonth's journey, bringing a beautiful diamond ring, which they had fetched for their little favorite from the Red Sea.

There she lay on the threshold of the nest, beautiful as ever, but cold and dead.

The Eagles could not bear the sight; so they placed the ring on her finger, and then, with loud cries, flew off to return no more.

But a little while after there chanced to come by a great Rajah, who was out on a hunting expedition. He came with hawks, and hounds, and attendants, and horses, and pitched his camp under the tree in which the Eagles' nest was built. Then looking up, he saw, amongst the topmost branches, what appeared like a queer little house; and he sent some of his attendants to see what it was. They soon returned, and told the

Rajah that up in the tree was a curious thing like a cage, having seven iron doors, and that on the threshold of the first door lay a fair maiden, richly dressed; that she was dead, and that beside her stood a little dog and a little cat.

At this the Rajah commanded that they should be fetched down, and when he saw Surya Bai he felt very sad to think that she was dead. And he took her hand to feel if it were already stiff; but all her limbs were supple, nor had she become cold, as the dead are cold; and, looking again at her hand, the Rajah saw that a sharp thing, like a long thorn, had run into the tender palm, almost far enough to pierce through to the back of her hand.

He pulled it out, and no sooner had he done so than Surya Bai opened her eyes, and stood up, crying, "Where am I? and who are you? Is it a dream, or true?"

The Rajah answered, "It is all true, beautiful lady. I am the Rajah of a neighboring land; pray tell me who are you;"

She replied, "I am the Eagles' child." But he laughed. "Nay," he said, "that cannot be; you are some great Princess." "No," she answered, "I am no royal lady; what I say is true. I have lived all my life in this tree. I am only the Eagles' child."

Then the Rajah said, "If you are not a Princess born, I will make you one, say only you will be my Queen."

Surya Bai consented, and the Rajah took her to his kingdom and made her his Queen. But Surya Bai was not his only wife, and the first Ranee, his other wife, was both envious and jealous of her.*

* See Notes at the end.

The Rajah gave Surya Bai many trustworthy attendants to guard her and be with her; and one old woman loved Surya Bai more than all the rest, and used to say to her, "Don't be too intimate with the first Ranee, dear lady, for she wishes you no good, and she has power to do you harm. Some day she may poison or otherwise injure you;" but Surya Bai would answer her, "Nonsense! what is there to be alarmed about? Why cannot we both live happily together like two sisters?" Then the old woman would rejoin, "Ah, dear lady, may you never live to rue your confidence! I pray my fears may prove folly." So Surya Bai went often to see the first Ranee, and the first Ranee also came often to see her.

One day they were standing in the palace court-yard, near a tank, where the Rajah's people used to bathe, and the first Ranee said to Surya Bai, "What pretty jewels you have, sister! let me try them on for a minute, and see how I look in them."

The old woman was standing beside Surya Bai, and she whispered to her, "Do not lend her your jewels." "Hush, you silly old woman," answered she. "What harm will it do?" and she gave the Ranee her jewels. Then the Ranee said, "How pretty all your things are! Do you not think they look well even on me? Let us come down to the tank; it is as clear as glass, and we can see ourselves reflected in it, and how these jewels will shine in the clear water!"

The old woman, hearing this, was much alarmed, and begged Surya Bai not to venture near the tank, but she said, "I bid you be silent; I will not distrust my sister." and she went down to the tank. Then, when no one was near, and they were both leaning over, looking at their reflections in the water, the first Ranee pushed Surya Bai into the tank, who, sinking under water, was drowned; and from the place where her body fell there sprang up a bright golden sunflower.

The Rajah shortly afterward inquired where Surya Bai was, but nowhere could she be found. Then, very angry, he came to the first Ranee and said, "Tell me where the child is? You have made away with her." But she answered, "You do me wrong; I know nothing of her. Doubtless that old woman, whom you allowed to be always with her, has done her some harm." So the Rajah ordered the poor old woman to be thrown into prison.

He tried to forget Surya Bai and all her pretty ways, but it was no good. Wherever he went he saw her face. Whatever he heard, he still listened for her voice. Every day he grew more miserable; he would not eat or drink; and as for the other Ranee, he could not bear to speak to her. All his people said, "He will surely die."

When matters were in this state, the Rajah one day wandered to the edge of the tank, and bending over the parapet, looked into the water. Then he was surprised to see, growing out of the tank close beside him, a stately golden flower; and as he watched it, the sunflower gently bent its head and leaned down toward him. The Rajah's heart was softened, and he kissed its leaves and murmured, "This flower reminds me of my lost wife. I love it, it is fair and gentle as she used to be." And every day he would go down to the tank; and sit and watch the flower. When the Ranee heard this, she ordered her servants to go and dig the sunflower up, and to take it far into the jungle and burn it

Next time the Rajah went to the tank he found his flower gone, and he was much grieved, but none dare say who had done it.

Then, in the jungle, from the place where the ashes of the sunflower had been thrown, there sprang up a young mango tree, tall and straight, that grew so quickly, and became such a beautiful tree, that it was the wonder of all the country round. At last, on its topmost bough, came one fair blossom; and the blossom fell, and the little mango grew rosier and rosier, and larger and larger, till so wonderful was it both for size and shape that people flocked from far and near only to look at it.

But none ventured to gather it, for it was to be kept for the Rajah himself.

Now one day, the poor Milkwoman, Surya Bai's mother, was returning homeward after her day's work with the empty milk cans, and being very tired with her long walk to the bazaar, she lay down under the mango tree and fell asleep. Then, right into her largest milk can, fell the wonderful mango! When the poor woman awoke and saw what had happened, she was dreadfully frightened, and thought to herself, "If any one sees me with this wonderful fruit, that all the Rajah's great people have been watching for so many, many weeks, they will never believe that I did not steal it, and I shall be put in prison, Yet it is no good leaving it here; besides, it fell off of itself into my milk can. I will therefore take it home as secretly as possible, and share it with my children."

So the Milkwoman covered up the can in which the mango was, and took it quickly to her home, where she placed it in the corner of the room, and put over it a dozen other milk cans, piled one above another. Then, as soon as it was dark, she called her husband and eldest son (for she had six or seven children), and said to them, "What good fortune do you think has befallen me to-day?"

"We cannot guess," they said. "Nothing less," she went on, "than the wonderful, wonderful mango falling into one of my milk cans while I slept! I have brought it home with me; it is in that lowest can. Go, husband, call all the children to have a slice; and you, my son, take down that pile of cans and fetch me the mango." "Mother," he said, when he got to the lowest can, "you were joking, I suppose, when you told us there was a mango here."

"No, not at all," she answered; "there is a mango there. I put it there myself an hour ago."

"Well, there's something quite different now," replied the son. "Come and see."

The Milkwoman ran to the place, and there, in the lowest can, she saw, not the mango, but a little tiny wee lady, richly dressed in red and gold, and no bigger than a mango! On her head shone a bright jewel like a little sun.

"This is very odd," said the mother. "I never heard of such a thing in my life! But since she has been sent to us, I will take care of her, as if she were my own child."

Every day the little lady grew taller and taller, until she was the size of an ordinary woman; she was gentle and lovable, but always sad and quiet, and she said her name was "Surya Bai."

The children were all very curious to know her history, but the Milkwoman and her husband would not let her be teased to tell who she was, and said to the children, "Let us wait. By and by, when she knows us better, she will most likely tell us her story of her own accord."

Now it came to pass that once, when Surya Bai was taking water from the well for the old Milkwoman, the Rajah rode by, and as he saw her walking along, he cried, "That is my wife," and rode after her as fast as possible. Surya Bai hearing a great clatter of horses' hoofs, was frightened, and ran home as fast as possible, and hid herself; and when the Rajah reached the place there was only the old Milkwoman to be seen standing at the door of her hut.

Then the Rajah said to her, "Give her up, old woman, you have no right to keep her; she is mine, she is mine!" But the old woman answered, "Are you mad? I don't know what you mean."

The Rajah replied, "Do not attempt to deceive me. I saw my wife go in at your door; she must be in the house."

"Your wife?" screamed the old woman—"your wife? you mean my daughter, who lately returned from the well! Do you think I am going to give my child up at your command? You are Rajah in your palace, but I am Rajah in my own house; and I won't give up my little daughter for any bidding of yours. Be off with you, or I'll pull out your beard." And so saying, she seized a long stick and attacked the Rajah, calling out loudly to her husband and sons, who came running to her aid.

The Rajah, seeing matters were against him, and having outridden his attendants (and not being quite certain moreover whether he had seen Surya Bai, or whether she might not have been really the poor Milkwoman's daughter), rode off and returned to his palace.

However, he determined to sift the matter. As a first step he went to see Surya Bai's old attendant, who was still in prison. From her he learnt enough to make him believe she was not only entirely innocent of Surya Bai's death, but gravely to suspect the first Rance of having caused it. He therefore ordered the old woman to be set at liberty, still keeping a watchful eye on her, and bade her prove her devotion to her long-lost mistress by going to the Milkwoman's house, and bringing him as much information as possible about the family, and more particularly about the girl he had seen returning from the well.

So the attendant went to the Milkwoman's house, and made friends with her, and bought some milk, and afterward she stayed and talked to her.

After a few days the Milkwoman ceased to be suspicious of her, and became quite cordial.

Surya Bai's attendant then told how she had been the late Ranee's waiting-woman, and how the Rajah had thrown her into prison on her mistress's death; in return for which intelligence the old Milkwoman imparted to her how the wonderful mango had tumbled into her can as she slept under the tree, and how it had miraculously changed in the course of an hour into a beautiful little lady. "I wonder why she should have chosen my poor house to live in, instead of any one else's," said the old woman.

Then Surya Bai's attendant said, "Have you ever asked her her history? Perhaps she would not mind telling it to you now."

So the Milkwoman called the girl, and as soon as the old attendant saw her, she knew it was none other than Surya Bai, and her heart jumped for joy; but she remained silent, wondering much, for she knew her mistress had been drowned in the tank.

The old Milkwoman turned to Surya Bai and said, "My child, you have lived long with us, and been a good daughter to me; but I have never asked you your history, because I thought it must be a sad one; but if you do not fear to tell it to me now, I should like to hear it."

Surya Bai answered, "Mother, you speak true; my story is sad. I believe my real mother was a poor Milkwoman like you, and that she took me with her one day when I was quite a little baby, as she was going to sell milk in the bazaar. But being tired with the long walk, she sat down to rest, and placed me also on the ground, when suddenly a great Eagle flew down and carried me away. But all the father and mother I ever knew were the two great Eagles."

"Ah, my child! my child!" cried the Milkwoman, "I was that poor woman; the Eagles flew away with my eldest girl when she was only a year old. Have I found you after these many years?"

And she ran and called all her children, and her husband, to tell them the wonderful news.

Then was there great rejoicing among them all.

When they were a little calmer, her mother said to Surya Bai, "Tell us, dear daughter, how your life has been spent since first we lost you." And Surya Bai went on:

"The old Eagles took me away to their home, and there I lived happily many years. They loved to bring me all the beautiful things they could find, and at last one day they both went to fetch me a diamond ring from the Red Sea; but while they were gone the fire went out in the nest: so I went to an old woman's hut, and got her to give me some fire; and next day (I don't know how it was), as I was opening the outer door of the cage, a sharp thing, that was sticking in it, ran into my hand and I fell down senseless.

"I don't know how long I lay there, but when I came to myself, I found the Eagles must have come back, and thought me dead, and gone away, for the diamond ring was on my little finger; a great many people were watching over me, and amongst them was a Rajah, who asked me to go home with him and be his wife, and he brought me to this place, and I was his Ranee.

"But his other wife, the first Ranee, hated me (for she was jealous), and desired to kill me; and one day she accomplished her purpose by pushing me into the tank, for I was young and foolish, and disregarded the warnings of my faithful old attendant, who begged me not to go near the place. Ah! if I had only listened to her words I might have been happy still."

At these words the old attendant, who had been sitting in the back ground, rushed forward and kissed Surya Bai's feet, crying, "Ah, my lady! my lady! have I found you at last!" and, without staying to hear more, she ran back to the palace to tell the Rajah the glad news.

Then Surya Bai told her parents how she had not wholly died in the tank, but became a sunflower; and how the first Ranee, seeing how fond the Rajah was of the plant, had caused it to be thrown away; and then how she had risen from the ashes of the sunflower, in the form of a mango tree; and how when the tree blossomed all her spirit went into the little mango flower, and she ended by saying: "And when the flower became fruit, I know not by what irresistible impulse I was induced to throw myself into your milk can. Mother, it was my destiny, and as soon as you took me into your house, I began to recover my human form."

"Why, then," asked her brothers and sisters, "why do you not tell the Rajah that you are living, and that you are the Ranee Surya Bai?"

"Alas," she answered, "I could not do that. Who knows but that he may be influenced by the first Ranee, and also desire my death. Let me rather be poor like you, but safe from danger."

Then her mother cried, "Oh, what a stupid woman I am! The Rajah one day came seeking you here, but I and your father and brothers drove him away, for we did not know you were indeed the lost Ranee."

As she spoke these words a sound of horses' hoofs was heard in the distance, and the Rajah himself appeared, having heard the good news of Surya Bai's being alive from her old attendant.

It is impossible to tell the joy of the Rajah at finding his long-lost wife, but it was not greater than Surya Bai's at being restored to her husband.

Then the Rajah turned to the old Milkwoman and said, "Old woman, you did not tell me true, for it was indeed my wife who was in your hut." "Yes, Protector of the Poor," answered the old Milkwoman, "but it was also my daughter." Then they told him how Surya Bai was the Milkwoman's child.

At hearing this the Rajah commanded them all to return with him to the palace. He gave Surya Bai's father a village, and ennobled the family; and he said to Surya Bai's old attendant, "For the good service you have done you shall be palace housekeeper," and he gave her great riches; adding, "I can never repay the debt I owe you, nor make you sufficient recompense for having caused you to be unjustly cast into prison." But she replied, "Sire, even in your anger you were temperate; if you had caused me to be put to death, as some would have done, none of this good might have come upon you; it is yourself you have to thank."

The wicked first Ranee was cast, for the rest of her life, into the prison in which the old attendant had been thrown; but Surya Bai lived happily with her husband the rest of her days; and in memory of her adventures, he planted round their palace a hedge of sunflowers and a grove of mango trees.

VII.

THE WANDERINGS OF VICRAM MAHARAJAH.

THERE was once upon a time a Rajah named Vicram Maharajah,* who had a Wuzeer named Butti.† Both the Rajah and his minister were left orphans when very young, and ever since their parents' death they had lived together: they were educated together, and they loved each other tenderly—like brothers.

Both were good and kind—no poor man coming to the Rajah was ever known to have been sent away disappointed, for it was his delight to give food and clothes to those in need. But whilst the Wuzeer had much judgment and discretion, as well as a brilliant fancy, the Rajah was too apt to allow his imagination to run away with his reason.

Under their united rule, however, the kingdom prospered greatly. The Rajah was the spur of every noble work, and the Wuzeer the curb to every rash or impracticable project.

In a country some way from Rajah Vicram's there lived a little Queen, called Anar Ranee (the Pomegranate Queen). Her father and mother reigned over the Pomegranate country, and for her they had made a beautiful garden. In the middle of the garden was a lovely pomegranate tree, bearing three large

* The great King Vicram. † Light.

pomegranates. They opened in the centre, and in each was a little bed. In one of them Anar Ranee used to sleep, and in the pomegranates on either side slept two of her maids.

Every morning early the pomegranate tree would gently bend its branches to the ground, and the fruit would open, and Anar Ranee and her attendants creep out to play under the shadow of the cool tree until the evening; and each evening the tree again bent down to enable them to get into their tiny, snug bed-rooms.

Many princes wished to marry Anar Ranee, for she was said to be the fairest lady upon earth: her hair was black as a raven's wing, her eyes like the eyes of a gazelle, her teeth two rows of exquisite pearls, and her cheeks the color of the rosy pomegranate. But her father and mother had caused her garden to be hedged around with seven hedges made of bayonets, so that none could go in or out; and they had published a decree that none should marry her but he who could enter the garden and gather the three pomegranates, in which she and her two maids slept. To do this, kings, princes and nobles innumerable had striven, but striven in vain.

Some never got past the first sharp hedge of bayonets; others, more fortunate, surmounted the second, the third, the fourth, the fifth, or even the sixth; but there perished miserably, being unable to climb the seventh. None had ever succeeded in entering the garden.

Before Vicram Maharajah's father and mother died, they had built, some way from their palace, a very beautiful temple. It was of marble, and in the centre stood an idol made of pure gold. But in course of time the jungle had grown up round it, and thick straggling plants of prickly pear had covered it, so that it was difficult even to find out whereabouts it was.

Then, one day, the Wuzeer Butti said to Vicram Maharajah, "The temple your father and mother built at so much pains and cost is almost lost in the jungle, and will probably ere long be in ruins. It would be a pious work to find it out and restore it." Vicram Maharajah agreed, and immediately sent for many workmen, and caused the jungle to be cut down and the temple restored. All were much astonished to find what a beautiful place it was! The floor was white marble, the walls exquisitely carved in bas-reliefs and gorgeously colored, while all over the ceiling was painted Vicram Maharajah's father's name, and in the centre was a golden image of Gunputti, to whom it was dedicated.

The Rajah Vicram was so pleased with the beauty of the place that on that account, as well as because of its sanctity, he and Butti used to go and sleep there every night.

One night Vicram had a wonderful dream. He dreamed his father appeared to him and said, "Arise, Vicram, go to the tower for lights* which is in front of this temple.

(For there was in front of the temple a beautiful tower or pyramid for lights, and all the way up it were projections on which to place candles on days dedicated to the idol; so that when the whole was lighted it looked like a gigantic candlestick, and to guard it there were around it seven hedges made of bayonets.)

"Arise. Vicram. therefore," said the vision; "go to

* See Notes at the end.

the tower for lights; below it is a vast amount of treasure, but you can only get it in one way without incurring the anger of Gunputti. You must first do in his honor an act of very great devotion, which if he graciously approve, and consent to preserve your life therein, you may with safety remove the treasure."

"And what is this act of devotion?" asked Vicram Maharajah.

"It is this," (he thought his father answered): "You must fasten a rope to the top of the tower, and to the other end of the rope attach a basket, into which you must get head downward, then twist the rope by which the basket is hung three times, and as it is untwisting, cut it, when you will fall head downward to the earth.

"If you fall on either of the hedges of bayonets, you will be instantly killed; but Gunputti is merciful—do not fear that he will allow you to be slain. If you escape unhurt, you will know that he has accepted your pious act, and may without danger take the treasure."*

The vision faded; Vicram saw no more, and shortly afterward he awoke.

Then, turning to the Wuzeer, he said, "Butti, I had a strange dream. I dreamed my father counseled me to do an act of great devotion; nothing less than fastening a basket by a rope to the top of the tower for lights, and getting into it head downward, then cutting the rope and allowing myself to fall; by which having propitiated the divinity, he promised me a vast treasure, to be found by digging under the tower! What do you think I had better do?"

"My advice," answered the Wuzeer, "is, if you care

* See Notes at the end.

to seek the treasure, to do entirely as your father commanded, trusting in the mercy of Gunputti."

So the Rajah caused a basket to be fastened by a rope to the top of the tower, and got into it head downward; then he called out to Butti, "How can I cut the rope?" "Nothing is easier," answered he; "take this sword in your hand. I will twist the rope three times, and as it untwists for the first time let the sword fall upon it." Vicram Maharajah took the sword, and Butti twisted the rope, and as it first began to untwist, the Rajah cut it, and the basket immediately fell. It would have certainly gone down among the bayonets, and he been instantly killed, had not Gunputti, seeing the danger of his devotee, rushed out of the temple at that moment in the form of an old woman, who, catching the basket in her arms before it touched the bayonets, brought it gently and safely to the ground; having done which she instantly returned into the temple. None of the spectators knew she was Gunputti himself in disguise; they only thought "What a clever old woman!"

Vicram Maharajah then caused excavations to be made below the tower, under which he found an immense amount of treasure. There were mountains of gold, there were diamonds, and rubies, and sapphires, and emeralds, and turquoises, and pearls; but he took none of them, causing all to be sold and the money given to the poor, so little did he care for the riches for which some men sell their bodies and souls.

Another day, the Rajah, when in the temple, dreamed again. Again his father appeared to him, and this time he said, "Vicram, come daily to this temple and Gunputti will teach you wisdom, and you shall get under-

12

standing. You may get learning in the world, but wisdom is the fruit of much learning and much experience, and much love to God and man; wherefore, come, acquire wisdom, for learning perishes, but wisdom never dies." When the Rajah awoke, he told his dream to the Wuzeer, and Butti recommended him to obey his father's counsel, which he accordingly did.

Daily he resorted to the temple and was instructed by Gunputti; and when he had learnt much, one day Gunputti said to him, "I have given you as much wisdom as is in keeping with man's finite comprehension; now, as a parting gift, ask of me what you will and it shall be yours—or riches, or power, or beauty, or long life, or health, or happiness—choose what you will have?" The Rajah was very much puzzled, and he begged leave to be allowed a day to think over the matter, and decide what he would choose, to which Gunputti assented.

Now it happened that near the palace there lived the son of a Carpenter, who was very cunning, and when he heard that the Rajah went to the temple to learn wisdom, he also determined to go and see if he could not learn it also; and each day, when Gunputti gave Vicram Maharajah instruction, the Carpenter's son would hide close behind the temple, and overhear all their conversation; so that he also became very wise. No sooner, therefore, did he hear Gunputti's offer to Vicram than he determined to return again when the Rajah did, and find out in what way he was to procure the promised gift, whatever it was.

The Rajah consulted Butti as to what he should ask for, saying, "I have riches more than enough; I have also sufficient power, and for the rest I had sooner take my chance with other men, which makes me much at a loss to know what to choose."

The Wuzeer answered, "Is there any supernatural power you at all desire to possess? If so, ask for that." "Yes," replied the Rajah, "it has always been a great desire of mine to have power to leave my own body when I will, and translate my soul and sense into some other body, either of man or animal. I would rather be able to do that than anything else." "Then," said the Wuzeer, "ask Gunputti to give you the power."

Next morning the Rajah, having bathed and prayed, went in great state to the temple to have his final interview with the idol. And the Carpenter's son went too, in order to overhear it.

Then Gunputti said to the Rajah, "Vicram, what gift do you choose?" "Oh, divine Power," answered the Rajah, "you have already given me a sufficiency of wealth and power, in making me Rajah; neither care I for more of beauty than I now possess; and of long life, health and happiness I had rather take my share with other men. But there is a power which I would rather own than all that you have offered."

"Name it, O good son of a good father," said Gunputti.

"Most Wise," replied Vicram, "give me the power to leave my own body when I will, and translate my soul, and sense, and thinking powers into any other body that I may choose, either of man, or bird, or beast—whether for a day, or a year, or for twelve years, or as long as I like; grant also, that however long the term of my absence, my body may not decay, but that, when I please to return to it again, I may find it still as when I left it."

"Vicram," answered Gunputti, "your prayer is heard," and he instructed Vicram Maharajah by what means he should translate his soul into another body, and also gave him something which, being placed within his own body when he left it, would preserve it from decay until his return.*

The Carpenter's son, who had been all this time listening outside the temple, heard and learnt the spell whereby Gunputti gave Vicram Maharajah power to enter into any other body; but he could not see nor find out what was given to the Rajah to place within his own body when he left it, to preserve it; so that he was only master of half the secret.

Vicram Maharajah returned home, and told the Wuzeer that he was possessed of the much-desired secret. "Then," said Butti, "the best use you can put it to is to fly to the Pomegranate country, and bring Anar Ranee here."

"How can that be done?" asked the Rajah. "Thus," replied Butti; "transport yourself into the body of a parrot, in which shape you will be able to fly over the seven hedges of bayonets that surround her garden. Go to the tree in the centre of it, bite off the stalks of the pomegranates and bring them home in your beak."

"Very well," said the Rajah, and he picked up a parrot which lay dead on the ground, and placing within his own body the beauty-preserving charm, transported his soul into the parrot, and flew off.

On, on, on he went, over the hills and far away, until he came to the garden. Then he flew over the seven hedges of bayonets, and with his beak broke off the

* See Notes at the end.

three pomegrantes (in which were Anar Ranee and her two ladies), and holding them by the stalks brought them safely home. He then immediately left the parrot's body and re-entered his own body.

When Butti saw how well he had accomplished the feat, he said, "Thank heaven! there's some good done already." All who saw Anar Ranee were astonished at her beauty, for she was fair as a lotus flower, and the color on her cheeks was like the deep rich color of a pomegranate, and all thought the Rajah very wise to have chosen such a wife.

They had a magnificent wedding, and were for a short time as happy as the day is long.

But within a little while Vicram Maharajah said to Butti, "I have again a great desire to see the world." "What!" said Butti, "so soon again to leave your home! So soon to care to go away from your young wife!"

"I love her and my people dearly," answered the Rajah; "but I cannot but feel that I have this supernatural power of taking any form I please, and longing to use it." "Where and how will you go?" asked the Wuzeer. "Let it be the day after to-morrow," answered Vicram Maharajah. "I shall again take the form of a parrot, and see as much of the world as possible."

So it was settled that the Rajah should go. He left his kingdom in the Wuzeer's sole charge, and also his wife, saying to her, "I don't know for how long I may be away; perhaps a day, perhaps a year, perhaps more. But if, while I am gone, you should be in any difficulty, apply to the Wuzeer. He has ever been like an elder brother or a father to me; do you therefore also regard him as a father. I have charged him to take care of you as he would of his own child."

Having said these words, the Rajah caused a beautiful parrot to be shot (it was a very handsome bird, with a tuft of bright feathers on its head and a ring about its neck). He then cut a small incision in his arm and rubbed into it some of the magic preservative given him by Gunputti to keep his body from decaying, and transporting his soul into the parrot's body, he flew away.

No sooner did the Carpenter's son hear that the Rajah was as dead, than, knowing the power of which Vicram Maharajah and he were alike possessed, he felt certain that the former had made use of it, and determined himself likewise to turn it to account. Therefore, directly the Rajah entered the parrot's body, the Carpenter's son entered the Rajah's body, and the world at large imagined that the Rajah had only swooned and recovered. But the Wuzeer was wiser than they, and immediately thought to himself, "Some one beside Vicram Maharajah must have become acquainted with this spell, and be now making use of it, thinking it would be very amusing to play the part of Rajah for a while; but I'll soon discover if this be the case or no."

So he called Anar Ranee and said to her, "You are as well assured as I am that your husband left us but now, in the form of a parrot; but scarcely had he gone before his deserted body arose, and he now appears walking about, and talking, and as much alive as ever; nevertheless, my opinion is, that the spirit animating the body is not the spirit of the Rajah, but that some one else is possessed of the power given to him by Gunputti, and has taken advantage of it to personate him.

But this it would be better to put to the proof. Do, therefore, as I tell you, that you may be assured of the truth of my words. Make to-day for your husband's dinner some very coarse and common currie, and give it to him. If he complains that it is not as good as usual, I am making a mistake; but if, on the contrary, he says nothing about it, you will know that my words are true, and that he is not Vicram Maharajah."

Anar Ranee did as the Wuzeer advised, and afterward came to him and said, "Father" (for so she always called him), "I have been much astonished at the result of the trial. I made the currie very carelessly, and it was as coarse and common as possible; but the Rajah did not even complain. I feel convinced it is as you say; but what can we do?"

"We will not," answered the Wuzeer, "cast him into prison, since he inhabits your husband's body; but neither you, nor any of the Rajah's relations, must have any friendship with, or so much as speak to him; and if he speak to any of you, let whoever it be, immediately begin to quarrel with him, whereby he will find the life of a rajah not so agreeable as he anticipated, and may be induced the sooner to return to his proper form.

Anar Ranee instructed all her husband's relations and friends as Butti had advised, and the Carpenter's son began to think the life of a rajah not at all as pleasant as he had fancied, and would, if he could, have gladly returned to his own body again; but, having no power to preserve it, his spirit had no sooner left it than it began to decay, and at the end of three days it was quite destroyed; so that the unhappy man had no alternative but to remain where he was.

Meantime, the real Vicram Maharajah had flown, in the form of a parrot, very far, far away, until he reached a large banyan tree, where there were a thousand other petty pollies, whom he joined, making their number a thousand and one. Every day the parrots flew away to get food, and every night they returned to roost in the great banyan tree.

Now it chanced that a hunter had often gone through that part of the jungle, and noticed the banyan tree and the parrots, and he said to himself, "If I could only catch the thousand and one parrots that nightly roost in that tree, I should not be so often hungry as I am now, for they would make plenty of very nice currie." But he could not do it, though he often tried; for the trunks of the tree were tall and straight, and very slippery, so that he no sooner climbed up a little way than he slid down again: however, he did not cease to look and long.

One day, a heavy shower of rain drove all the parrots back earlier than usual to their tree, and when they got there they found a thousand crows who had come on their homeward flight to shelter themselves there till the storm was over.

Then Vicram Maharajah Parrot said to the other parrots, "Do you not see these crows have all sorts of seeds and fruits in their beaks, which they are carrying home to their little ones? Let us quickly drive them away, lest some of these fall down under our tree, which, being sown there, will spring up strong plants and twine round the trunks, and enable our enemy the hunter to climb up with ease and kill us all."

But the other parrots answered, "That is a very far-fetched idea! Do not let us hunt the poor birds away from shelter in this pouring rain, they will get so wet." So the crows were not molested. It turned out, however, just as Vicram Maharajah had foretold; for some of the fruits and seeds they were taking home to their young ones fell under the tree, and the seeds took root and sprang up, strong creeping plants, which twined all round the straight trunks of the banyan tree, and made it very easy to climb.

Next time the hunter came by he noticed this, and saying, "Ah, my fine friends, I've got you at last," he, by the help of the creepers, climbed the tree, and set one thousand and one snares of fine thread among the branches; having done which he went away.

That night, when the parrots flew down on the branches as usual, they found themselves all caught fast prisoners by the feet.

"Crick! crick! crick!" cried they, "crick! crick! crick! Oh dear! oh dear! what shall we do? what can we do? Oh, Vicram Maharajah, you were right and we were wrong. Oh dear! oh dear! crick! crick! crick!"

Then Vicram said, "Did I not tell you how it would be? But do as I bid you, and we may yet be saved. So soon as the hunter comes to take us away, let every one hang his head down on one side, as if he were dead; then, thinking us dead, he will not trouble himself to wring our necks, or stick the heads of those he wishes to keep alive through his belt, as he otherwise would; but will merely release us, and throw us on the ground. Let each one when there, remain perfectly still, till the whole thousand and one are set free, and the hunter begins to descend the tree; then we will all fly up over his head and far out of sight."

The parrots agreed to do as Vicram Maharajah Parrot proposed, and when the hunter came next morning to take them away, every one had his eyes shut and his head hanging down on one side, as if he were dead. Then the hunter said, "All dead, indeed! Then I shall have plenty of nice currie." And so saying, he cut the noose that held the first, and threw him down. The parrot fell like a stone to the ground, so did the second, the third, the fourth, the fifth, the sixth, the seventh, the eighth, the ninth, the tenth, and so on—up to the thousandth parrot. Now the thousandth and first chanced to be none other than Vicram; all were released but he. But, just as the hunter was going to cut the noose round his feet, he let his knife fall, and had to go down and pick it up again. When the thousand parrots who were on the ground, heard him coming down, they thought, "The thousand and one are all released, and here comes the hunter; it is time for us to be off." And with one accord they flew up into the air and far out of sight, leaving poor Vicram Maharajah still a prisoner.

The hunter, seeing what had happened, was very angry, and seizing Vicram, said to him, "You wretched bird! it's you that have worked all this mischief. I know it must be, for you are a stranger here, and different to the other parrots. I'll strangle you, at all events—that I will." But to his surprise, the parrot answered him, "Do not kill me. What good will that do you? Rather sell me in the next town. I am very handsome. You will get a thousand gold mohurs* for me."

"A thousand gold mohurs!" answered the hunter,

* About $7,500.

much astonished. "You silly bird, who'd be so foolish as to give a thousand gold mohurs for a parrot?" "Never mind," said Vicram, "only take me and try."

So the hunter took him into the town, crying "Who'll buy? who'll buy? Come buy this pretty polly that can talk so nicely. See how handsome he is—see what a great red ring he has round his neck. Who'll buy? who'll buy?"

Then several people asked how much he would take for the parrot; but when he said a thousand gold mohurs, they all laughed and went away, saying "None but a fool would give so much for a bird."

At last the hunter got angry, and he said to Vicram, "I told you how it would be. I shall never be able to sell you." But he answered, "Oh yes, you will. See here comes a merchant down this way; I dare say he will buy me." So the hunter went to the merchant and said to him, "Pray, sir, buy my pretty parrot." "How much do you want for him?" asked the merchant—"two rupees?"* "No, sir," answered the hunter; "I cannot part with him for less than a thousand gold mohurs." "A thousand gold mohurs!" cried the merchant, "a thousand gold mohurs! I never heard of such a thing in my life! A thousand gold mohurs for one little wee polly! Why, with that sum you might buy a house, or gardens, or horses, or ten thousand yards of the best cloth. Who's going to give you such a sum for a parrot? Not I, indeed. I'll give you two rupees and no more." But Vicram called out, "Merchant, merchant, do not fear to buy me. I am Vicram Maharajah Parrot. Pay what the hunter

* About $1.

asks, and I will repay it to you—buy me only, and I will kéep your shop."

"Polly," answered the merchant, "what nonsense you talk!" But he took a fancy to the bird, and paid the hunter a thousand gold mohurs, and taking Vicram Maharajah home, hung him up in his shop.

Then the Parrot took on him the duties of shopman, and talked so much and so wisely that every one in the town soon heard of the merchant's wonderful bird. Nobody cared to go to any other shop—all came to his shop, only to hear the Parrot talk; and he sold them what they wanted, and they did not care how much he charged for what he sold, but gave him whatever he asked; insomuch, that in one week the merchant had made a thousand gold mohurs over and above his usual weekly profits; and there Vicram Maharajah Parrot lived for a long time, made much of by everybody, and very happy.

It happened in the town where the merchant lived there was a very accomplished Nautch girl,* named Champa Ranee.† She danced so beautifully that the people of the town used always to send for her to dance on the occasion of any great festival.

There also lived in the town a poor wood-cutter, who earned his living by going out far into the jungle to cut wood, and bringing it in every day, into the bazaar to sell.

One day he went out as usual into the jungle to cut wood, and being tired, he fell asleep under a tree and began to dream; and he dreamed that he was a very

* Dancing girl.

† The Champa Queen. "The Champa" (*Michelia champaca*) is a beautiful, sweet-scented yellow flower.

rich man, and that he married the beautiful Nautch girl, and that he took her home to his house, and gave his wife, as a wedding present, a thousand gold mohurs!

When he went into the bazaar that evening as usual to sell wood, he began telling his dream to his friends, saying, "While I was in the jungle I had such an absurd dream; I dreamed that I was a rich man, and that I married the Champa Ranee, and gave her as a wedding present a thousand gold mohurs!" "What a funny dream!" they cried, and thought no more of it.

But it happened that the house under which he was standing whilst talking to his friends was Champa Ranee's house, and Champa Ranee herself was near the window, and heard what he said, and thought to herself, "For all that man looks so poor, he has then a thousand gold mohurs, or he would not have dreamed of giving them to his wife; if that is all, I'll go to law about it, and see if I can't get the money."

So she sent out her servants and ordered them to catch the poor wood-cutter; and when they caught him, she began crying out, "Oh husband! husband! here have I been waiting ever so long, wondering what has become of you; where have you been all this time?" He answered, "I'm sure I don't know what you mean. You're a great lady and I'm a poor wood-cutter; you must mistake me for somebody else."

But she answered, "Oh no! don't you remember we were married on such and such a day! Have you forgotten what a grand wedding it was, and you took me home to your palace, and promised to give me as a wedding present a thousand gold mohurs? But you quite forgot to give me the money, and you went away, and I returned to my father's house till I could learn tidings of you; how can you be so cruel?"

The poor wood-cutter thought he must be dreaming, but all Champa Ranee's friends and relations declared that what she said was true. Then, after much quarreling, they said they would go to law about it; but the judge could not settle the matter, and referred it to the Rajah himself. The Rajah was no less puzzled than the judge. The wood-cutter protested that he was only a poor wood-cutter; but Champa Ranee and her friends asserted that he was, on the contrary, a rich man, her husband, and had had much money, which he must have squandered. She offered, however, to give up all claim to that, if he would only give her a thousand gold mohurs, which he had promised; and so suggested a compromise. The wood-cutter replied that he would gladly give the gold mohurs if he had them; but that (as he brought witnesses to prove) he was really and truly what he professed to be—only a poor wood-cutter, who earned two annas* a day cutting wood, and had neither palace nor riches nor wife in the world! The whole city was interested in this curious case, and all wondered how it would end; some being sure one side was right, and some equally certain of the other.

The Rajah could make nothing of the matter, and at last he said: "I hear there is a merchant in this town who has a very wise parrot, wiser than most men are; let him be sent for to decide this business, for it is beyond me; we will abide by his decision."

So Vicram Maharajah Parrot was sent for, and

* Six cents.

placed in the court of justice, to hear and judge the case.

First he said to the wood-cutter, "Tell me your version of the story." And the wood-cutter answered, "Polly, Sahib, what I tell is true. I am a poor man. I live in the jungle, and earn my living by cutting wood and selling it in the bazaar. I never get more than two annas a day. One day I fell asleep and dreamed a silly dream—how I had become rich and married the Champa Ranee, and had given her as a wedding present a thousand gold mohurs; but it is no more true that I owed her a thousand gold mohurs, or have them to pay, than that I married her.

"That is enough," said Vicram Maharajah. "Now, dancing girl, tell us your story." And Champa Ranee gave her version of the matter. Then the Parrot said to her, "Tell me now where was the house of this husband of yours, to which he took you?" "Oh!" she answered; "very far away, I don't know how far, in the jungles." "How long ago was it?" asked he. "At such and such a time," she replied. Then he called credible and trustworthy witnesses, who proved that Champa Ranee had never left the city at the time she mentioned. After hearing whom, the Parrot said to her, "Is it possible that you can have the folly to think any one would believe that you would leave your rich and costly home to go a long journey into the jungle? It is now satisfactorily proved that you did not do it; you had better give up all claim to the thousand gold mohurs."

But this the Nautch girl would not do. The Parrot then called for a money-lender, and begged of him the loan of a thousand gold mohurs, which he placed in a great bottle, putting the stopper in, and sealing it securely down; he then gave it to the Nautch girl, and said, "Get this money if you can, without breaking the seal or breaking the bottle." She answered, "It cannot be done." "No more," replied Vicram Maharajah, "can what you desire be done. You cannot force a poor man, who has no money in the world, to pay you a thousand gold mohurs.

"Let the prisoner go free! Begone, Champa Ranee. Dancing girl! you are a liar and a thief; go rob the rich if you will, but meddle no more with the poor."

All applauded Vicram Maharajah Parrot's decision, and said, "Was ever such a wonderful bird!" But Champa Ranee was extremely angry, and said to him, "Very well, nasty polly; nasty, stupid polly! be assured before long I will get you in my power, and when I do, I will bite off your head!"

"Try your worst, madam," answered Vicram; "but in return, I tell you this—I will live to make you a beggar. Your house shall be, by your own order, laid even with the ground, and you for grief and rage shall kill yourself."

"Agreed," said Champa Ranee; "we will soon see whose words come true—mine or yours;" and so saying, she returned home.

The merchant took Vicram Maharajah back to his shop, and a week passed without adventure; a fortnight passed, but still nothing particular happened. At the end of this time the merchant's eldest son was married, and in honor of the occasion, the merchant ordered that a clever dancing-girl should be sent for, to dance before the guests. Champa Ranee came, and danced so beautifully that every one was delighted;

and the merchant was much pleased, and said to her, "You have done your work very well, and in payment you may choose what you like out of my shop or house, and it shall be yours—whether jewels or rich cloth, or whatever it is."

She replied, "I desire nothing of the kind: of jewels and rich stuffs I have more than enough, but you shall give me your pretty little parrot; I like it much, and that is the only payment I will take."

The merchant felt very much vexed, for he had never thought the Nautch girl would ask for the parrot which he was so fond of, and which had been so profitable to him; he felt he would rather have parted with anything he possessed than that; nevertheless, having promised, he was bound to keep his word, so, with many tears, he went to fetch his favorite. But Polly cried, "Don't be vexed, master; give me to the girl; I can take good care of myself."

So Champa Ranee took Vicram Maharajah Parrot home with her; and no sooner did she get there than she sent for one of her maids, and said, "Quick, take this parrot and boil him for my supper; but first cut off his head and bring it to me on a plate, grilled; for I will eat it before tasting any other dish."

"What nonsensical idea is this of our mistress," said the maid to another, as she took the parrot into the kitchen; "to think of eating a grilled parrot's head!" "Never mind," said the other; "you'd better prepare it as she bids you, or she'll be very cross." Then the maid who had received the order began plucking the long feathers out of Vicram Maharajah's wings, he all the time hanging down his head, so that she thought he was dead. Then, going to fetch some water in which to boil him, she laid him down close to the place where they washed the dishes. Now, the kitchen was on the ground floor, and there was a hole right through the wall, into which the water used in washing the dishes ran, and through which all the scraps, bones, peelings and parings were washed away after the daily cooking; and in this hole Vicram Maharajah hid himself, quick as thought.

"Oh dear! oh dear!" cried the maid when she returned. "What can I do? what will my mistress say? I only turned my back for one moment, and the parrot's gone." "Very likely," answered the other maid, "some cat has taken it away. It could not have been alive, and flown or run away, or I should have seen it go; but never fear, a chicken will do very well for her instead."

Then they took a chicken and boiled it, and grilled the head and took it to their mistress; and she eat it, little bit by little bit, saying as she did so—

"Ah, pretty polly! so here's the end of you! This is the brain that thought so cunningly and devised my overthrow! this is the tongue that spoke against me! this is the throat through which came the threatening words! Aha! who is right now, I wonder?"

Vicram, in the hole close by, heard her and felt very much alarmed; for he thought, "If she should catch me after all!" He could not fly away, for all his wing feathers had been pulled out; so there he had to stay some time, living on the scraps that were washed into the hole in the washing of the plates, and perpetually exposed to danger of being drowned in the streams of water that were poured through it. At last, however, his new feathers were sufficiently grown to bear him, and he flew away to a little temple in the jungle some way off, where he perched behind the idol.

It happened that Champa Ranee used to go to that temple, and he had not been there long before she came there to worship her idol.

She fell on her knees before the image, and began to pray. Her prayer was that the god would transport her body and soul to heaven (for she had a horror of dying), and she cried, "Only grant my prayer—only let this be so, and I will do anything you wish—anything—anything."

Vicram Maharajah was hidden behind the image and heard her, and said—

"Champa Ranee Nautch girl, your prayer is heard!" (She thought the idol himself was speaking to her, and listened attentively.) "This is what you must do: sell all you possess, and give the money to the poor; you must also give money to all your servants and dismiss them. Level also your house to the ground, that you may be wholly separated from earth. Then you will be fit for heaven. Come, having done all I command you, on this day week to this place, and you shall be transported thither body and soul."

Champa Ranee believed what she heard, and forgetful of Vicram Maharajah Parrot's threat, hastened to do as she was bidden. She sold her possessions, and gave all the money to the poor; razed her house to the ground, and dismissed her servants; which being accomplished, on the day appointed she went to the temple, and sat on the edge of a well outside it, explaining to the assembled people how the idol himself haa spoken to her, and how they would shortly see her caught up to heaven, and thus her departure from the world would be even more celebrated than her doings whilst in it. All the people listened eagerly to her words, for they believed her inspired, and to see her ascension the whole city had come out, with hundreds and hundreds of strangers and travelers, princes, merchants and nobles, from far and near, all full of expectation and curiosity.

Then, as they waited, a fluttering of little wings was heard, and a parrot flew over Champa Ranee's head, calling out, "Nautch girl! Nautch girl! what have you done?" Champa Ranee recognized the voice as Vicram's; he went on: "Will you go body and soul to heaven? have you forgotten polly's words?"

Champa Ranee rushed into the temple, and, falling on her knees before the idol, cried out, "Gracious Power, I have done all as you commanded; let your words come true; save me; take me to heaven."

But the Parrot above her cried, "Good-bye, Champa Ranee, good-bye; you ate a chicken's head, not mine. Where is your house now? where your servants and all your possessions? Have my words come true, think you, or yours?"

Then the woman saw all, and in her rage and despair, cursing her own folly, she fell violently down on the floor of the temple, and dashing her head against the stone, killed herself.

It was now two years since the Rajah Vicram left his kingdom; and about six months before, Butti, in despair of his ever returning, had set out to seek for him. Up and down through many countries had he gone, searching for his master, but without success. As good fortune would have it, however, he chanced to be one of those strangers who had come to witness the Nautch girl's translation, and no sooner did he see the Parrot which spoke to her than in him he recognized Vicram. The Rajah also saw him, and flew on to his shoulder, upon which Butti caught him, put him in a cage and took him home.

Now was a puzzling problem to be solved. The Rajah's soul was in the Parrot's body, and the Carpenter's son's soul in the Rajah's body. How was the the latter to be expelled to make way for the former? He could not return to his own body, for that had perished long before. The Wuzeer knew not how to manage the matter, and determined therefore to await the course of events.

It happened that the pretended Rajah and Butti each had a fighting ram, and one day the Rajah said to the Wuzeer, "Let us set our rams to fight to-day, and try the strength of mine against yours." "Agreed," answered the Wuzeer; and they set them to fight. But there was much difference in the two rams; for when Butti's ram was but a lamb, and his horns were growing, Butti had tied him to a lime tree, and his horns had got very strong indeed by constantly rubbing against its tender stem and butting against it; but the Carpenter's son had tied his ram, when a lamb, to a young teak tree, the trunk of which was so stout and strong that the little creature, butting against it, could make no impression on it, but only damaged and loosened his own horns.

The pretended Rajah soon saw, to his vexation, that his favorite's horns being less strong than its opponent's, he was getting tired, and beginning to lose courage, would certainly be worsted in the fight; so, quick as thought, he left his own body and transported his soul into the ram's body, in order to give it an increase of courage and resolution, and enable it to win.

No sooner did Vicram Maharajah, who was hanging up in a cage, see what had taken place, than he left the parrot's body and re-entered his own body. Then Butti's ram pushed the other down on its knees and the Wuzeer ran and fetched a sword, and cut off its head; thus putting an end, with the life of the ram, to the life of the Carpenter's son.

Great was the joy of Anar Ranee and all the household at recovering the Rajah after his long absence; and Anar Ranee prayed him to fly away no more as a parrot, which he promised her he would not do.

But the taste for wandering and love of an unsettled life did not leave him on his resuming his proper form; and one of the things in which he most delighted was to roam about the jungles near the palace by himself, without attendant or guide. One very sultry day, when he was thus out by himself, he wandered over a rocky part of the country, which was flat and arid, without a tree upon it to offer shelter from the burning sun. Vicram, tired with his walk, threw himself down by the largest piece of rock he could find to rest. As he lay there, half asleep, a little Cobra came out of a hole in the ground, and seeing his mouth wide open (which looked like some shady cranny in a rock), crept in and curled himself up in the Rajah's throat.

Vicram Maharajah called out to the Cobra, "Get out of my throat." But the Cobra said, "No, I won't go; I like being here better then under ground;" and there he stayed. Vicram didn't know what to do, for the Cobra lived in his throat and could not be got out.

At times it would peep out of his mouth, but the moment the Rajah tried to catch it, it ran back again.

"Who ever heard of a Rajah in such a miserable plight?" sighed he to Butti—"to think of having this Cobra in my throat!"

"Ah, my dear friend," Butti would answer, "why will you go roaming about the country by yourself? Will you never be cured of it?"

"If one could only catch this Cobra, I'd be content to wander no more," said the Rajah, "for my wandering has not brought me much good of late." But to catch the Cobra was more than any man could do. At last, one day, Vicram, driven nearly mad in this perplexity, ran away into the jungle. Tidings of this were soon brought to Butti, who was much grieved to hear it, and sighed, saying, "Alas! alas! of what avail to Vicram Maharajah is his more than human wisdom, when the one unlucky self-chosen gift neutralizes all the good he might do with it! It has given him a love of wandering hither and thither, minding everybody's business but his own; his kingdom is neglected, his people uncared for, and he, that used to be the pride of all Rajahs, the best, the noblest, has finally slunk out of his country, like a thief escaping from jail."

Butti sent messengers far and wide seeking Vicram Maharajah, but they could not find him; he then determined to go himself in search of his lost friend; and having made proper arrangements for the government of the country during his absence, he set off on his travels.

Meantime Vicram wandered on and on until at last, one day, he came to the palace of a certain Rajah, who reigned over a country very far from his own, and he sat down with the beggars at the palace gate.

Now, the Rajah at whose gate Vicram Maharajah sat had a good and lovely daughter, named Buccoulee.* Many Princes wished to marry this Princess, but she would marry none of them. Her father and mother said to her, "Why will you not choose a husband? Among all these Princes who ask you in marriage there are many rich and powerful—many handsome and brave—many wise and good; why will you refuse them all?" The Princess replied, "It is not my destiny to marry any of them; continually in my dreams I see my destined husband, and I wait for him." "Who is he?" they asked. "His name," she answered, "is the Rajah Vicram; he will come from a very far country; he has not come yet." They replied, "There is no Rajah, far or near, that we know of, of this name; give over this fancy of yours and marry some one else."

But she constantly refused, saying, "No, I will wait for the Rajah Vicram." Her parents thought, "It may be even as she says. Who knows but perhaps some day a great King, greater than any we know, may come to this country and wish to marry the girl; we shall then be glad that we had not obliged her to marry any of her present suitors?"

No sooner had Vicram Maharajah come to the palace gate, and sat down there with the beggars, than the Princess Buccoulee, looking out of the window, saw him and cried, "There is the husband I saw in my dreams; there is the Rajah Vicram." "Where, child, where?" said her mother; "there's no Rajah there; only a parcel of beggars."

But the Princess persisted that one of them was the

* Said to mean some sort of water-plant.

Rajah Vicram. Then the Ranee sent for Vicram Maharajah and questioned him.

He said his name was "Rajah Vicram." But the Rajah and Ranee did not believe him; and they were very angry with the Princess because she persisted in saying that he, and no other, would she marry. At last they got so enraged with her that they said, "Well, marry your beggar husband, if you will, but don't think to remain any longer our daughter after becoming his wife; if you marry him it shall be to follow his fortunes in the jungle; we shall soon see you repent your obstinacy."

"I will marry him and follow him wherever he goes," said the Princess.

So Vicram Maharajah and the Princess Buccoulee were married, and her parents turned her out of the house; nevertheless, they allowed her a little money. "For" they said, "she will fast enough find the difference between a king's daughter and a beggar's wife, without wanting food."

Vicram built a little hut in the jungle, and there they lived; but the poor Princess had a sad time of it, for she was neither accustomed to cook nor wash, and the hard work tired her very much. Her chief grief, however, was that Vicram should have such a hideous tormenter as the Cobra in his throat; and often and often of a night she sat awake, trying to devise some means for catching it, but all in vain.

At last, one night, when she was thinking about it, she saw close by two Cobras come out of their holes, and as they began to talk, she listened to hear what they would say.

"Who are these people?" said the first Cobra.

"These," said the second, "are the Rajah Vicram, and his wife the Princess Buccoulee." "What are they doing here? why is the Rajah so far from his kingdom?" asked the first Cobra.

"Oh, he ran away because he was so miserable; he has a Cobra that lives in his throat," answered the second.

"Can no one get it out?" said the first.

"No," replied the other; "because they do not know the secret." "What secret?" asked the first Cobra. "Don't you know?" said the second; "why, if his wife only took a few marking nuts,* and pounded them well, and mixed them in cocoa-nut oil, and set the whole on fire, and hung the Rajah, her husband, head downward up in a tree above it, the smoke, rising upward, would instantly kill the Cobra in his mouth, which would tumble down dead."

"I never heard of that before," said the first Cobra.

"Didn't you?" exclaimed the second. "Why, if they did the same thing at the mouth of your hole, they'd kill you in no time; and then, perhaps, they might find all the fine treasure you have there!" "Don't joke in that way," said the first Cobra; "I don't like it;" and he crawled away quite offended, and the second Cobra followed him.

No sooner had the Princess heard this than she determined to try the experiment. So next morning she sent for all the villagers living near (who all knew and loved her, and would do anything she told them, because she was the Rajah's daughter), and bade them take a great cauldron and fill it with cocoa-nut oil, and pound down an immense number of marking nuts and

***Semecarpus anacardium.*

throw them into it, and then bring the cauldron to her. They did so, and she set the whole on fire, and caused Vicram to be hung up in a tree overhead; and as soon as the smoke from the cauldron rose in the air it suffocated the Cobra in Vicram Maharajah's throat, which fell down quite dead. Then the Rajah Vicram said to his wife, "O worthy Buccoulee! what a noble woman you are! You have delivered me from this torment, which was more than all the wise men in my kingdom could do."

Buccoulee then caused the cauldron of oil to be placed close to the hole of the first Cobra, which she had heard speaking the night before, and he was suffocated.

She then ordered the people to dig him out of his hole, and in it they found a vast amount of treasure—gold, silver and jewels. Then Buccoulee sent for royal robes for herself and her husband, and bade him cut his hair and shave him; and when they were all ready, she took the remainder of the treasure and returned with it to her father's house; and her father and mother, who had repented of their harshness, gladly welcomed her back, and were both surprised and delighted to see all the vast treasures she had, and what a handsome, princely-looking man her husband was.

Then one day news was brought to Vicram that a stranger Wuzeer had arrived in the palace as the Rajah's guest, and that this Wuzeer had for twelve years been wandering round the world in search of his master, but, not having found him, was returning to his own home. Vicram thought to himself, "Can this possibly be Butti?" and he ran to see.

It was indeed Butti, who cried for joy to see him,

saying, "Oh Vicram, Vicram! do you know it is twelve years since you left us all?"

Then Vicram Maharajah told Butti how the good Princess Buccoulee had married him and succeeded in killing the Cobra, and how he was then on the point of returning to his own country. So they all set out together, being given many rich presents by Buccoulee's father and mother. At last after a long, long journey, they reached home. Anar Ranee was overjoyed to see them again, for she had long mourned her husband as dead. When Buccoulee Ranee was told who Anar Ranee was and taken to see her, she felt very much frightened, for she thought, "Perhaps she will be jealous of me and hate me." But with a gentle smile Anar Ranee came to meet her, saying, "Sister, I hear it is to you we owe the preservation of the Rajah, and that it was you who killed the Cobra; I can never be sufficiently grateful to you, nor love you enough, as long as I live."

From that day Vicram Maharajah stayed in his own kingdom, ruling it wisely and well, and beloved by all. He and Butti lived to a good old age, and their affection for each other lasted as long as they lived. So that it became a proverb it that country, and instead of saying, "So-and-so love each other like brothers" (when speaking of two who were much attached), the people would say, "So-and-so love each other like the Rajah and the Wuzeer."

VIII.

LESS INEQUALITY THAN MEN DEEM.

A YOUNG Rajah once said to his Wuzeer, "How is it that I am so often ill? I take care of myself; I never go out in the rain; I wear warm clothes; I eat good food. Yet I am always catching cold or getting fever, in spite of all precautions."

"Overmuch care is worse than none at all," answered the Wuzeer, "which I will soon prove to you."

So he invited the Rajah to accompany him for a walk in the fields. Before they had gone very far they met a poor Shepherd. The Shepherd was accustomed to be out all day long, tending his flock; he had only a coarse cloak on, which served but insufficiently to protect him from the rain and the cold—from the dews by night and the sun by day; his food was parched corn, his drink water; and he lived out in the fields in a small hut made of plaited palm branches. The Wuzeer said to the Rajah, "You know perfectly well what hard lives these poor shepherds lead. Accost this one, and ask him if he often suffers from the exposure which he is obliged to undergo."

The Rajah did as the Wuzeer told him, and asked the Shepherd whether he did not often suffer from rheumatism, cold and fever. The Shepherd answered, "Perhaps it will surprise you, sire, to hear that I never suffer from either the one or the other. From childhood I have been accustomed to endure the extremes of heat and cold, and I suppose that is why they never affect me."

At this the Rajah was very much astonished, and he said to the Wuzeer, "I own I am surprised; but doubtless this Shepherd is an extraordinarily strong man, whom nothing would ever affect." "We shall see," said the Wuzeer; and he invited the Shepherd to the palace. There, for a long time, the Shepherd was taken great care of; he was never permitted to go out in the sun or rain, he had good food and good clothes, and he was not allowed to sit in a draught or get his feet wet. At the end of some months the Wuzeer sent for him into a marble courtyard, the floor of which he caused to be sprinkled with water.

The Shepherd had been for some time so little used to exposure of any kind that wetting his feet caused him to take cold; the place felt to him chilly and damp after the palace; he rapidly became worse, and in a short time, in spite of all the doctors' care, he died. "Where is our friend the Shepherd?" asked the Rajah, a few days afterward; "he surely could not have caught cold merely by treading on the marble floor you had caused to be sprinkled with water?"

"Alas!" answered the Wuzeer, "the result was more disastrous than I had anticipated; the poor Shepherd caught cold and is dead. Having been lately accustomed to overmuch care, the sudden change of temperature killed him.

"You see now to what dangers we are exposed from which the poor are exempt. It is thus that Nature equalizes her best gifts; wealth and opulence tend too frequently to destroy health and shorten life, though they may give much enjoyment to it whilst it lasts."

IX.

PANCH-PHUL RANEE.

A CERTAIN Rajah had two wives, of whom he preferred the second to the first; the first Ranee had a son, but, because he was not the child of the second Ranee, his father took a great dislike to him, and treated him so harshly that the poor boy was very unhappy.

One day, therefore, he said to his mother: "Mother, my father does not care for me, and my presence is only a vexation to him. I should be happier anywhere than here; let me therefore go and seek my fortune in other lands."

So the Ranee asked her husband if he would allow their son to travel. He said, "The boy is free to go, but I don't see how he is to live in any other part of the world, for he is too stupid to earn his living, and I will give him no money to squander on senseless pleasures." Then the Ranee told her son that he had his father's permission to travel, and said to him, "You are going out into the world now to try your luck; take with you the food and clothes I have provided for your journey." And she gave him a bundle of clothes and several small loaves, and in each loaf she placed a gold mohur, that on opening it, he might find money as well as food inside; and he started on his journey.

When the young Rajah had traveled a long way, and left his father's kingdom far behind, he one day came upon the outskirts of a great city, where (instead of taking the position due to his rank, and sending to inform the Rajah of his arrival) he went to a poor Carpenter's house, and begged of him a lodging for the night. The Carpenter was busy making wooden clogs in the porch of his house, but he looked up and nodded, saying, "Young man, you are welcome to any assistance a stranger may need and we can give. If you are in want of food, you will find my wife and daughter in the house: they will be happy to cook for you." The Rajah went inside and said to the Carpenter's daughter, "I am a stranger, and have traveled a long way; I am both tired and hungry: cook me some dinner as fast as you can, and I will pay you for your trouble." She answered, "I would willingly cook you some dinner at once, but I have no wood to light the fire, and the jungle is some way off." "It matters not," said the Rajah; "this will do to light the fire, and I'll make the loss good to your father;" and taking a pair of new clogs which the Carpenter had just finished making, he broke them up and lighted the fire with them.

Next morning he went into the jungle, cut wood, and, having made a pair of new clogs—better than those with which he had lighted the fire the evening before—placed them with the rest of the goods for sale in the Carpenter's shop. Shortly afterward, one of the servants of the Rajah of that country came to buy a pair of clogs for his master, and seeing these new ones, said to the Carpenter, "Why, man, these clogs are better than all the rest put together. I will take none other to the Rajah. I wish you would always make such clogs as these." And throwing down ten gold mohurs on the floor of the hut, he took up the clogs and went away.

The Carpenter was much surprised at the whole business. In the first place, he usually received only two or three rupees for each pair of clogs; and in the second, he knew that these which the Rajah's servant had judged worth ten gold mohurs had not been made by him; and how they had come there he could not think, for he felt certain they were not with the rest of the clogs the night before. He thought and thought, but the more he thought about the matter the more puzzled he got, and he went to talk about it to his wife and daughter. Then his daughter said, "Oh, those must have been the clogs the stranger made!" And she told her father how he had lighted the fire the night before with two of the clogs which were for sale, and had afterward fetched wood from the jungle and made another pair to replace them.

The Carpenter at this news was more astonished than ever, and he thought to himself, "Since this stranger seems a quiet, peaceable sort of man, and can make clogs so well, it is a great pity he should leave this place: he would make a good husband for my daughter;" and, catching hold of the young Rajah, he propounded his scheme to him. (But all this time he had no idea that his guest was a Rajah.)

Now the Carpenter's daughter was a very pretty girl—as pretty as any Ranee you ever saw; she was also good-tempered, clever, and could cook extremely well. So when the Carpenter asked the Rajah to be his son-in-law, he looked at the father, the mother and the girl, and thinking to himself that many a better man had a worse fate, he said, "Yes, I will marry your daughter, and stay here and make clogs." So the Rajah married the Carpenter's daughter.

This Rajah was very clever at making all sorts of things in wood. When he had made all the clogs he wished to sell next day, he would amuse himself in making toys; and in this way he made a thousand wooden parrots. They were as like real parrots as possible. They had each two wings, two legs, two eyes and a sharp beak. And when the Rajah had finished them all, he painted and varnished them and put them one afternoon outside the house to dry.

Night came on, and with it came Parbuttee and Mahdeo,* flying round the world to see the different races of men. Amongst the many places they visited was the city where the Carpenter lived; and in the garden in front of the house they saw the thousand wooden parrots which the Rajah had made and painted and varnished, all placed out to dry. Then Parbuttee turned to Mahdeo, and said, "These parrots are very well made—they need nothing but life. Why should not we give them life?" Mahdeo answered, "What would be the use of that? It would be a strange freak, indeed!" "Oh," said Parbuttee, "I only meant you to do it as an amusement. It would be so funny to see the wooden parrots flying about! But do not do it if you don't like." "You would like it then?" answered Mahdeo. "Very well, I will do it." And he endowed the thousand parrots with life.

Parbuttee and Mahdeo then flew away.

Next morning the Rajah got up early to see if the

* The god Mahdeo is an incarnation of Siva the Destroyer. The goddess Parbuttee is his wife.

varnish he had put on the wooden parrots was dry; but no sooner did he open the door than—marvel of marvels!—the thousand wooden parrots all came walking into the house, flapping their wings and chattering to each other.

Hearing the noise, the Carpenter and the Carpenter's wife and daughter came running out to see what was the matter, and were not less astonished than the Rajah himself at the miracle which had taken place. Then the Carpenter's wife turned to her son-in-law, and said, "It is all very well that you should have made these wooden parrots; but I don't know where we are to find food for them! Great, strong parrots like these will eat not less than a pound of rice a-piece every day. Your father-in-law and I cannot afford to procure as much as that for them in this poor house. If you wish to keep them, you must live elsewhere, for we cannot provide for you all."

"Very well," said the Rajah; "you shall not have cause to accuse me of ruining you, for from henceforth I will have a house of my own." So he and his wife went to live in a house of their own, and he took the thousand parrots with him, and his mother-in-law gave her daughter some corn and rice and money to begin housekeeping with. Moreover, he found that the parrots, that instead of being an expense, were the means of increasing his fortune; for they flew away every morning early to get food, and spent the whole day out in the fields; and every evening, when they returned home, each parrot brought in his beak a stalk of corn or rice, or whatever it had found good to eat. So that their master was regularly supplied with more food than enough; and what with selling what he did not require, and working at his trade, he soon became quite a rich carpenter.

After he had been living in this way very happily for some time, one night, when he fell asleep, the Rajah dreamed a wonderful dream, and this was the dream:

He thought that very, very far away beyond the Red Sea was a beautiful kingdom surrounded by seven other seas; and that it belonged to a Rajah and Ranee who had one lovely daughter, named Panch-Phul Ranee (the Five Flower Queen), after whom the whole kingdom was called Panch-Phul Ranee's country; and that this Princess lived in the centre of her father's kingdom, in a little house round which were seven wide ditches, and seven great hedges made of spears; and that she was called Panch-Phul Ranee because she was so light and delicate that she weighed no more than five white lotus flowers! Moreover, he dreamed that this Princess had vowed to marry no one who could not cross the seven seas, and jump the seven ditches, and seven hedges made of spears.

After dreaming this the young Rajah awoke, and feeling much puzzled, got up, and sitting with his head in his hands, tried to think the matter over and discover if he had ever heard anything like his dream before; but he could make nothing of it.

Whilst he was thus thinking, his wife awoke and asked him what was the matter. He told her, and she said, "That is a strange dream. If I were you, I'd ask the old parrot about it; he is a wise bird, and perhaps he knows." This parrot of which she spoke was the most wise of all the thousand wooden parrots. The Rajah took his wife's advice, and when all the birds came home that evening, he called the old parrot and told him his dream, saying, "Can this be true?" To which the parrot replied, "It is all true. The Panch-Phul Ranee's country lies beyond the Red Sea, and is surrounded by seven seas, and she dwells in a house built in the centre of her father's kingdom. Round her house are seven ditches, and seven hedges made of spears, and she has vowed not to marry any man who cannot jump these seven ditches and seven hedges; and because she is very beautiful many great and noble men have tried to do this, but in vain.

"The Rajah and Ranee, her father and mother, are very fond of her and proud of her. Every day she goes to the palace to see them, and they weigh her in a pair of scales. They put her in one scale and five lotus flowers in the other, and she's so delicate and fragile she weighs no heavier than the five little flowers, so they call her the Panch-Phul Ranee. Her father and mother are very proud of this."

"I should like to go to that country and see the Panch-Phul Ranee," said the Rajah; "but I don't know how I could cross the seven seas." "I will show you how to manage that," replied the old parrot. "I and another parrot will fly close together, I crossing my left over his right wing; so that we will move along as if we were one bird (using only our outside wings to fly with), and on the chair made of our interlaced wings you shall sit, and we will carry you safely across the seven seas. On the way we will every evening alight in some high tree and rest, and every morning we can go on again." "That sounds a good plan; I have a great desire to try it," said the Rajah. "Wife, what should you think of my going to the Panch-Phul Ranee's country, and seeing if I can jump the seven ditches, and seven hedges made of spears? Will you let me try?"

"Yes," she answered. "If you like to go and marry her, go; only take care that you do not kill yourself; and mind you come back some day." And she prepared food for him to take with him, and took off her gold and silver bangles, which she placed in a bundle of warm things, that he might be in need neither of money nor clothes on the journey. He then charged the nine hundred and ninety-eight parrots he left behind him to bring her plenty of corn and rice daily (that she might never need food while he was away), and took her to the house of her father, in whose care she was to remain during his absence; and he wished her good-bye, saying, "Do not fear but that I will come back to you, even if I do win the Panch-Phul Ranee, for you will always be my first wife, though you are the Carpenter's daughter."

The old parrot and another parrot then spread their wings, on which the Rajah seated himself as on a chair, and rising up in the air, they flew away with him out of sight.

Far, far, far they flew, as fast as parrots can fly, over hills, over forests, over rivers, over valleys, on, on, on, hour after hour, day after day, week after week, only staying to rest every night when it got too dark to see where they were going. At last they reached the seven seas which surrounded the Panch-Phul Ranee's country. When once they began crossing the seas they could not rest (for there was neither rock nor island on which to alight), so they were obliged to fly straight across them, night and day, until they gained the shore.

By reason of this the parrots were too exhausted on their arrival to go as far as the city where the Rajah,

Panch-Phul Ranee's father, lived, but they flew down to rest on a beautiful banyan tree, which grew not far from the sea, close to a small village. The Rajah determined to go into the village and get food and shelter there. He told the parrots to stay in the banyan tree till his return; then, leaving his bundle of clothes and most of his money in their charge, he set off on foot toward the nearest house.

After a little while he reached a Malee's cottage, and giving a gold mohur to the Malee's wife, got her to provide him with food and shelter for the night.

Next morning he rose early, and said to his hostess, "I am a stranger here, and know nothing of the place. What is the name of your country?" "This," she said, "is Panch-Phul Ranee's country."

"And what is the last news in your town?" he asked. "Very bad news indeed," she replied. "You must know our Rajah has one only daughter—a most beautiful Princess—and her name is Panch-Phul Ranee, for she is so light and delicate that she weighs no heavier than five lotus flowers. After her this whole country is called Panch-Phul Ranee's country. She lives in a small bungalow* in the centre of the city you see yonder; but, unluckily for us, she has vowed to marry no man who cannot jump on foot over the seven hedges made of spears, and across the seven great ditches that surround her house. This cannot be done, Babamah! † I don't know how many hundreds of thousands of Rajahs have tried to do it and died in the attempt! Yet the Princess will not break her vow. Daily, worse and worse tidings come from the city of fresh people having been killed in trying to jump the seven hedges

* House. † Oh, my child.

and seven ditches, and I see no end to the misfortunes that will arise from it. Not only are so many brave men lost to the world, but, since the Princess will marry no one who does not succeed in this, she stands a chance of not marrying at all; and if that be so, when the Rajah dies there will be no one to protect her and claim the right to succeed to the throne. All the nobles will probably fight for the Raj, and the whole kingdom be turned topsy-turvy."

"Mahi,"* said the Rajah, "if that is all there is to do, I will try and win your Princess, for I can jump right well."

"Baba,"† answered the Malee's wife, "do not think of such a thing; are you mad? I tell you, hundreds of thousands of men have said these words before, and been killed for their rashness. What power do you think you possess to succeed where all before you have failed? Give up all thought of this, for it is utter folly."

"I will not do it," answered the Rajah, "before going to consult some of my friends."

So he left the Malee's cottage, and returned to the banyan tree to talk over the matter with the parrots; for he thought they would be able to carry him on their wings across the seven ditches and seven hedges made of spears. When he reached the tree the old parrot said to him, "It is two days since you left us; what news have you brought from the village?" The Rajah answered, "The Panch-Phul Ranee still lives in the house surrounded by the seven ditches, and seven hedges made of spears, and has vowed to marry no man who cannot jump over them; but cannot you parrots, who

* Woman or mother. † Child.

brought me all the way over the seven seas, carry me on your wings across these great barriers?"

"You stupid man!" answered the old parrot; "of course we could; but what would be the good of doing so? If we carried you across, it would not be at all the same thing as your jumping across, and the Princess would no more consent to marry you than she would now; for she has vowed to marry no one who has not jumped across *on foot*. If you want to do the thing, why not do it yourself, instead of talking nonsense. Have you forgotten how, when you were a little boy, you were taught to jump by conjurors and tumblers (for the parrot knew all the Rajah's history)? Now is the time to put their lessons in practice. If you can jump the seven ditches, and seven hedges made of spears, you will have done a good work, and be able to marry the Panch-Phul Ranee; but if not, this is a thing in which we cannot help you."

"You reason justly," replied the Rajah. "I will try to put in practice the lessons I learnt when a boy; meantime, do you stay here till my return."

So saying, he went away to the city, which he reached by nightfall. Next morning early he went to where the Princess' bungalow stood, to try and jump the fourteen great barriers. He was strong and agile, and he jumped the seven great ditches, and six of the seven hedges made of spears; but in running to jump the seventh hedge he hurt his foot, and, stumbling, fell upon the spears and died—run through and through with the cruel iron spikes.

When Panch-Phul Ranee's father and mother got up that morning and looked out, as their custom was, toward their daughter's bungalow, they saw something transfixed upon the seventh hedge of spears, but what it was they could not make out, for it dazzled their eyes. So the Rajah called his Wuzeer and said to him, "For some days I have seen no one attempt to jump the seven hedges and seven ditches round Panch-Phul Ranee's bungalow; but what is that which I now see upon the seventh hedge of spears?" The Wuzeer answered, "That is a Rajah's son, who has failed like all who have gone before him." "But how is it," asked the Rajah, "that he thus dazzles our eyes?"

"It is," replied the Wuzeer, "because he is so beautiful. Of all that have died for the sake of Panch-Phul Ranee, this youth is, beyond doubt, the handsomest." "Alas!" cried the Rajah, "how many and how many brave men has my daughter killed? I will have no more die for her. Let us send her and the dead man together away into the jungle."

Then he ordered the servants to fetch the young Rajah's body. There he lay, still and beautiful, with a glory shining round him as the moonlight shines round the clear bright moon, but without a spark of life.

When the Rajah saw him, he said, "Oh pity, pity, that so brave and handsome a boy should have come dying after this girl! Yet he is but one of the thousands of thousands who have died thus to no purpose. Pull up the spears and cast them into the seven ditches, for they shall remain no longer."

Then he commanded two palanquins to be prepared and men in readiness to carry them, and said, "Let the girl be married to the young Rajah, and let both be taken far away into the jungle, that we may never see them more. Then there will be quiet in the land again."

The Ranee, Panch-Phul Ranee's mother, cried bitterly at this, for she was very fond of her daughter, and she begged her husband not to send her away so cruelly—the living with the dead; but the Rajah was inexorable. "That poor boy died," he said: "let my daughter die too. I'll have no more men killed here."

So the two palanquins were prepared. Then he placed his daughter in the one, and her dead husband in the other, and said to the palkee-bearers, "Take these palkees and go out into the jungle until you have reached a place so desolate that not so much as a sparrow is to be seen, and there leave them both."

And so they did. Deep down in the jungle, where no bright sun could pierce the darkness, nor human voice be heard, far from any habitation of man or means of supporting life, on the edge of a dank, stagnant morass that was shunned by all but noisome reptiles and wandering beasts of prey, they set them down and left them, the dead husband and the living wife, alone to meet the horrors of the coming night—alone, without a chance of rescue.

Panch-Phul Ranee heard the bearers' retreating footsteps, and their voices getting fainter and fainter in the distance, and felt that she had nothing to hope for but death.

Night seemed coming on apace, for though the sun had not set, the jungle was so dark that but little light pierced the gloom; and she thought she would take a last look at the husband her vow had killed, and sitting beside him wait till starvation should make her as he was, or some wild animal put a more speedy end to her sufferings.

She left her palkee and went toward his. There

he lay with closed eyes and close-shut lips: black curling hair, which escaped from under his turban, concealed a ghastly wound on his temple. There was no look of pain on the face, and the long, sweeping eyelashes gave it such a tender, softened expression she could hardly believe that he was dead. He was, in truth, very beautiful; and watching him she said to herself, "Alas, what a noble being is here lost to the world! what an earth's joy is extinguished! Was it for this that I was cold, and proud, and stern—to break the cup of my own happiness and to be the death of such as you? Must you now never know that you won your wife? Must you never hear her ask your pardon for the past, nor know her cruel punishment? Ah, if you had but lived, how dearly I would have loved you! Oh my husband! my husband!" And sinking down on the ground, she buried her face in her hands and cried bitterly.

While she was sitting thus night closed over the jungle, and brought with it wild beasts that had left their dens and lairs in search of prey—to roam about, as the heat of the day was over. Tigers, lions, elephants and bison, all came by turns crushing through the underwood which surrounded the place where the palkees were, but they did no harm to Panch-Phul Ranee, for she was so fair that not even the cruel beasts of the forest would injure her. At last, about four o'clock in the morning, all the wild animals had gone, except two little jackals, who had been very busy watching the rest and picking the bones left by the tigers. Tired with running about, they lay down to rest close to the palkees. Then one little jackal said to the other, who was her husband, "Do tell me a little story." "Dear me!" he exclaimed, "what people you women are for stories! Well, look just in front of you; do you see those two?" "Yes," she answered; "what of them?" "That woman you see sitting on the ground," he said, "is the Panch-Phul Ranee." "And what son of a Rajah is the man in the palkee?" asked she. "That," he replied, "is a very sorrowful son. His father was so unkind to him that he left his own home, and went to live in another country very far from this; and there he dreamed about the Panch-Phul Ranee, and came to our land in order to marry her, but he was killed in jumping the seventh hedge of spears, and all he gained was to die for her sake."

"That is very sad," said the first little jackal; "but could he never by any chance come to life again?" "Yes," answered the other; "may be he could, if only some one knew how to apply the proper remedies." "What are the proper remedies, and how could he be cured?" asked the lady jackal. (Now all this conversation had been heard by Panch-Phul Ranee, and when this question was asked she listened very eagerly and attentively for the answer.)

"Do you see this tree?" replied her husband. "Well, if some of its leaves were crushed, and a little of the juice put into the Rajah's two ears and upon his upper lip, and some upon his temples also, and some upon the spear-wounds in his side, he would come to life again and be as well as ever."

At this moment day dawned, and the two little jackals ran away. Panch-Phul Ranee did not forget their words. She, a Princess born, who had never put her foot to the ground before (so delicately and tenderly had she been reared), walked over the rough clods of earth and the sharp stones till she reached the place where the tree grew of which the jackals had spoken. She gathered a number of its leaves, and, with hands and feet that had never before done coarse or common work, beat and crushed them down. They were so stiff and strong that it took her a long time. At last, after tearing them, and stamping on them, and pounding them between two stones, and biting the hardest parts, she thought they were sufficiently crushed; and rolling them up in a corner of her saree, she squeezed the juice through it on to her husband's temples, and put a little on his upper lip and into his ears, and some also on the spear-wound in his side. And when she had done this, he awoke as if he had been only sleeping, and sat up, wondering where he was. Before him stood Panch-Phul Ranee shining like a glorious star, and all around them was the dark jungle.

It would be hard to say which of them was the most astonished—the Rajah or the Princess. She was surprised that the remedy should have taken such speedy effect, and could hardly believe her eyes when she saw her husband get up. And if he looked beautiful when dead, much more handsome did he seem to her now, so full of life and animation and power—the picture of health and strength. And he in his turn was lost in amazement at the exquisite loveliness of the lady who stood before him. He did not know who she could be, for he had never seen her like except in a dream. Could she be really the world-renowned Panch-Phul Ranee, or was he dreaming still? He feared to move lest he should break the spell. But as he sat there wondering, she spoke, saying, "You marvel at what has taken place. You do not know me—I am Panch-Phul Ranee, your wife."

Then he said, "Ah, Princess, is it indeed you? You have been very hard to me." "I know, I know," she answered; "I caused your death, but I brought you to life again. Let the past be forgotten; come home with me, and my father and mother will welcome you as a son."

He replied, "No, I must first return to my own home a while. Do you rather return there now with me, for it is a long time since I left it, and afterward we will come again to your father's kingdom."

To this Panch-Phul Ranee agreed. It took them, however, a long time to find their way out of the jungle. At last they succeeded in doing so, for none of the wild animals in it attempted to injure them, so beautiful and royal did they both look.

When they reached the banyan tree, where the Rajah had left the two parrots, the old parrot called out to him, "So you have come back at last! We thought you never would, you were such a long time away! There you went, leaving us here all the time, and after all doing no good, but only getting yourself killed. Why didn't you do as we advised you, and jump up nicely?"

"Well, I'm sure," said the Rajah, "yours is a hard case; but I beg your pardon for keeping you waiting so long, and now I hope you'll take me and my wife home."

"Yes, we will do that," answered the parrots; "but you had better get some dinner first, for it's a long journey over the seven seas."

So the Rajah went to the village close by and bought

food for himself and the Panch-Phul Ranee. When he returned with it, he said to her, "I fear the long journey before us for you: had you not better let me make it alone, and return here for you when it is over?" But she answered, "No! what could I, a poor, weak woman, do here alone? and I will not return to my father's house till you can come too. Take me with you, however far you go; only promise me you will never leave me." So he promised her, and they both, mounting the parrots, were carried up in the air across the seven seas, across the Red Sea, on, on, on, a whole year's journey, until they reached his father's kingdom, and alighted to rest at the foot of the palace garden. The Rajah, however, did not know where he was, for all had much changed since he left it some years before.

Then a little son was born to the Rajah and Panch-Phul Ranee. He was a beautiful child, but his father was grieved to think that in that bleak place there was no shelter for the mother or the baby. So he said to his wife, "I will go to fetch food for us both, and fire to cook it with, and inquire what this country is, and seek out a place of rest for you. Do not be afraid; I shall soon return." Now, far off in the distance smoke was to be seen rising from tents which belonged to some conjurors and dancing-people, and thither the Rajah bent his steps, feeling certain he should be able to get fire, and perhaps food also, from the inhabitants. When he got there, he found the place was much larger than he had expected—quite a good-sized village in fact—the abode of Nautch-people and conjurors. In all the houses the people were busy, some dancing, some singing, others trying various conjuring tricks or practising beating the drum, and all seemed happy and joyful.

When the conjurors saw him, they were so much struck with his appearance (for he was very handsome) that they determined to make him, if possible, stay among them and join their band. And they said one to another, "How well he would look beating the drum for the dancers! All the world would come to see us dance, if we had such a handsome man as that to beat the drum."

The Rajah, unconscious of their intentions, went into the largest hut he saw, and said to a woman who was grinding corn, "Bai,* give me a little rice, and some fire from your hearth." She immediately consented, and got up to fetch the burning sticks he asked for; but before she gave them to him, she and her companions threw upon them a certain powder, containing a very potent charm; and no sooner did the Rajah receive them than he forgot about his wife and little child, his journey, and all that had ever happened to him in his life before; such was the peculiar property of the powder. And when the conjurors said to him, "Why should you go away? stay with us, and be one of us," he willingly consented to do so.

All this time Panch-Phul Ranee waited and waited for her husband, but he never came. Night approached without his having brought her any food or news of having found a place of shelter for her and the baby. At last, faint and weary, she swooned away.

It happened that that very day the Ranee (Panch-Phul Ranee's husband's mother) lost her youngest child, a fine little boy of only a day old; and her servants

* Woman.

took its body to the bottom of the garden to bury it. Just as they were going to do so, they heard a low cry, and, looking round, saw close by a beautiful woman lying on the ground, dead, or apparently so, and beside her a fine little baby boy. The idea immediately entered their heads of leaving the dead baby beside the dead woman, and taking her living baby back with them to the palace; and so they did.

When they returned, they said to their mistress, "Your child did not die; see here it is—it got well again," and showed her Panch-Phul Ranee's baby; but after a time, when the Ranee questioned them about it, they told her the whole truth, but she had become meanwhile very fond of the little boy, and so he continued in the palace and was brought up as her son; being, in truth, her grandson, though she did not know it.

Meantime the palace Malee's wife went out, as her custom was every morning, and evening, to gather flowers. In search of them she wandered as far as the jungle at the bottom of the garden, and there she found the Panch-Phul Ranee lying as dead, and the dead baby beside her.

The good woman felt very sorry, and rubbed the Ranee's cold hands and gave her sweet flowers to smell, in hopes that she might revive. At last she opened her eyes, and seeing the Malee's wife, said, "Where am I? has not my husband come back? and who are you?"

"My poor lady," answered the Malee's wife, "I do not know where your husband is. I am the Malee's wife, and coming here to gather flowers, I found you lying on the ground, and this your little baby, which is dead; but come home with me, I will take care of you."

Panch-Phul Ranee answered, "Kind friend, this is

not my baby; he did not die; he was the image of his father, and fairer than this child. Some one must have taken him away, for but a little while ago I held him in my arms, and he was strong and well, while this one could never have been more than a puny, weakly infant. Take me away; I will go home with you."

So the Malee's wife buried the dead child and took the Panch-Phul Ranee to her house, where she lived for fourteen years; but all that time she could learn no tidings of her husband or her lost little boy. The child, meanwhile, grew up in the palace, and became a very handsome youth. One day he was wandering round the garden and chanced to pass the Malee's house. The Panch-Phul Ranee was sitting within, watching the Malee's wife cook their dinner.

The young Prince saw her, and calling the Malee's wife, said to her, "What beautiful lady is that in your house? and how did she come there?" She answered, "Little Prince, what nonsense you talk! there is no lady here." He said again, "I know there is a beautiful lady here, for I saw her as I passed the open door." She replied, "If you come telling such tales about my house, I'll pull your tongue out." For she thought to herself, "Unless I scold him well, the boy'll go talking about what he's seen in the palace, and then perhaps some of the people from there will come and take the poor Panch-Phul Ranee away from my care." But whilst the Malee's wife was talking to the young Prince, the Panch-Phul Ranee came from the inner room to watch and listen to him unobserved; and no sooner did she see him than she could not forbear crying out, "Oh, how like he is to my husband! The same eyes, the same shaped face and the same king-like bearing! Can he be my son? He is just the age my son would have been had he lived."

The young Prince heard her speaking and asked what she said, to which the Malee's wife replied, "The woman you saw, and who just now spoke, lost her child fourteen years ago, and she was saying to herself how like you were to that child, and thinking you must be the same; but she is wrong, for we know you are the Ranee's son." Then Panch-Phul Ranee herself came out of the house, and said to him, "Young Prince, I could not, when I saw you, help exclaiming how like you are to what my lost husband was, and to what my son might have been; for it is now fourteen years since I lost them both." And she told him how she had been a great Princess, and was returning with her husband to his own home (to which they had got halfway in reaching that place), and how her little baby had been born in the jungle, and her husband had gone away to seek shelter for her and the child, and fire and food, and had never returned; and also how, when she had fainted away, some one had certainly stolen her baby and left a dead child in its place; and how the good Malee's wife had befriended her, and taken her ever since to live in her house. And when she had ended her story she began to cry.

But the Prince said to her, "Be of good cheer; I will endeavor to recover your husband and child for you: who knows but I may indeed be your son, beautiful lady?" And running home to the Ranee (his adopted mother), he said to her, "Are you really my mother? Tell me truly; for this I must know before the sun goes down." "Why do you ask foolish questions?" she replied; "have I not always treated you as a son?"

"Yes," he said; "but tell me the very truth, am I your own child, or the child of some one else, adopted as yours? If you do not tell me, I will kill myself." And so saying, he drew his sword. She replied, "Stay, stay, and I will tell you the whole truth: the day before you were born I had a little baby, but it died; and my servants took it to the bottom of the garden to bury it, and there they found a beautiful woman lying as dead, and beside her a living infant. You were that child. They brought you to the palace, and I adopted you as my son, and left my baby in your stead." "What became of my mother?" he asked. "I cannot tell," answered the Ranee; "for, two days afterward, when I sent to the same place, she and the baby had both disappeared, and I have never since heard of her."

The young Prince, on hearing this, said, "There is in the head Malee's house a beautiful lady, whom the Malee's wife found in the jungle, fourteen years ago; that must be my mother. Let her be received here this very day with all honor, for that is the only reparation that can now be made to her."

The Ranee consented, and the young Prince went down to the Malee's house himself to fetch his mother to the palace.

With him he took a great retinue of people, and a beautiful palanquin for her to go in, covered with rich trappings; also costly things for her to wear, and many jewels and presents for the good Malee's wife.

When Panch-Phul Ranee had put on her son's gifts, and come out of the Malee's poor cottage to meet him, all the people said there had never been so royal-looking a queen. As gold and clear crystal are lovely, as mother-of-pearl is exquisitely fair and delicate-looking, so beautiful, so fair, so delicate appeared Panch-Phul Ranee.

Her son conducted her with much pomp and state to the palace, and did all in his power to honor her; and there she lived long very happily, and beloved by all.

One day the young Prince begged her to tell him again, from the beginning, the story of her life, and as much as she knew of his father's life; and so she did. And after that, he said to her, "Be no longer sad, dear mother, regarding my father's fate; for I will send into all lands to gather tidings of him, and maybe in the end we shall find him." And he sent people out to hunt for the Rajah all over the kingdom, and in all neighboring countries—to the north, to the south, to the east and to the west—but they found him not.

At last (after four years of unsuccessful search), when there seemed no hope of ever learning what had become of him, Panch-Phul Ranee's son came to see her, and said, "Mother, I have sent into all lands seeking my father, but can hear no news of him. If there were only the slightest clue as to the direction in which he went, there would still be some chance of tracing him, but that, I fear, cannot be got. Do you not remember his having said anything of the way which he intended to go when he left you?" She answered, "When your father went away, his words to me were, 'I will go to fetch food for us both, and fire to cook it with, and inquire what this country is, and seek out a place of shelter for you. Do not be afraid—I shall soon return.' That was all he said, and then he went away, and I never saw him more."

"In what direction did he go from the foot of the garden?" asked the Prince. "He went," answered the

Panch-Phul Ranee, "toward that village of conjurors close by. I thought he was intending to ask some of them to give us food. But had he done so, he would certainly have returned in a very short time."

"Do you think you should know my father, mother darling, if you were to see him again?" asked the Prince. "Yes," answered she, "I should know him again." "What!" he said, "even though eighteen years have gone by since you saw him last? Even though age and sickness and want had done their utmost to change him?" "Yes!" she replied; "his every feature is so impressed on my heart that I should know him again anywhere or in any disguise."

"Then let us," he said, "send for all those people in the direction of whose houses he went away. Maybe they have detained him among them to this day. It is but a chance, but we can hope for nothing more certain."

So the Panch-Phul Ranee and her son sent down orders to the conjurors' village that every one of the whole band should come up to the palace that afternoon—not a soul was to stay behind. And the dancers were to dance and the conjurors to play all their tricks for the amusement of the palace inmates.

The people came. The nautch girls began to dance—running, jumping and flying here, there and everywhere, some up, some down, some round and round. The conjurors conjured and all began in different ways to amuse the company. Among the rest was one wild, ragged-looking man, whose business was to beat the drum. No sooner did the Panch-Phul Ranee set eyes on him than she said to her son, "Boy, that is your father!" "What, mother!" he said, "that wretched-looking man who is beating the drum?" "The same," she answered.

The Prince said to his servants, "Fetch that man here." And the Rajah came toward them, so changed that not even his own mother knew him—no one recognized him but his wife. For eighteen years he had been among the nautch people; his hair was rough, his beard untrimmed, his face thin and worn, sunburnt and wrinkled; he wore a nose-ring and heavy ear-rings, such as the nautch people have; and his dress was a rough, common cumlee.* All traces of his former self seemed to have disappeared. They asked him if he did not remember he had been a Rajah once, and about his journey to Panch-Phul Ranee's country. But he said, No, he remembered nothing but how to beat the drum—Rub-a-dub! tat-tat! tom-tum! tom-tum! He thought he must have beaten it all his life.

Then the young Prince gave orders that all the nautch people should be put into jail until it could be discovered what part they had taken in reducing his father to so pitiable a state. And sending for the wisest doctors in the kingdom, he said to them, "Do your best and restore the health of this Rajah, who has to all appearance lost both memory and reason; and discover, if possible, what has caused these misfortunes to befall him." The doctors said, "He has certainly had some potent charm given to him, which has destroyed both his memory and reason, but we will do our best to counteract its influence."

And so they did. And their treatment succeeded so well that, after a time, the Rajah entirely recovered his former senses. And they took such good care of him that in a little while he regained his health and strengh also, and looked almost as well as ever.

* A coarse woolen blanket.

He then found to his surprise that he, Panch-Phul Ranee, and their son, had all this time been living in his father's kingdom. His father was so delighted to see him again that he was no longer unkind to him, but treated him as a dearly beloved, long-lost son. His mother also was overjoyed at his return, and they said to him, "Since you have been restored to us again, why should you wander any more? Your wife and son are here; do you also remain here, and live among us for the rest of your days." But he replied, "I have another wife—the Carpenter's daughter—who first was kind to me in my adopted country. I also have there nine hundred and ninety-eight talking wooden parrots, which I greatly prize. Let me first go and fetch them."

They said, "Very well; go quickly and then return." So he mounted the two wooden parrots which had brought him from the Panch-Phul Ranee's country (and which had for eighteen years lived in the jungle close to the palace), and returned to the land where his first wife lived, and fetched her and the nine hundred and ninety-eight remaining wooden parrots to his father's kingdom. Then his father said to him, "Don't have any quarreling with your half-brother after I am dead (for his half-brother was son of the old Rajah's favorite wife). "I love you both dearly, and will give each of you half of my kingdom." So he divided the kingdom into two halves, and gave the one half to the Panch-Phul Ranee's husband, who was the son of his first wife, and the other half to the eldest son of his second but favorite wife.

A short time after this arrangement was made, Panch-Phul Ranee said to her husband, "I wish to see my father and mother again before I die; let me go and see them." He answered, "You shall go, and I and our son will also go." So he called four of the wooden parrots—two to carry himself and the Ranee, and two to carry their son. Each pair of parrots crossed their wings; the young Prince sat upon the two wings of one pair, and on the wings of the other pair sat his father and mother. Then they all rose up in the air, and the parrots carried them (as they had before carried the Rajah alone), up, up, up, on, on, on, over the Red Sea, and across the seven seas, until they reached the Panch-Phul Ranee's country.

Panch-Phul Ranee's father saw them come flying through the air as quickly as shooting stars, and much wondering who they were, he sent out many of his nobles and chief officers to inquire.

The nobles went out to meet them, and called out, "What great Rajah is this who is dressed so royally, and comes flying through the air so fast? Tell us, that we may tell our Rajah."

The Rajah answered, "Go and tell your master that this is Panch-Phul Ranee's husband, come to visit his father-in-law." So they took that answer back to the palace, but when the Rajah heard it, he said, "I cannot tell what this means, for the Panch-Phul Ranee's husband died long ago. It is twenty years since he fell upon the iron spears and died; let us, however, all go and discover who this great Rajah really is." And he and all his court went out to meet the new-comers, just as the parrots had alighted close to the palace gate. The Panch-Phul Ranee took her son by the one hand and her husband by the other, and walking to meet her father, said, "Father, I have come to see you again. This is my husband who died, and this boy is my son." Then all the land was glad to see the Panch-Phul Ranee back, and the people said, "Our Princess is the most beautiful Princess in the world, and her husband is as handsome as she is, and her son is a fair boy; we will that they should always live among us and reign over us."

When they had rested a little, the Panch-Phul Ranee told her father and mother the story of all her adventures from the time she and her husband were left in the palkees in the jungle. And when they had heard it, her father said to the Rajah, her husband, "You must never go away again; for see, I have no son but you. You and your son must reign here after me. And behold all this great kingdom will I now give you, if you will only stay with us; for I am old and weary of governing the land."

But the Rajah answered, "I must return once again to my own country, and then I will stay with you as long as I live."

So, leaving the Panch-Phul Ranee and her son with the old Rajah and Ranee, he mounted his parrots and once more returned to his father's land. And when he had reached it, he said to his mother, "Mother, my father-in-law has given me a kingdom ten thousand times larger than this. So I have but returned to bid you farewell and fetch my first wife, and then I must go back to live in that other land." She answered, "Very well; so you are happy anywhere, I am happy too."

He then said to his half-brother, "Brother, my father-in-law has given me all the Panch-Phul Ranee's country, which is very far away; therefore I give up to you the half of this kingdom that my father gave to me." Then, bidding his father farewell, he took the Carpenter's daughter back with him (riding through the air on two of the wooden parrots, and followed by the rest) to the Panch-Phul Ranee's country, and there he and his two wives and his son lived very happily all their mortal days.

X.

HOW THE SUN, THE MOON AND THE WIND WENT OUT TO DINNER.

ONE day the Sun, the Moon and the Wind went out to dine with their uncle and aunt, the Thunder and Lightning. Their mother (one of the most distant Stars you see far up in the sky) waited alone for her children's return.

Now both the Sun and the Wind were greedy and selfish. They enjoyed the great feast that had been prepared for them, without a thought of saving any of it to take home to their mother; but the gentle Moon did not forget her. Of every dainty dish that was brought round she placed a small portion under one of her beautiful long finger-nails, that the Star might also have a share in the treat.*

On their return, their mother, who had kept watch for them all night long with her little bright eye, said, "Well, children, what have you brought home for me?" Then the Sun (who was eldest) said, "I have brought nothing home for you. I went out to enjoy myself with my friends, not to fetch a dinner for my mother!" And the Wind said, "Neither have I brought anything home for you, mother. You could hardly expect me to bring a collection of good things for you,

* See Notes at the end.

when I merely went out for my own pleasure." But the Moon said, "Mother, fetch a plate; see what I have brought you." And shaking her hands she showered down such a choice dinner as never was seen before.

Then the Star turned to the Sun and spoke thus: "Because you went out to amuse yourself with your friends, and feasted and enjoyed yourself without any thought of your mother at home, you shall be cursed. Henceforth, your rays shall ever be hot and scorching, and shall burn all that they touch. And men shall hate you and cover their heads when you appear."

(And that is why the Sun is so hot to this day.)

Then she turned to the Wind and said: "You also, who forgot your mother in the midst of your selfish pleasures, hear your doom. You shall always blow in the hot, dry weather, and shall parch and shrivel all living things. And men shall detest and avoid you from this very time."

(And that is why the Wind in the hot weather is still so disagreeable.)

But to the Moon she said: "Daughter, because you remembered your mother, and kept for her a share in your own enjoyment, from henceforth you shall be ever cool and calm and bright. No noxious glare shall accompany your pure rays, and men shall always call you 'blessed.'"

(And that is why the Moon's light is so soft and cool and beautiful even to this day.)

XI.

SINGH RAJAH AND THE CUNNING LITTLE JACKALS.

ONCE upon a time, in a great jungle, there lived a great Lion. He was Rajah of all the country round; and every day he used to leave his den, in the deepest shadow of the rocks, and *roar* with a loud, angry voice; and when he roared, the other animals in the jungle, who were all his subjects, got very much frightened and ran here and there; and Singh Rajah would pounce upon them and kill them, and gobble them up for his dinner.

This went on for a long, long time, until, at last, there were no living creatures left in the jungle but two little Jackals—a Rajah Jackal and a Ranee Jackal—husband and wife.

A very hard time of it the poor little Jackals had, running this way and that to escape the terrible Singh Rajah; and every day the little Ranee Jackal would say to her husband, "I am afraid he will catch us to-day; do you hear how he is roaring? Oh dear! oh dear!" And he would answer her, "Never fear; I will take care of you. Let us run on a mile or two. Come, come quick, quick, quick." And they would both run away as fast as they could.

After some time spent in this way, they found, however, one fine day, that the Lion was so close upon them that they could not escape. Then the little Rance Jackal said, "Husband, husband, I feel much frightened. The Singh Rajah is so angry he will certainly kill us at once. What can we do?" But he answered, "Cheer up; we can save ourselves yet. Come, and I'll show you how we may manage it."

So what did these cunning little Jackals do but they went to the great Lion's den; and when he saw them coming, he began to roar and shake his mane, and he said, "You little wretches, come and be eaten at once! I have had no dinner for three whole days, and all that time I have been running over hill and dale to find you. Ro-a-ar! Ro-a-ar! Come and be eaten, I say!" and he lashed his tail and gnashed his teeth, and looked very terrible indeed. Then the Jackal Rajah, creeping quite close up to him, said, "Oh, great Singh Rajah, we all know you are our master, and we would have come at your bidding long ago; but indeed, sir, there is a much bigger Rajah even than you in this jungle, and he tried to catch hold of us and eat us up, and frightened us so much that we were obliged to run away."

"What do you mean?" growled Singh Rajah. "There is no king in this jungle but me!" "Ah, sire," answered the Jackal, "in truth one would think so, for you are very dreadful. Your very voice is death. But it is as we say, for we, with our own eyes, have seen one with whom you could not compete—whose equal you can no more be than we are yours—whose face is as flaming fire, his step as thunder, and his power supreme." "It is impossible!" interrupted the old Lion; "but show me this Rajah of whom you speak so much, that I may destroy him instantly!"

Then the little Jackals ran on before him until they reached a great well, and pointing down to his own reflection in the water, they said, "See, sire, there lives the terrible king of whom we spoke." When Singh Rajah looked down the well, he became very angry, for he thought he saw another Lion there. He roared and shook his great mane, and the shadow Lion shook his and looked terribly defiant. At last, beside himself with rage at the violence of his opponent, Singh Rajah sprang down to kill him at once, but no other Lion was there—only the treacherous reflection—and the sides of the well were so steep that he could not get out again to punish the two Jackals, who peeped over the top. After struggling for some time in the deep water, he sank to rise no more. And the little Jackal threw stones down upon him from above, and danced round and round the well, singing, "Ao! Ao! Ao! Ao! The King of the Forest is dead, is dead! We have killed the great Lion who would have killed us! Ao! Ao! Ao! Ao! Ring-a-ting—ding-a-ting! Ring-a-ting—ding-a-ting! Ao! Ao! Ao!"*

* See Notes at the end.

XII.

THE JACKAL, THE BARBER AND THE BRAHMIN WHO HAD SEVEN DAUGHTERS.

A BARBER and a Jackal once struck up a great friendship, which might have continued to this day, had not the Jackal been so clever that the Barber never felt quite on equal terms with him, and suspected his friend of playing him many tricks. But this he was not able to prove.

One day the Jackal said to the Barber, "It would be a nice thing for us to have a garden of our own, in which we might grow as many cucumbers, pumpkins and melons as we like. Why should we not buy one?"

The Barber answered, "Very well; here is money. Do you go and buy us a garden." So the Jackal took the Barber's money, and with it bought a fine garden, in which were cucumbers, pumpkins, melons, figs, and many other good fruits and vegetables. And he used to go there every day and feast to his heart's content. When, however, the Barber said to him, "What is the garden like which you bought with the money I gave you?" he answered, "There are very fine plants in it, but there is no fruit upon them; when the fruit is ripe I will let you know." This reply satisfied the Barber, who inquired no further at that time.

A little while afterward, the Barber again asked the Jackal about the garden, saying, "I see you go down to that garden every day; is the fruit getting ripe?" "Oh dear no, not yet," answered the Jackal; "why, the plants are only just coming into blossom."

But all this time there was a great deal of fruit in the garden, and the Jackal went there every day and ate as much as he could.

Again, a third time, when some weeks had passed, the Barber said to him, "Is there no ripe fruit in our garden yet?" "No," said the Jackal; "the blossoms have only just fallen, but the fruit is forming. In time we shall have a fine show of melons and figs there."

Then the Barber began to think the Jackal was deceiving him, and determined to see and judge for himself. So next day, without saying anything about it, he followed him down to the garden.

Now it happened that very day the Jackal had invited all his friends to come and feast there. All the animals in the neighboring jungle had accepted the invitation; there they came trooping by hundreds and dozens, and were very-merry indeed—running here and there, and eating all the melons and cucumbers and figs and pumpkins in the place.

The Barber peeped over the hedge, and saw the assembled wild beasts, and his friend the Jackal entertaining them—talking to this one, laughing with that, and eating with all. The good man did not dare to attack the intruders, as they were many and powerful. But he went home at once, very angry, muttering to himself, "I'll be the death of that young jackanapes; he shall play no more pranks in my garden." And, watching his opportunity, he returned there when the

Jackal and all his friends had left, and tied a long knife to the largest of the cucumbers that still remained; then he went home and said nothing of what he had seen.

Early next morning the Jackal thought to himself, "I'll just run down to the garden and see if there are no cucumbers or melons left." So he went there, and, picking out the largest of the cucumbers, began to eat it. Quick as thought, the long knife, that was concealed by the cucumber leaves, ran into him, cutting his muzzle, his neck and his side.

"Ah, that nasty Barber!" he cried; "this must be his doing!" And instead of going home, he ran as fast as he could, very far, far, away into the jungle, and stretching himself out on a great flat rock, prepared to die.

But he did not die. Only for three whole days the pain in his neck and side was so great that he could not move; moreover, he felt very weak from loss of blood.

At the end of the third day he tried to get up, but his own blood had sealed him to the stone! He endeavored to move it by his struggles, but could not succeed. "Oh dear! oh dear!" he murmured; "to think that I should recover from my wound, only to die such a horrible death as this! Ah me! here is the punishment of dishonesty!" And, having said this, he began to weep. It chanced, however, that the god of Rain heard his lamentations, and taking pity on the unfortunate animal, he sent a kindly shower, which, wetting the stone, effected his release.

No sooner was the Jackal set free than he began to think what he could do to earn a livelihood, since he did not dare return to the Barber's house. It was not long before a feasible plan struck him: all around was the mud made by the recent rain; he placed a quantity of it in a small chattee, covered the top over carefully with leaves (as people do jars of fresh butter), and took it into a neighboring village to sell.

At the door of one of the first houses to which he came stood a woman, to whom the Jackal said, "Mahi, here is butter—beautiful fresh butter! won't you buy some fresh butter?" She answered, "Are you sure it is quite fresh? Let me see it." But he replied, "It is perfectly fresh; but if you open the chattee now, it will be all spoilt by the time you want it. If you like to buy it, you may take it; if not, I will sell it to some one else." The woman did want some fresh butter, and the chattee the Jackal carried on his head was carefully fastened up, as if what it contained was of the best; and she knew if she opened it, it might spoil before her husband returned home; besides, she thought, if the Jackal had intended to deceive her, he would have been more pressing in asking her to buy it. So she said, "Very well, give me the chattee; here is money for you. You are sure it is the best butter?" "It is the best of its kind," answered the Jackal; "only be sure you put it in some cool place, and don't open it till it is wanted." And taking the money, he ran away.

A short time afterward the woman discovered how she had been cheated, and was very angry; but the Jackal was by that time far away, out of reach of punishment.

When his money was spent, the Jackal felt puzzled as to how to get a living, since no one would give him food and he could buy none. Fortunately for him, just then one of the bullocks belonging to the village died. The Jackal found it lying dead by the road-side, and he began to eat it, and ate, and ate so much that at last he had got too far into the animal's body to be seen by passers-by. Now the weather was hot and dry. Whilst the Jackal was in it, the bullock's skin crinkled up so tightly with the heat that it became too hard for him to bite through, and so he could not get out again.

The Mahars* of the village all came out to bury the dead bullock. The Jackal, who was inside it, feared that if they caught him they would kill him, and that if they did not discover him, he would be buried alive; so on their approach he called out, "People, people, take care how you touch me, for I am a great saint." The poor people were very much frightened when they heard the dead bullock talking, and thought that some mighty spirit must indeed possess it.† "Who are you, sir, and what do you want?" they cried. "I," answered the Jackal, "am a very holy saint. I am also the god of your village, and I am very angry with you because you never worship me nor bring me offerings." "O my Lord," they cried, "what offerings will please you? Tell us only, and we will bring you whatever you like." "Good," he replied. "Then you must fetch here plenty of rice, plenty of flowers and a nice fat chicken; place them as an offering beside me, and pour a great deal of water over them, as you do at your most solemn feasts, and I will forgive you your sins." The Mahars did as they were commanded. They placed some rice and flowers, and the best chicken they

* The lowest caste, employed as scavengers in every village.

† See Notes at the end.

could procure, beside the bullock, and poured water over it and the offering. Then, no sooner did the dry, hard bullock's skin get wetted than it split in many places, and to the surprise of all his worshipers, the Jackal jumped out, seized the chicken in his mouth, and ran away with it through the midst of them into the jungle. The Mahars ran after him over hedges and ditches for many, many miles, but he got away in spite of them all.

On, on he ran—on, on, for a very long way—until at last he came to a place where a little kid lived under a little sicakai* tree. All her relations and friends were away, and when she saw him coming she thought to herself, "Unless I frighten this Jackal, he will eat me." So she ran as hard as she could up against the sicakai tree, which made all the branches shake and the leaves go rustle, rustle, rustle. And when the Jackal heard the rustling noise he got frightened, and thought it was all the little kid's friends coming to help her. And she called out to him, "Run away, Jackal, run away. Thousands and thousands of Jackals have run away at that sound—run away for your life." And the Jackal was so frightened that he ran away. So, he who had deceived so many was outwitted by a simple little kid!

After this the Jackal found his way back to his own village, where the Barber lived, and there for some time he used to prowl round the houses every night and live upon any bones he could find. The villagers did not like his coming, but did not know how to catch him, until one night his old friend the Barber (who had never forgiven him for stealing the fruit from the

* *Acacia concinna.*

garden) caught him in a great net, having before made many unsuccessful attempts to do so. "Aha!" cried the Barber, "I've got you at last, my friend. You did not escape death from the cucumber-knife for nothing! you won't get away this time. Here, wife! wife! see what a prize I've got." The Barber's wife came running to the door, and the Barber gave her the Jackal (after he had tied all his four legs firmly together with a strong rope), and said to her, "Take this animal into the house, and be sure you don't let him escape, while I go and get a knife to kill him with."

The Barber's wife did as she was bid, and taking the Jackal into the house, laid him down on the floor. But no sooner had the Barber gone than the Jackal said to her, "Ah, good woman, your husband will return directly and put me to death. For the love of heaven, loosen the rope round my feet before he comes, for one minute only, and let me drink a little water from that puddle by the door, for my throat is parched with thirst." "No, no, friend Jackal," answered the Barber's wife. "I know well enough what you'll do. No sooner shall I have untied your feet than you will run away, and when my husband returns and finds you are gone, he will beat me."

"Indeed, indeed, I will not run away," he replied. "Ah, kind mother, have pity on me, only for one little moment." Then the Barber's wife thought, "Well, it is hard not to grant the poor beast's last request; he will not live long enough to have many more pleasures." So she untied the Jackal's legs and held him by a rope, that he might drink from the puddle. But quick as possible, he gave a jump and a twist and a pull, and, jerking the rope out of her hand, escaped once more into the jungle.

For some time he roamed up and down, living on what he could get in this village or that, until he had wandered very far away from the country where the Barber lived. At last one day, by chance, he passed a certain cottage, in which there dwelt a very poor Brahmin, who had seven daughters.

As the Jackal passed by, the Brahmin was saying to himself, "Oh dear me! what can I do for my seven daughters? I shall have to support them all my life, for they are much too poor ever to get married. If a dog or a jackal were to offer to take one off my hands, he should have her." Next day the Jackal called on the Brahmin, and said to him, "You said yesterday, if a jackal or a dog were to offer to marry one of your daughters, you would let him have her; will you, therefore accept me as a son-in-law?"

The poor Brahmin felt very much embarrassed, but it was certain he had said the words, and therefore he felt in honor bound not to retract, although he had little dreamed of ever being placed in such a predicament. Just at that moment all the seven daughters began crying for bread, and the father had no bread to give them. Observing this, the Jackal continued, "Let me marry one of your seven daughters and I will take care of her. It will at least leave you one less to provide for, and I will see that she never needs food." Then the Brahmin's heart was softened, and he gave the Jackal his eldest daughter in marriage, and the Jackal took her home to his den in the high rocks.

Now you will say there never was a Jackal so clever as this. Very true, for this was not a common Jackal, or he could never have done all that I have told you This Jackal was, in fact, a great Rajah in disguise, who, to amuse himself, took the form of a Jackal; for he was a great magician as well as a great prince.

The den to which he took the Brahmin's daughter looked like quite a common hole in the rocks on the outside, but inside it was a splendid palace, adorned with silver, and gold, and ivory and precious stones. But even his own wife did not know that he was not always a Jackal, for the Rajah never took his human form except every morning very early, when he used to take off the jackal skin and wash it and brush it, and put it on again.

After he and his wife, the Brahmin's daughter, had lived up in their home in the rocks happily for some time, who should the Jackal see one day but his father-in-law, the old Brahmin, climbing up the hill to come and pay him a visit. The Jackal was vexed to see the Brahmin, for he knew he was very poor, and thought he had most likely come to beg; and so it was. The Brahmin said to him, "Son-in-law, let me come into your cave and rest a little while. I want to ask you to help me, for I am very poor and much in need of help."

"Don't go into my cave," said the Jackal; "it is but a poor hole, not fit for you to enter" (for he did not wish his father-in-law to see his fine palace); "but I will call my wife, that you may see I have not eaten her up, and she and you and I will talk over the matter, and see what we can do for you."

So the Brahmin, the Brahmin's daughter and the Jackal all sat down on the hill-side together, and the Brahmin said, "I don't know what to do to get food for myself, my wife and my six daughters. Son-in-law Jackal, cannot you help me?" "It is a difficult business," answered the Jackal, "but I'll do what I can for you;" and he ran to his cave and fetched a large melon, and gave it to the Brahmin, saying, "Father-in-law, you must take this melon, and plant it in your garden, and when it grows up sell all the fruit you find upon it, and that will bring you in some money." So the Brahmin took the melon home with him and planted it in his garden.

By next day the melon that the Jackal had given him had grown up in the Brahmin's garden into a fine plant, covered with hundreds of beautiful ripe melons. The Brahmin, his wife and family were overjoyed at the sight. And all the neighbors were astonished, and said, "How fast that fine melon plant has grown in the Brahmin's garden!"

Now it chanced that a woman who lived in a house close by wanted some melons, and seeing what fine ones these were, she went down at once to the Brahmin's house and bought two or three from the Brahmin's wife. She took them home with her and cut them open; but then, lo and behold! marvel of marvels! what a wonderful sight astonished her! Instead of the thick white pulp she expected to see, the whole of the inside of the melon was composed of diamonds, rubies and emeralds, and all the seeds were enormous pearls. She immediately locked her door, and taking with her all the money she had, ran back to the Brahmin's wife and said to her, "Those were very good melons you sold me; I like them so much that I will buy all the others on your melon plant." And giving her the money, she took home all the rest of the melons. Now this cunning woman told none of her friends of the treasure she had found, and the poor, stupid Brahmin and his family did not know what they had lost, for they had never thought of opening any of the melons; so that for all the precious stones they sold they only got a few pice, which was very hard. Next day, when they looked out of the window, the melon plant was again covered with fine ripe melons, and again the woman who had bought those which had grown the day before came and bought them all. And this went on for several days. There were so many melons, and all the melons were so full of precious stones, that the woman who bought them had enough to fill the whole of one room in her house with diamonds, rubies, emeralds and pearls.

At last, however, the wonderful melon plant began to wither, and when the woman came to buy melons one morning, the Brahmin's wife was obliged to say to her, in a sad voice, "Alas! there are no more melons on our melon plant." And the woman went back to her own house very much disappointed.

That day the Brahmin and his wife and children had no money in the house to buy food with, and they all felt very unhappy to think that the fine melon plant had withered. But the Brahmin's youngest daughter, who was a clever girl, thought, "Though there are no more melons fit to sell on our melon plant, perhaps I may be able to find one or two shriveled ones, which, if cooked, will give us something for dinner." So she went out to look, and searching carefully amongst the thick leaves, found two or three withered little melons still remaining. These she took into the house and began cutting them up to cook, when—more wonderful than wonderful!—

within each little melon she found a number of small emeralds, rubies, diamonds and pearls! The girl called her father and mother, and her five sisters, crying, "See what I have found! See these precious stones and pearls. I dare say inside all the melons we sold there were as good or better than these. No wonder that woman was so anxious to buy them all! See, father—see, mother—see, sisters!"

Then they were all overjoyed to see the treasure, but the Brahmin said, "What a pity we have lost all the benefit of my son-in-law the Jackal's good gift by not knowing its worth! I will go at once to that woman, and try and make her give us back the melons she took."

So he went to the melon-buyer's house, and said to her, "Give me back the melons you took from me, who did not know their worth." She answered, "I don't know what you mean." He replied, "You were very deceitful; you bought melons full of precious stones from us poor people, who did not know what they were worth, and you only paid for them the price of common melons: give me some of them back, I pray you." But she said, "I bought common melons from your wife, and made them all into common soup long ago; therefore talk no further nonsense about jewels, but go about your business." And she turned him out of the house. Yet all this time she had a whole roomful of the emeralds, diamonds, rubies and pearls that she had found in the melons the Brahmin's wife had sold her.

The Brahmin returned home and said to his wife, "I cannot make that woman give me back any of the melons you sold her; but give me the precious stones our daughter has just found, and I will sell them to a jeweler and bring home some money." So he went to the town, and took the precious stones to a jeweler, and said to him, "What will you give me for these?" But no sooner did the jeweler see them than he said, "How could such a poor man as you become possessed of such precious stones? You must have stolen them: you are a thief! You have stolen these from my shop, and now come to sell them to me!"

"No, no, sir; indeed no, sir," cried the Brahmin. "Thief, thief!" shouted the jeweler. "In truth, no sir," said the Brahmin; "my son-in-law, the Jackal, gave me a melon plant, and in one of the melons I found these jewels." "I don't believe a word you say," screamed the jeweler (and he began beating the Brahmin, whom he held by the arm); "give up those jewels which you have stolen from my shop." "No, I won't," roared the Brahmin; "oh! oh-o! oh-o-o! don't beat me so; I didn't steal them." But the jeweler was determined to get the jewels; so he beat the Brahmin and called the police, who came running up to his assistance, and shouted till a great crowd of people had collected round his shop. Then he said to the Brahmin, "Give me up the jewels you stole from me, or I'll give you to the police, and you shall be put in jail." The Brahmin tried to tell his story about his son-in-law, the Jackal, but of course nobody believed him; and he was obliged to give the precious stones to the jeweler in order to escape the police, and to run home as fast as he could. And every one thought the jeweler was very kind to let him off so easily.

All his family were very unhappy when they heard what had befallen him. But his wife said, "You had better go again to our son-in-law, the Jackal, and see what he can do for us." So next day the Brahmin climbed the hill again, as he had done before, and went to call upon the Jackal. When the Jackal saw him coming he was not very well pleased. So he went to meet him, and said, "Father-in-law, I did not expect to see you again so soon." "I merely came to see how you were," answered the Brahmin, "and to tell you how poor we are; and how glad we should be of any help you can give us." "What have you done with all the melons I gave you?" asked the Jackal. "Ah," answered the Brahmin, "that is a sad story!" And beginning at the beginning, he related how they had sold almost all the melons without knowing their value; and how the few precious stones they had found had been taken from him by the jeweler. When the Jackal heard this he laughed very much, and said, "I see it is no use giving such unfortunate people as you gold or jewels, for they will only bring you into trouble. Come, I'll give you a more useful present." So, running into his cave, he fetched thence a small chattee, and gave it to the Brahmin, saying, "Take this chattee; whenever you or any of the family are hungry, you will always find in it as good a dinner as this." And putting his paw into the chattee, he extracted thence currie and rice, pilau,* and all sorts of good things, enough to feast a hundred men; and the more he took out of the chattee, the more remained inside.

When the Brahmin saw the chattee and smelt the good dinner, his eyes glistened for joy; and he embraced the Jackal, saying, "Dear son-in-law, you are the only support of our house." And he took his new present carefully home with him.

* Meat cooked with almonds, raisins and spice.

After this, for some time, the whole family led a very happy life, for they never wanted good food; every day the Brahmin, his wife and his six daughters found inside the chattee a most delicious dinner; and every day, when they had dined, they placed it on a shelf, to find it replenished when next it was needed.

But it happened that hard by there lived another Brahmin, a very great man, who was much in the Rajah's confidence; and this man smelt daily the smell of a very nice dinner, which puzzled him a good deal. The rich Brahmin thought it smelt even nicer than his own dinner, for which he paid so much, and yet it seemed to come from the poor Brahmin's little cottage. So one day he determined to find out all about it; and, going to call on his neighbor, he said to him, "Every day, at about twelve o'clock, I smell such a very nice dinner—much nicer than my own; and it seems to come from your house. You must live on very good things, I think, although you seem to every one to be so very poor."

Then, in the pride of his heart, the poor Brahmin invited his rich neighbor to come and dine with him, and lifting the magic chattee down from the shelf, took out of it such delicate fare as the other had never before tasted. And in an evil hour he proceeded to tell his friend of the wondrous properties of the chattee, which his son-in-law, the Jackal, had given him, and how it never was empty. No sooner had the great man learnt all this than he went to the Rajah, and said to him, "There is a poor Brahmin in the town who possesses a wonderful chattee, which is always filled with the most delicious dinner. I should not feel authorized to deprive him of it; but if it pleased your Highness to take it from him, he could not complain." The Rajah, hearing this, determined to see and taste for himself. So he said, "I should very much like to see this chattee with my own eyes." And he accompanied the rich Brahmin to the poor Brahmin's house. The poor Brahmin was overjoyed at being noticed by the Rajah himself, and gladly exhibited the various excellences of the chattee; but no sooner did the Rajah taste the dinner it contained than he ordered his guards to seize it and take it away to the palace, in spite of the Brahmin's tears and protestations. Thus, for a second time, he lost the benefit of his son-in-law's gift.

When the Rajah had gone, the Brahmin said to his wife, "There is nothing to be done but to go again to the Jackal, and see if he can help us." "If you don't take care, you'll put him out of all patience at last," answered she. "I can't think why you need have gone talking about our chattee!"

When the Jackal heard the Brahmin's story, he became very cross, and said, "What a stupid old man you were to say anything about the chattee! But see, here is another, which may aid you to get back the first. Take care of it, for this is the last time I will help you." And he gave the Brahmin a chattee, in which was a stout stick tied to a very strong rope. "Take this," he said, "into the presence of those who deprived you of my other gifts, and when you open the chattee, command the stick to beat them; this it will do so effectually that they will gladly return you what you have lost; only take care not to open the chattee when you are alone, or the stick that is in it will punish your rashness."

The Brahmin thanked his son-in-law, and took away

the chattee, but he found it hard to believe all that had been said. So, going through the jungle on his way home, he uncovered it, just to peep in and see if the stick were really there. No sooner had he done this than out jumped the rope, out jumped the stick; the rope seized him and bound him to a tree, and the stick beat him, and beat him, and beat him, until he was nearly killed. "Oh dear! oh dear!" screamed the Brahmin; "what an unlucky man I am! Oh dear! oh dear! stop, please stop! good stick, stop! what a very good stick this is!" But the stick would not stop, but beat him so much that he could hardly crawl home again.

Then the Brahmin put the rope and stick back again into the chattee, and sent to his rich neighbor and to the Rajah, and said to them, "I have a new chattee, much better than the old one; do come and see what a fine one it is." And the rich Brahmin and the Rajah thought, "This is something good; doubtless there is a choice dinner in this chattee also, and we will take it from this foolish man, as we did the other." So they went down to meet the Brahmin in the jungle, taking with them all their followers and attendants. Then the Brahmin uncovered his chattee, saying, "Beat, stick, beat! beat them every one!" and the stick jumped out, and the rope jumped out, and the rope caught hold of the Rajah and the rich Brahmin and all their attendants, and tied them fast to the trees that grew around, and the stick ran from one to another, beating, beating, beating—beating the Rajah, beating his courtiers—beating the rich Brahmin, beating his attendants, and beating all their followers; while the poor Brahmin cried with all his might,

"Give me back my chattee! give me back my chattee!"

At this the Rajah and his people were very much frightened, and thought they were going to be killed. And the Rajah said to the Brahmin, "Take away your stick, only take away your stick, and you shall have back your chattee." So the Brahmin put the stick and rope back into the chattee, and the Rajah returned him the dinner-making chattee. And all the people felt very much afraid of the Brahmin, and respected him very much.

Then he took the chattee containing the rope and stick to the house of the woman who had bought the melons, and the rope caught her and the stick beat her; and the Brahmin cried, "Return me those melons! return me those melons!" And the woman said, "Only make your stick stop beating me and you shall have back all the melons." So he ordered the stick back into the chattee, and she returned him them forthwith —a whole roomful of melons full of diamonds, pearls, emeralds and rubies.

The Brahmin took them home to his wife, and going into the town, with the help of his good stick, forced the jeweler who had deprived him of the little emeralds, rubies, diamonds and pearls he had taken to sell to give them back to him again, and having accomplished this, he returned to his family; and from that time they all lived very happily. Then, one day, the Jackal's wife invited her six sisters to come and pay her a visit. Now the youngest sister was more clever than any of the others; and it happened that, very early in the morning, she saw her brother-in-law, the Jackal, take off the jackal skin and wash it and brush it, and hang it up to dry; and when he had taken off the jackal-skin coat, he looked the handsomest prince that ever was seen. Then his little sister-in-law ran, quickly and quietly, and stole away the jackal-skin coat, and threw it on the fire and burnt it. And she awoke her sister, and said, "Sister, sister, your husband is no longer a jackal; see, that is he standing by the door." So the Jackal Rajah's wife ran to the door to meet her husband, and because the jackal's skin was burnt, and he could wear it no longer, he continued to be a man for the rest of his life, and gave up playing all jackal-like pranks; and he and his wife, and his father and mother and sisters-in-law, lived very happily all the rest of their days.

XIII.

TIT FOR TAT.

THERE once lived a Camel and a Jackal who were great friends. One day the Jackal said to the Camel, "I know that there is a fine field of sugar-cane on the other side of the river. If you will take me across, I'll show you the place. This plan will suit me as well as you. You will enjoy eating the sugar-cane, and I am sure to find many crabs, bones and bits of fish by the river-side, on which to make a good dinner."

The Camel consented and swam across the river, taking the Jackal, who could not swim, on his back. When they reached the other side, the Camel went to eating the sugar-cane, and the Jackal ran up and down the river bank devouring all the crabs, bits of fish and bones he could find.

But being so much smaller an animal, he had made an excellent meal before the Camel had eaten more than two or three mouthfuls; and no sooner had he finished his dinner than he ran round and round the sugar-cane field, yelping and howling with all his might.

The villagers heard him, and thought, "There is a Jackal among the sugar-canes; he will be scratching holes in the ground and spoiling the roots of the plants." And they all went down to the place to drive him away. But when they got there they found to their surprise not only a Jackal, but a Camel who was eating the sugar-canes! This made them very angry, and they caught the poor Camel and drove him from the field and beat him and beat him, until he was nearly dead.

When they had gone, the Jackal said to the Camel, "We had better go home." And the Camel said, "Very well; then jump upon my back, as you did before."

So the Jackal jumped upon the Camel's back, and the Camel began to recross the river. When they had got well into the water, the Camel said, "This is a pretty way in which you have treated me, friend Jackal. No sooner had you finished your own dinner than you must go yelping about the place loud enough to arouse the whole village, and bring all the villagers down to beat me black and blue, and turn me out of the field before I had eaten two mouthfuls! What in the world did you make such a noise for?"

"I don't know," said the Jackal. "It is a custom I have. I always like to sing a little after dinner."

The Camel waded on through the river. The water reached up to his knees—then above them—up, up, up, higher and higher, until he was obliged to swim. Then turning to the Jackal, he said, "I feel very anxious to roll." "Oh, pray don't; why do you wish to do so?" asked the Jackal. "I don't know," answered the Camel. "It is a custom I have. I always like to have a little roll after dinner." So saying, he rolled over in the water, shaking the Jackal off as he did so. And the Jackal was drowned, but the Camel swam safely ashore.

XIV.

THE BRAHMIN, THE TIGER AND THE SIX JUDGES.

ONCE upon a time, a Brahmin, who was walking along the road, came upon an iron cage, in which a great Tiger had been shut up by the villagers who caught him.

As the Brahmin passed by, the Tiger called out and said to him, "Brother Brahmin, brother Brahmin, have pity on me, and let me out of this cage for one minute only to drink a little water, for I am dying of thirst." The Brahmin answered, "No, I will not; for if I let you out of the cage you will eat me."

"Oh, father of mercy," answered the Tiger, "in truth that will I not. I will never be so ungrateful; only let me out, that I may drink some water and return." Then the Brahmin took pity on him and opened the cage door; but no sooner had he done so than the Tiger, jumping out, said, "Now, I will eat you first and drink the water afterward." But the Brahmin said, "Only do not kill me hastily. Let us first ask the opinion of six, and if all of them say it is just and fair that you should put me to death, then I am willing to die." "Very well," answered the Tiger, "it shall be as you say; we will first ask the opinion of six."

So the Brahmin and the Tiger walked on till they

came to a Banyan tree; and the Brahmin said to it, "Banyan tree, Banyan tree, hear and give judgment." "On what must I give judgment?" asked the Banyan tree. "This Tiger," said the Brahmin, "begged me to let him out of his cage to drink a little water, and he promised not to hurt me if I did so; but now, that I have let him out, he wishes to eat me. Is it just that he should do so or no?"

The Banyan tree answered, "Men often come to take shelter in the cool shade under my boughs from the scorching rays of the run; but when they have rested, they cut and break my pretty branches and wantonly scatter my leaves. Let the Tiger eat the man, for men are an ungrateful race."

At these words the Tiger would have instantly killed the Brahmin; but the Brahmin said, "Tiger, Tiger, you must not kill me yet, for you promised that we should first hear the judgment of six." "Very well," said the Tiger, and they went on their way. After a little while they met a Camel. "Sir Camel, Sir Camel," cried the Brahmin, "hear and give judgment." "On what shall I give judgment?" asked the Camel. And the Brahmin related how the Tiger had begged him to open the cage door, and promised not to eat him if he did so; and how he had afterward determined to break his word, and asked if that were just or not. The Camel replied, "When I was young and strong, and could do much work, my master took care of me and gave me good food; but now that I am old, and have lost all my strength in his service, he overloads me and starves me, and beats me without mercy. Let the Tiger eat the man, for men are an unjust and cruel race."

The Tiger would then have killed the Brahmin, but the latter said, "Stop, Tiger, for we must first hear the judgment of six."

So they both went again on their way. At a little distance they found a Bullock lying by the roadside. The Brahmin said to him, "Brother Bullock, brother Bullock, hear and give judgment." "On what must I give judgment?" asked the Bullock. The Brahmin answered, "I found this Tiger in a cage, and he prayed me to open the door and let him out to drink a little water, and promised not to kill me if I did so; but when I had let him out he resolved to put me to death. Is it fair he should do so or no?" The Bullock said, "When I was able to work my master fed me well and tended me carefully, but now I am old he has forgotten all I did for him, and left me by the roadside to die. Let the Tiger eat the man, for men have no pity."

Three out of the six had given judgment against the Brahmin, but still he did not lose all hope, and determined to ask the other three.

They next met an Eagle flying through the air, to whom the Brahmin cried, "O Eagle, great Eagle, hear and give judgment?" "On what must I give judgment?" asked the Eagle. The Brahmin stated the case, but the Eagle answered, "Whenever men see me they try to shoot me; they climb the rocks and steal away my little ones. Let the Tiger eat the man, for men are the persecutors of the earth."

Then the Tiger began to roar, and said, "The judgment of all is against you, O Brahmin." But the Brahmin answered, "Stay yet a little longer, for two others must first be asked." After this they saw an Alligator, and the Brahmin related the matter to him, hoping for a more favorable verdict. But the Alligator said, "Whenever I put my nose out of the water men torment me and try to kill me. Let the Tiger eat the man, for as long as men live we shall have no rest."

The Brahmin gave himself up as lost; but again he prayed the Tiger to have patience and let him ask the opinion of the sixth judge. Now the sixth was a Jackal. The Brahmin told his story, and said to him, "Mama* Jackal, mama Jackal, say what is your judgment?" The Jackal answered, "It is impossible for me to decide who is in the right and who in the wrong unless I see the exact position in which you were when the dispute began. Show me the place." So the Brahmin and the Tiger returned to the place where they first met, and the Jackal went with them. When they got there, the Jackal said, "Now, Brahmin, show me exactly where you stood." "Here," said the Brahmin, standing by the iron tiger-cage. "Exactly there, was it?" asked the Jackal. "Exactly here," replied the Brahmin. "Where was the Tiger, then?" asked the Jackal. "In the cage," answered the Tiger. "How do you mean?" said the Jackal; "how were you within the cage? which way were you looking?" "Why, I stood so," said the Tiger, jumping into the cage, "and my head was on this side." "Very good," said the Jackal, "but I cannot judge without understanding the whole matter exactly. Was the cage door open or shut?" "Shut and bolted," said the Brahmin. "Then shut and bolt it," said the Jackal.

When the Brahmin had done this, the Jackal said, "Oh, you wicked and ungrateful Tiger! when the

* Uncle.

good Brahmin opened your cage door, is to eat him the only return you would make? Stay there, then, for the rest of your days, for no one will ever let you out again. Proceed on your journey, friend Brahmin. Your road lies that way and mine this."

So saying, the Jackal ran off in one direction, and the Brahmin went rejoicing on his way in the other.

XV.

THE SELFISH SPARROW AND THE HOUSELESS CROWS.

A SPARROW once built a nice little house for herself, and lined it well with wool and protected it with sticks, so that it equally resisted the summer sun and the winter rains. A Crow who lived close by had also built a house, but it was not such a good one, being only made of a few sticks laid one above another on the top of a prickly pear hedge. The consequence was, that one day, when there was an unusually heavy shower, the Crow's nest was washed away, while the Sparrow's was not at all injured.

In this extremity the Crow and her mate went to the Sparrow, and said, "Sparrow, Sparrow, have pity on us and give us shelter, for the wind blows and the rain beats, and the prickly pear hedge thorns stick into our eyes." But the Sparrow answered, "I'm cooking the dinner; I cannot let you in now; come again presently." In a little while the Crows returned, and said, "Sparrow, Sparrow, have pity on us and give us shelter, for the wind blows and the rain beats, and the prickly pear hedge thorns stick into our eyes." The Sparrow answered, "I'm eating my dinner; I cannot let you in now; come again presently." The Crows flew away, but in a little while returned, and cried once more, "Sparrow, Sparrow, have pity on us and give us shelter, for the wind blows and the rain beats, and the prickly pear hedge thorns stick into our eyes." The Sparrow replied, "I'm washing the dishes; I cannot let you in now; come again presently." The Crows waited a while and then called out, "Sparrow, Sparrow, have pity on us and give us shelter, for the wind blows and the rain beats, and the prickly pear hedge thorns stick into our eyes." But the Sparrow would not let them in; she only answered, "I'm sweeping the floor; I cannot let you in now; come again presently." Next time the Crows came and cried, "Sparrow, Sparrow, have pity on us and give us shelter, for the wind blows and the rain beats, and the prickly pear hedge thorns stick into our eyes." She answered, "I'm making the beds; I cannot let you in now; come again presently." So, on one pretence or another, she refused to help the poor birds. At last, when she and her children had had their dinner, and she had prepared and put away the dinner for next day, and had put all the children to bed and gone to bed herself, she cried to the Crows, "You may come in now, and take shelter for the night." The Crows came in, but they were much vexed at having been kept out so long in the wind and the rain, and when the Sparrow and all her family were asleep, the one said to the other, "This selfish Sparrow had no pity on us; she gave us no dinner, and would not let us in till she and all her children were comfortably in bed; let us punish her." So the two Crows took all the nice dinner the Sparrow had prepared for herself and her chil dren to eat next day, and flew away with it.

XVI.

THE VALIANT CHATTEE-MAKER.

ONCE upon a time, in a violent storm of thunder, lightning, wind and rain, a Tiger crept for shelter close to the wall of an old woman's hut. This old woman was very poor, and her hut was but a tumble-down place, through the roof of which the rain came drip, drip, drip on more sides than one. This troubled her much, and she went running about from side to side, dragging first one thing and then another out of the way of the leaky places in the roof, and as she did so she kept saying to herself, "Oh dear! oh dear! how tiresome this is! I'm sure the roof will come down! If an elephant, or a lion, or a tiger were to walk in, he wouldn't frighten me half so much as this perpetual dripping." And then she would begin dragging the bed and all the other things in the room about again, to get them out of the way of the wet. The Tiger, who was crouching down just outside, heard all that she said, and thought to himself, "This old woman says she would not be afraid of an elephant, or a lion, or a tiger, but that this perpetual dripping frightens her more than all. What can this 'perpetual dripping' be?—it must be something very dreadful." And hearing her immediately afterward dragging all the things about the room again, he said to himself, "What a terrible noise! Surely that must be the '*perpetual dripping.*'"

At this moment a Chattee-maker,* who was in search of his donkey, which had strayed away, came down the road. The night being very cold, he had, truth to say, taken a little more toddy than was good for him, and seeing, by the light of a flash of lightning, a large animal lying down close to the old woman's hut, he mistook it for the donkey he was looking for. So, running up to the Tiger, he seized hold of it by one ear, and commenced beating, kicking and abusing it with all his might and main. "You wretched creature!" he cried, "is this the way you serve me, obliging me to come out and look for you in such pouring rain and on such a dark night as this? Get up instantly, or I'll break every bone in your body;" so he went on scolding and thumping the Tiger with his utmost power, for he had worked himself up into a terrible rage. The Tiger did not know what to make of it all, but he began to feel quite frightened, and said to himself, "Why, this must be the 'perpetual dripping;' no wonder the old woman said she was more afraid of it than of an elephant, a lion, or a tiger, for it gives most dreadfully hard blows."

The Chattee-maker, having made the Tiger get up, got on his back and forced him to carry him home, kicking and beating him the whole way, for all this time he fancied he was on his donkey; and then he tied his fore feet and his head firmly together, and fastened him to a post in front of his house, and when he had done this he went to bed.

* Potter.

Next morning, when the Chattee-maker's wife got up and looked out of the window, what did she see but a great big Tiger tied up in front of their house, to the post to which they usually fastened the donkey: she was very much surprised, and running to her husband, awoke him, saying, "Do you know what animal you fetched home last night?" "Yes, the donkey to be sure," he answered. "Come and see," said she, and she showed him the great Tiger tied to the post. The Chattee-maker at this was no less astonished than his wife, and felt himself all over to find if the Tiger had not wounded him. But, no! there he was safe and sound, and there was the Tiger tied to the post, just as he had fastened it up the night before.

News of the Chattee-maker's exploit soon spread through the village, and all the people came to see him and hear him tell how he had caught the Tiger and tied it to the post; and this they thought so wonderful that they sent a deputation to the Rajah, with a letter to tell him how a man of their village had, alone and unarmed, caught a great Tiger and tied it to a post.

When the Rajah read the letter he also was much surprised, and determined to go in person and see this astonishing sight. So he sent for his horses and carriages, his lords and attendants, and they all set off together to look at the Chattee-maker and the Tiger he had caught.

Now the Tiger was a very large one, and had long been the terror of all the country round, which made the whole matter still more extraordinary; and all this being represented to the Rajah, he determined to confer all possible honor on the valiant Chattee-maker. So he gave him houses and lands, and as much money as would fill a well, made him a lord of his court, and conferred on him the command of ten thousand horse.

It came to pass, shortly after this, that a neighboring Rajah, who had long had a quarrel with this one, sent to announce his intention of going instantly to war with him; and tidings were at the same time brought that the Rajah who sent the challenge had gathered a great army together on the borders, and was prepared at a moment's notice to invade the country.

In this dilemma no one knew what to do. The Rajah sent for all his generals, and inquired of them which would be willing to take command of his forces and oppose the enemy. They all replied that the country was so ill-prepared for the emergency, and the case was apparently so hopeless, that they would rather not take the responsibility of the chief command. The Rajah knew not whom to appoint in their stead. Then some of his people said to him, "You have lately given the command of ten thousand horse to the valiant Chattee-maker who caught the Tiger: why not make him commander-in-chief? A man who could catch a Tiger and tie him to a post, must surely be more courageous and clever than most." "Very well," said the Rajah, "I will make him commander-in-chief." So he sent for the Chattee-maker and said to him, "In your hands I place all the power of the kingdom; you must put our enemies to flight for us." "So be it," answered the Chattee-maker; "but, before I lead the whole army against the enemy, suffer me to go by myself and examine their position, and, if possible, find out their numbers and strength."

The Rajah consented, and the Chattee-maker returned home to his wife. and said: "Thev have made me commander-in-chief, which is a very difficult post for me to fill, because I shall have to ride at the head of all the army, and you know I never was on a horse in my life. But I have succeeded in gaining a little delay, as the Rajah has given me permission to go first alone and reconnoitre the enemy's camp. Do you therefore provide a very quiet pony, for you know I cannot ride, and I will start to-morrow morning."

But, before the Chattee-maker had started, the Rajah sent over to him a most magnificent charger richly caparisoned, which he begged he would ride when going to see the enemy's camp. The Chattee-maker was frightened almost out of his life, for the charger that the Rajah had sent him was very powerful and spirited, and he felt sure that even if he ever got on it, he should very soon tumble off; however, he did not dare to refuse it, for fear of offending the Rajah by not accepting his present. So he sent back to him a message of thanks, and said to his wife, "I cannot go on the pony, now that the Rajah has sent me this fine horse; but how am I ever to ride it?" "Oh, don't be frightened," she answered; "you've only got to get upon it, and I will tie you firmly on, so that you cannot tumble off, and if you start at night, no one will see that you are tied on." "Very well," he said. So that night his wife brought the horse that the Rajah had sent him to the door. "Indeed," said the Chattee-maker, "I can never get into that saddle, it is so high up." "You must jump," said his wife. So he tried to jump several times, but each time he jumped he tumbled down again. "I always forget when I am jumping," said he, "which way I ought to turn." "Your face must be toward the horse's head," she answered. "To be sure, of course," he cried, and giving one great jump he jumped into the saddle, but with his face toward the horse's tail. "This won't do at all," said his wife as she helped him down again; "try getting on without jumping." "I never can remember," he continued, "when I have got my left foot in the stirrup, what to do with my right foot or where to put it." "That must go in the other stirrup," she answered; "let me help you." So, after many trials, in which he tumbled down very often, for the horse was fresh and did not like standing still, the Chattee-maker got into the saddle; but no sooner had he got there than he cried, "Oh, wife, wife! tie me very firmly as quickly as possible, for I know I shall jump down if I can." Then she fetched some strong rope and tied his feet firmly into the stirrups, and fastened one stirrup to the other, and put another rope round his waist and another round his neck, and fastened them to the horse's body and neck and tail.

When the horse felt all these ropes about him he could not imagine what queer creature had got upon his back, and he began rearing and kicking and prancing, and at last set off full gallop, as fast as he could tear, right across country. "Wife, wife!" cried the Chattee-maker, "you forgot to tie my hands." "Never mind," said she; "hold on by the mane." So he caught hold of the horse's mane as firmly as he could. Then away went horse, away went Chattee-maker—away, away, away, over hedges, over ditches, over rivers, over plains—away, away, like a flash of lightning—now this way, now that—on, on, on, gallop, gallop, gallop—until they came in sight of the enemy's camp.

The Chattee-maker did not like his ride at all, and when he saw where it was leading him he liked it still less, for he thought the enemy would catch him and very likely kill him. So he determined to make one desperate effort to be free, and stretching out his hand as the horse shot past a young banyan tree, seized hold of it with all his might, hoping that the resistance it offered might cause the ropes that tied him to break. But the horse was going at his utmost speed, and the soil in which the banyan tree grew was loose, so that when the Chattee-maker caught hold of it and gave it such a violent pull, it came up by the roots, and on he rode as fast as before, with the tree in his hand.

All the soldiers in the camp saw him coming, and having heard that an army was to be sent against them, made sure that the Chattee-maker was one of the van-guard. "See," cried they, "here comes a man of gigantic stature on a mighty horse! He rides at full speed across the country, tearing up the very trees in his rage! He is one of the opposing force; the whole army must be close at hand. If they are such as he, we are all dead men." Then, running to their Rajah, some of them cried again, "Here comes the whole force of the enemy" (for the story had by this time become exaggerated); "they are men of gigantic stature, mounted on mighty horses; as they come they tear up the very trees in their rage; we can oppose men, but not monsters such as these." These were followed by others, who said, "It is all true," for by this time the Chattee-maker had got pretty near the camp; "they're coming! they're coming! let us fly! let us fly! fly, fly for your lives!" And the whole panic-stricken multitude fled from the camp (those who had seen no cause for alarm going because the others did, or because they did not care to stay by themselves), after having obliged their Rajah to write a letter to the one whose country he was about to invade to say that he would not do so, and propose terms of peace, and to sign it and seal it with his seal. Scarcely had all the people fled from the camp when the horse on which the Chattee-maker was came galloping into it, and on his back rode the Chattee-maker, almost dead from fatigue, with the banyan tree in his hand: just as he reached the camp the ropes by which he was tied broke, and he fell to the ground. The horse stood still, too tired with his long run to go farther. On recovering his senses, the Chattee-maker found, to his surprise, that the whole camp, full of rich arms, clothes and trappings, was entirely deserted. In the principal tent, moreover, he found a letter addressed to his Rajah, announcing the retreat of the invading army and proposing terms of peace.

So he took the letter, and returned home with it as fast as he could, leading his horse all the way, for he was afraid to mount him again. It did not take him long to reach his house by the direct road, for whilst riding he had gone a more circuitous journey than was necessary, and he got there just at nightfall. His wife ran out to meet him, overjoyed at his speedy return. As soon as he saw her, he said, "Ah, wife, since I saw you last I've been all round the world, and had many wonderful and terrible adventures. But never mind that now: send this letter quickly to the Rajah by a messenger, and send the horse also that he sent for me to ride. He will then see, by the horse looking so tired, what a long ride I've had; and if he is sent on beforehand, I shall not be obliged to ride him up to the palace door to-morrow morning, as I otherwise should, and that would be very tiresome, for most likely I should tumble off." So his wife sent the horse and the letter to the Rajah, and a message that her husband would be at the palace early next morning, as it was then late at night. And next day he went down there, as he had said he would; and when the people saw him coming, they said, "This man is as modest as he is brave; after having put our enemies to flight, he walks quite simply to the door, instead of riding here in state, as another man would." For they did not know that the Chattee-maker walked because he was afraid to ride.

The Rajah came to the palace door to meet him, and paid him all possible honor. Terms of peace were agreed upon between the two countries, and the Chatte-maker was rewarded for all he had done by being given twice as much rank and wealth as he had before, and he lived very happily all the rest of his life.

XVII.

THE RAKSHAS' PALACE.

ONCE upon a time there lived a Rajah who was left a widower with two little daughters. Not very long after his first wife died he married again, and his second wife did not care for her step-children, and was often unkind to them; and the Rajah, their father, never troubled himself to look after them, but allowed his wife to treat them as she liked. This made the poor girls very miserable, and one day one of them said to the other, "Don't let us remain any longer here; come away into the jungle, for nobody here cares whether we go or stay." So they both walked off into the jungle, and lived for many days on the jungle fruits. At last, after they had wandered on for a long while, they came to a fine palace which belonged to a Rakshas, but both the Rakshas and his wife were out when they got there. Then one of the Princesses said to the other, "This fine palace, in the midst of the jungle, can belong to no one but a Rakshas, but the owner has evidently gone out; let us go in and see if we can find anything to eat." So they went into the Rakshas' house, and finding some rice, boiled and ate it. Then they swept the room and arranged all the furniture in the house tidily. But hardly had they finished doing so when the Rakshas and his wife returned home.

Then the two Princesses were so frightened that they ran up to the top of the house and hid themselves on the flat roof, from whence they could look down on one side into the inner courtyard of the house, and from the other could see the open country. The house-top was a favorite resort of the Rakshas and his wife. Here they would sit upon the hot summer evenings; here they winnowed the grain and hung out the clothes to dry; and the two Princesses found a sufficient shelter behind some sheaves of corn that were waiting to be threshed. When the Rakshas came into the house, he looked round and said to his wife, "Somebody has been arranging the house, everything in it is so clean and tidy. Wife, did you do this?" "No," she said; "I don't know who can have done all this." "Some one also has been sweeping the courtyard," continued the Rakshas. "Wife, did you sweep the courtyard?' "No." she answered, "I did not do it. I don't know who did." Then the Rakshas walked round and round several times with his nose up in the air, saying, "Some one is here now. I smell flesh and blood! Where can they be?" "Stuff and nonsense!" cried his wife. "You smell blood indeed! Why, you have just been killing and eating a hundred thousand people. I should wonder if you didn't still smell flesh and blood!" They went on quarreling thus until the Rakshas said, "Well, never mind; I don't know how it is, but I'm very thirsty; let's come and drink some water." So both the Rakshas and his wife went to a well which was close to the house, and began letting down jars into it, and drawing up the water and drinking it. And the Princesses, who were on the top of the house, saw them. Now the youngest of the two Princesses was a very wise girl, and when she saw the Rakshas and his wife by the well, she said to her sister, "I will do something now that will be good for us both;" and, running down quickly from the top of the house, she crept close behind the Rakshas and his wife as they stood on tip-toe more than half over the side of the well, and, catching hold of one of the Rakshas' heels and one of his wife's, gave each a little push, and down they both tumbled into the well and were drowned—the Rakshas and the Rakshas' wife! The Princess then returned to her sister and said, "I have killed the Rakshas." "What, both?" cried her sister. "Yes, both," she said. "Won't they come back?" said her sister. "No, never," answered she.

The Rakshas being thus killed, the two Princesses took possession of the house, and lived there very happily for a long time. In it they found heaps and heaps of rich clothes and jewels, and gold and silver, which the Rakshas had taken from people he had murdered; and all round the house were folds for the flocks and sheds for the herds of cattle which the Rakshas owned. Every morning the youngest Princess used to drive out the flocks and herds to pasturage, and return home with them every night, while the eldest stayed at home, cooked the dinner and kept the house; and the youngest Princess, who was the cleverest, would often say to her sister, on going away for the day, "Take care, if you see any stranger (be it man, woman or child) come by the house, to hide, if possible, that nobody may know of our living here; and if any one should call out and ask for a drink of water, or any poor beggar pray for food, before you give it him be sure you put on ragged clothes and cover your face with charcoal, and make yourself look as ugly as possible, lest, seeing how fair you are, he should steal you away, and we never meet again." "Very well," the other Princess would answer, "I will do as you advise."

But a long time passed, and no one ever came by that way. At last one day, after the youngest Princess had gone out, a young Prince, the son of a neighboring Rajah, who had been hunting with his attendants for many days in the jungles, came near the place when searching for water (for he and his people were tired with hunting, and had been seeking all through the jungle for a stream of water, but could find none). When the Prince saw the fine palace standing all by itself, he was very much astonished, and said, "It is a strange thing that any one should have built such a house as this in the depths of the forest. Let us go in; the owners will doubtless give us a drink of water." "No, no, do not go," cried his attendants; "this is most likely the house of a Rakshas." "We can but see," answered the Prince. "I should scarcely think anything very terrible lived here, for there is not a sound stirring nor a living creature to be seen." So he began tapping at the door, which was bolted, and crying, "Will whoever owns this house give me and my people some water to drink, for the sake of kind charity?" But nobody answered, for the Princess, who heard him, was busy up in her room, blacking her face with charcoal and covering her rich dress with rags. Then the Prince got impatient and shook the door, saying, angrily, "Let me in, whoever you are! If you don't, I'll force the door open." At this the poor little Princess got dreadfully frightened; and having blacked her face and made herself look as ugly as possible, she ran down stairs with a pitcher of water, and unbolting the door, gave the Prince the pitcher to drink from; but she did not speak, for she was afraid. Now the Prince was a very clever man, and as he raised the pitcher to his mouth to drink the water, he thought to himself, "This is a very strange-looking creature who has brought me this jug of water. She would be pretty, but that her face seems to want washing, and her dress also is very untidy. What can that black stuff be on her face and hands? it looks very unnatural." And so thinking to himself, instead of drinking the water, he threw it in the Princess' face! The Princess started back with a little cry, whilst the water, trickling down her face, washed off the charcoal, and showed her delicate features and beautiful, fair complexion. The Prince caught hold of her hand, and said, "Now tell me true, who are you? where do you come from? Who are your father and mother? and why are you here alone by yourself in the jungle? Answer me, or I'll cut your head off." And he made as if he would draw his sword. The Princess was so terrified she could hardly speak, but as best she could she told how she was the daughter of a Rajah, and had run away into the jungle because of her cruel stepmother, and, finding the house, had lived there ever since; and having finished her story, she began to cry. Then the Prince said to her, "Pretty lady, forgive me for my roughness; do not fear; I will take you home with me, and you shall be my wife." But the more he spoke to her the more frightened she got. So frightened that she did not understand what he said, and could do nothing but cry. Now she had said nothing to the Prince about her sister, nor even told him that she had one, for she thought, "This man says he will kill me; if he hears that I have a sister, he will kill her too." So the Prince, who was really kind-hearted, and would never have thought of separating the two little sisters who had been together so long, knew nothing at all of the matter, and only seeing she was too much alarmed even to understand gentle words, said to his servants, "Place this lady in one of the palkees, and let us set off home." And they did so. When the Princess found herself shut up in the palkee, and being carried she knew not where, she thought how terrible it would be for her sister to return home and find her gone, and determined, if possible, to leave some sign to show her which way she had been taken. Round her neck were many strings of pearls. She untied them, and tearing her saree into little bits, tied one pearl in each piece of the saree, that it might be heavy enough to fall straight to the ground; and so she went on, dropping one pearl and then another and another and another, all the way she went along, until they reached the palace where the Rajah and Ranee, the Prince's father and mother, lived. She threw the last remaining pearl down just as she reached the palace gate. The old Rajah and Ranee were delighted to see the beautiful Princess their son had brought home; and when they heard her story they said, "Ah, poor thing! what a sad story! but now she has come to live with us, we will do all we can to make her happy." And they married her to their son with great pomp and ceremony, and gave her rich dresses and jewels, and were very kind to her. But the Princess remained sad and unhappy, for she was always thinking about her sister, and yet she could not summon courage to beg the Prince or his father to send and fetch her to the palace.

Meantime the youngest Princess, who had been out with her flocks and herds when the Prince took her sister away, had returned home. When she came back she found the door wide open and no one standing there. She thought it very odd, for her sister always came every night to the door to meet her on her return. She went up stairs; her sister was not there; the whole house was empty and deserted. There she must stay all alone, for the evening had closed in, and it was impossible to go outside and seek her with any hope of success. So all the night long she waited, crying, "Some one has been here, and they have stolen her away; they have stolen my darling away. O sister! sister!" Next morning, very early, going out to continue the search, she found one of the pearls belonging to her sister's necklace tied up in a small piece of saree; a little farther on lay another, and yet another, all along the road the Prince had gone. Then the Princess understood that her sister had left this clue to guide her on her way, and she at once set off to find her again. Very, very far she went—a six months' journey through the jungle, for she could not travel fast, the many days' walking tired her so much—and sometimes it took her two or three days to find the next piece of saree with the pearl. At last she came near a large town, to which it was evident her sister had been taken. Now this young Princess was very beautiful indeed—as beautiful as she was wise—and when she got near the town she thought to herself, "If people see me, they may steal me away, as they did my sister, and then I shall never find her again. I will therefore disguise myself." As she was thus thinking she saw by the side of the road the corpse of a poor old beggar woman, who had evidently died from want and poverty. The body was shriveled up, and nothing of it remained but the skin and bones. The Princess took the skin and washed it, and drew it on over her own lovely face and neck, as one draws a glove on one's hand. Then she took a long stick and began hobbling along, leaning on it, toward the town. The old woman's skin was all crumpled and withered, and people who passed by only thought, "What an ugly old woman!" and never dreamed of the false skin and the beautiful, handsome girl inside. So on she went, picking up the pearls—one here, one there—until she found the last pearl just in front of the palace gate. Then she felt certain her sister must be somewhere near, but where she did not know. She longed to go into the palace and ask for her, but no guards would have let such a wretched-looking old woman enter, and she did not dare offer them any of the pearls she had with her, lest they should think she was a thief. So she determined merely to remain as close to the palace as possible, and wait till fortune favored her with the means of learning something further about her sister. Just opposite the palace was a small house belonging to a farmer, and the Princess went up to it and stood by the door. The farmer's wife saw her and said, "Poor old woman, who are you? what do you want? why are you here? Have you no friends?" "Alas, no!" answered the Princess. "I am a poor old woman, and have neither father nor mother, son nor daughter, sister nor brother, to take care of me; all are gone? and I can only beg my bread from door to door."

"Do not grieve, good mother," answered the farmer's wife, kindly. "You may sleep in the shelter of our porch, and I will give you some food." So the Princess stayed there for that night and for many more; and every day the good farmer's wife gave her food. But all this time she could learn nothing of her sister.

Now there was a large tank near the palace, on which grew some fine lotus plants, covered with rich crimson lotuses—the royal flower—and of these the Rajah was very fond indeed, and prized them very much. To this tank (because it was the nearest to the farmer's house) the Princess used to go every morning, very early, almost before it was light, at about three o'clock, and take off the old woman's skin and wash it, and hang it out to dry, and wash her face and hands, and bathe her feet in the cool water, and comb her beautiful hair. Then she would gather a lotus flower (such as she had been accustomed to wear in her hair from a child) and put it on, so as to feel for a few minutes like herself again! Thus she would amuse herself. Afterward, as soon as the wind had dried the old woman's skin, she put it on again, threw away the lotus flower, and hobbled back to the farmer's door before the sun was up.

After a time the Rajah discovered that some one had plucked some of his favorite lotus flowers. People were set to watch, and all the wise men in the kingdom put their heads together to try and discover the thief, but without avail. At last the excitement about this matter being very great, the Rajah's second son, a brave and noble young Prince (brother to him who had found the eldest Princess in the forest) said, "I will certainly discover this thief." It chanced that several fine trees grew around the tank. Into one of these the young Prince climbed one evening (having made a sort of light thatched roof across two of the boughs, to keep off the heavy dews), and there he watched all the night through, but with no more success than his predecessors. There lay the lotus plants, still in the moonlight, without so much as a thieving wind coming by to break off one of the flowers. The Prince began to get very sleepy, and thought the delinquent, whoever he might be, could not intend to return, when, in the very early morning, before it was light, who should come down to the tank but an old woman he had often seen near the palace gate. "Aha!" thought the Prince, "this then is the thief; but what can this queer old woman want with lotus flowers?" Imagine his astonishment when the old woman sat down on the steps of the tank and began pulling the skin off her face and arms, and from underneath the shriveled yellow skin came the loveliest face he had ever beheld! So fair, so fresh, so young, so gloriously beautiful, that, appearing thus suddenly, it dazzled the Prince's eyes like a flash of golden lightning. "Ah," thought he, "can this be a woman or a spirit? a devil or an angel in disguise?"

The Princess twisted up her glossy black hair, and, plucking a red lotus, placed it in it, and dabbled her feet in the water, and amused herself by putting round her neck a string of pearls that had been her sister's necklace. Then, as the sun was rising, she threw away the lotus, and covering her face and arms again with the withered skin, went hastily away. When the

Prince got home, the first thing he said to his parents was, "Father, mother! I should like to marry that old woman who stands all day at the farmer's gate, just opposite." "What!" cried they, "the boy is mad!" Marry that skinny old thing! You cannot—you are a King's son. Are there not enough Queens and Princesses in the world, that you should wish to marry a wretched old beggar-woman?" But he answered, "Above all things I should like to marry that old woman. You know that I have ever been a dutiful and obedient son. In this matter, I pray you, grant me my desire." Then, seeing he was really in earnest about the matter, and that nothing they could say would alter his mind, they listened to his urgent entreaties—not, however, without much grief and vexation—and sent out the guards, who fetched the old woman (who was really the Princess in disguise) to the palace, where she was married to the Prince as privately and with as little ceremony as possible, for the family were ashamed of the match.

As soon as the wedding was over, the Prince said to his wife, "Gentle wife, tell me how much longer you intend to wear that old skin? You had better take it off; do be so kind." The Princess wondered how he knew of her disguise, or whether it was only a guess of his; and she thought, "If I take this ugly skin off, my husband will think me pretty, and shut me up in the palace and never let me go away, so that I shall not be able to find my sister again. No, I had better not take it off." So she answered, "I don't know what you mean. I am as all these years have made me; nobody can change their skin." Then the Prince pretended to be very angry, and said, "Take off that hideous disguise this instant, or I'll kill you." But she only bowed her head, saying, "Kill me, then, but nobody can change their skin." And all this she mumbled as if she were a very old woman indeed, and had lost all her teeth and could not speak plain. At this the Prince laughed very much to himself, and thought, "I'll wait and see how long this freak lasts." But the Princess continued to keep on the old woman's skin; only every morning, at about three o'clock, before it was light, she would get up and wash it and put it on again. Then, some time afterward, the Prince, having found this out, got up softly one morning early, and followed her to the next room, where she had washed the skin and placed it on the floor to dry, and stealing it, he ran away with it and threw it on the fire. So the Princess, having no old woman's skin to put on, was obliged to appear in her own likeness. As she walked forth, very sad at missing her disguise, her husband ran to meet her, smiling and saying, "How do you do, my dear? Where is your skin now? Can't you take it off, dear?" Soon the whole palace had heard the joyful news of the beautiful young wife that the Prince had won; and all the people, when they saw her, cried, "Why she is exactly like the beautiful Princess our young Rajah married, the jungle lady." The old Rajah and Ranee were prouder than all of their daughter-in-law, and took her to introduce her to their eldest son's wife. Then no sooner did the Princess enter her sister-in-law's room then she saw that in her she had found her lost sister, and they ran into each other's arms. Great then was the joy of all, but the happiest of all these happy people were the two Princesses.

XVIII.

THE BLIND MAN, THE DEAF MAN AND THE DONKEY.

A BLIND Man and a Deaf Man once entered into partnership. The Deaf Man was to see for the Blind Man, and the Blind Man was to hear for the Deaf Man.

One day both went to a nautch* together. The Deaf Man said, "The dancing is very good, but the music is not worth listening to;" and the Blind Man said, "On the contrary, I think the music very good, but the dancing is not worth looking at."

After this they went together for a walk in the jungle, and there they found a Dhobee's donkey that had strayed away from its owner, and a great big chattee (such as Dhobees boil clothes in), which the donkey was carrying with him.

The Deaf Man said to the Blind Man, "Brother, here are a donkey and a Dhobee's great big chattee, with nobody to own them! Let us take them with us—they may be useful to us some day." "Very well," said the Blind Man, "we will take them with us." So the Blind Man and the Deaf Man went on their way, taking the donkey and the great big chattee with them. A little farther on they came to an ant's nest, and the

* Musical and dancing entertainment.

Deaf Man said to the Blind Man, "Here are a number of very fine black ants, much larger than any I ever saw before. Let us take some of them home to show our friends." "Very well," answered the Blind Man; "we will take them as a present to our friends." So the Deaf Man took a silver snuff-box out of his pocket, and put four or five of the finest black ants into it; which done, they continued their journey.

But before they had gone very far a terrible storm came on. It thundered and lightened and rained and blew with such fury that it seemed as if the whole heavens and earth were at war. "Oh dear! oh dear!" cried the Deaf Man, "how dreadful this lightning is! Let us make haste and get to some place of shelter." "I don't see that it's dreadful at all," answered the Blind Man, "but the thunder is very terrible; we had better certainly seek some place of shelter."

Now, not far off was a lofty building, which looked exactly like a fine temple. The Deaf Man saw it, and he and the Blind Man resolved to spend the night there; and having reached the place, they went in and shut the door, taking the donkey and the great big chattee with them. But this building, which they mistook for a temple, was in truth no temple at all, but the house of a very powerful Rakshas; and hardly had the Blind Man, the Deaf Man and the donkey got inside and fastened the door than the Rakshas, who had been out, returned home. To his surprise, he found the door fastened and heard people moving about inside his house. "Ho! ho!" cried he to himself, "some men have got in here, have they! I'll soon make mince-meat of them." So he began to roar in a voice louder than the thunder, and he cried, "Let me into my house this minute, you wretches; let me in, let me in, I say," and to kick the door and batter it with his great fists. But though his voice was very powerful, his appearance was still more alarming, insomuch that the Deaf Man, who was peeping at him through a chink in the wall, felt so frightened that he did not know what to do. But the Blind Man was very brave (because he couldn't see), and went up to the door and called out, "Who are you? and what do you mean by coming battering at the door in this way and at this time of night?"

"I'm a Rakshas," answered the Rakshas, angrily, "and this is my house. Let me in this instant, or I'll kill you." All this time the Deaf Man, who was watching the Rakshas, was shivering and shaking in a terrible fright, but the Blind Man was very brave (because he couldn't see), and he called out again, "Oh, you're a Rakshas, are you! Well, if you're Rakshas, I'm Bakshas; and Bakshas is as good as Rakshas." "Bakshas!" roared the Rakshas. "Bakshas! Bakshas! What nonsense is this? There is no such creature as a Bakshas!" "Go away," replied the Blind Man, "and don't dare to make any further disturbance, lest I punish you with a vengeance; for know that I'm Bakshas! and Bakshas is Rakshas' father." "My father?" answered the Rakshas. "Heavens and earth! Bakshas and my father! I never heard such an extraordinary thing in my life. You my father; and in there! I never knew my father was called Bakshas!"

"Yes," replied the Blind Man; "go away instantly, I command you, for I am your father Bakshas." "Very well," answered the Rakshas (for he began to get puzzled and frightened), "but if you are my father, let me first see your face." (For he thought, "Perhaps they are deceiving me.") The Blind Man and the Deaf Man didn't know what to do; but at last they opened the door a very tiny chink and poked the donkey's nose out. When the Rakshas saw it he thought to himself, "Bless me, what a terribly ugly face my father Bakshas has!" He then called out, "O father Bakshas, you have a very big, fierce face; but people have sometimes very big heads and very little bodies. Pray let me see your body as well as head before I go away." Then the Blind Man and the Deaf Man rolled the great, big Dhobee's chattee with a thundering noise past the chink in the door, and the Rakshas, who was watching attentively, was very much surprised when he saw this great black thing rolling along the floor, and he thought, "In truth, my father Bakshas has a very big body as well as a big head. He's big enough to eat me up altogether. I'd better go away." But still he could not help being a little doubtful, so he cried, "O Bakshas, father Bakshas! you have indeed got a very big head and a very big body; but do, before I go away, let me hear you scream" (for all Rakshas scream fearfully). Then the cunning Deaf Man (who was getting less frightened) pulled the silver snuff-box out of his pocket, and took the black ants out of it, and put one black ant in the donkey's right ear, and another black ant in the donkey's left ear, and another and another. The ants pinched the poor donkey's ears dreadfully, and the donkey was so hurt and frightened he began to bellow as loud as he could, "Eh augh! eh augh! eh augh! augh! augh!" and at this terrible noise the Rakshas fled away in a great fright, saying, "Enough, enough, father Bakshas! the sound of your voice would make the most refractory obedient." And no sooner had he gone than the Deaf Man took the ants out of the donkey's ears, and he and the Blind Man spent the rest of the night in peace and comfort.

Next morning the Deaf Man woke the Blind Man early, saying, "Awake, brother, awake; here we are indeed in luck! the whole floor is covered with heaps of gold and silver and precious stones." And so it was, for the Rakshas owned a vast amount of treasure, and the whole house was full of it. "That is a good thing," said the Blind Man. "Show me where it is and I will help you to collect it." So they collected as much treasure as possible and made four great bundles of it. The Blind Man took one great bundle, the Deaf Man took another, and, putting the other two great bundles on the donkey, they started off to return home. But the Rakshas, whom they had frightened away the night before, had not gone very far off, and was waiting to see what his father Bakshas might look like by daylight. He saw the door of his house open and watched attentively, when out walked—only a Blind Man, a Deaf Man and a donkey, who were all three laden with large bundles of his treasure. The Blind Man carried one bundle, the Deaf Man carried another bundle, and two bundles were on the donkey.

The Rakshas was extremely angry, and immediately called six of his friends to help him kill the Blind Man, the Deaf Man and the donkey, and recover the treasure.

The Deaf Man saw them coming (seven great Rakshas, with hair a yard long and tusks like an elephant's), and was dreadfully frightened; but the Blind Man was very brave (because he couldn't see), and said, "Brother, why do you lag behind in that way?" "Oh!" answered the Deaf Man, "there are seven great Rakshas with tusks like an elephant's coming to kill us; what can we do?" "Let us hide the treasure in the bushes," said the Blind Man; "and do you lead me to a tree; then I will climb up first, and you shall climb up afterward, and so we shall be out of their way." The Deaf Man thought this good advice; so he pushed the donkey and the bundles of treasure into the bushes, and led the Blind Man to a high soparee tree that grew close by; but he was a very cunning man, this Deaf Man, and instead of letting the Blind Man climb up first and following him, he got up first and let the Blind Man clamber after, so that he was farther out of harm's way than his friend.

When the Rakshas arrived at the place and saw them both perched out of reach in the soparee tree, he said to his friends, "Let us get on each other's shoulders; we shall then be high enough to pull them down." So one Rakshas stooped down, and the second got on his shoulders, and the third on his, and the fourth on his, and the fifth on his, and the sixth on his; and the seventh and the last Rakshas (who had invited all the others) was just climbing up when the Deaf Man (who was looking over the Blind Man's shoulder) got so frightened that in his alarm he caught hold of his friend's arm, crying, "They're coming, they're coming!" The Blind Man was not in a very secure position, and was sitting at his ease, not knowing how close the Rakshas were. The consequence was, that when the Deaf Man gave him this unexpected push, he lost his balance and tumbled down on to the neck of the seventh Rakshas, who was just then climbing up. The Blind Man had no idea where he was, but thought he had got on to the branch of some other tree; and, stretching out his hand for something to catch hold of, caught hold of the Rakshas' two great ears, and pinched them very hard in his surprise and fright. The Rakshas couldn't think what it was that had come tumbling down upon him; and the weight of the Blind Man upsetting his balance, down he also fell to the ground, knocking down in their turn the sixth, fifth, fourth, third, second and first Rakshas, who all rolled one over another, and lay in a confused heap at the foot of the tree together. Meanwhile the Blind Man called out to his friend, "Where am I? what has happened? Where am I? where am I?" The Deaf Man (who was safe up in the tree) answered, "Well done, brother! never fear! never fear! You're all right, only hold on tight. I'm coming down to help you." But he had not the least intention of leaving his place of safety. However, he continued to call out, "Never mind, brother; hold on as tight as you can. I'm coming, I'm coming," and the more he called out, the harder the Blind Man pinched the Rakshas' ears, which he mistook for some kind of palm branches. The six other Rakshas, who had succeeded, after a good deal of kicking, in extricating themselves from their unpleasant position, thought they had had quite enough of helping their friend, and ran away as fast as they could; and the seventh, thinking from their going that the danger must be greater than he imagined, and being moreover very much afraid of the mysterious creature that sat on his shoulders, put his hands to the back of his ears and pushed off the Blind

Man, and then (without staying to see who or what he was) followed his six companions as fast as he could.

As soon as all the Rakshas were out of sight, the Deaf Man came down from the tree, and, picking up the Blind Man, embraced him, saying, "I could not have done better myself. You have frightened away all our enemies, but you see I came to help you as fast as possible." He then dragged the donkey and the bundles of treasure out of the bushes, gave the Blind Man one bundle to carry, took the second himself, and put the remaining two on the donkey, as before. This done, the whole party set off to return home. But when they had got nearly out of the jungle the Deaf Man said to the Blind Man, "We are now close to the village, but if we take all this treasure home with us, we shall run great risk of being robbed. I think our best plan would be to divide it equally; then you shall take care of your half, and I will take care of mine, and each one can hide his share here in the jungle, or wherever pleases him best." "Very well," said the Blind Man; "do you divide what we have in the bundles into two equal portions, keeping one-half yourself and giving me the other." But the cunning Deaf Man had no intention of giving up half of the treasure to the Blind Man; so he first took his own bundle of treasure and hid it in the bushes, and then he took the two bundles off the donkey and hid them in the bushes; and he took a good deal of treasure out of the Blind Man's bundle, which he also hid. Then, taking the small quantity that remained, he divided it into two equal portions, and placing half before the Blind Man and half in front of himself, said, "There, brother, is your share to do what you please with." The Blind Man put out his hand, but when he felt what a very little heap of treasure it was, he got very angry, and cried, "This is not fair—you are deceiving me; you have kept almost all the treasure for yourself and only given me a very little." "Oh, oh! how can you think so?" answered the Deaf Man; "but if you will not believe me, feel for yourself. See, my heap of treasure is no larger than yours." The Blind Man put out his hands again to feel how much his friend had kept; but in front of the Deaf Man lay only a very small heap, no larger than what he had himself received. At this he got very cross, and said, "Come, come, this won't do. You think you can cheat me in this way because I am blind; but I'm not so stupid as all that. I carried a great bundle of treasure, you carried a great bundle of treasure, and there were two great bundles on the donkey. Do you mean to pretend that all that made no more treasure than these two little heaps! No, indeed; I know better than that." "Stuff and nonsense!" answered the Deaf Man. "Stuff or no stuff," continued the other, "you are trying to take me in, and I won't be taken in by you." "No, I'm not," said the Deaf Man. "Yes, you are," said the Blind Man; and so they went on bickering, scolding, growling, contradicting, until the Blind Man got so enraged that he gave the Deaf Man a tremendous box on the ear. The blow was so violent that it made the Deaf Man hear! The Deaf Man, very angry, gave his neighbor in return so hard a blow in the face that it opened the Blind Man's eyes!

So the Deaf Man could hear as well as see! and the Blind Man could see as well as hear! This astonished them both so much that they became good friends at once. The Deaf Man confessed to having hidden the bulk of the treasure, which he thereupon dragged forth from its place of concealment, and, having divided it equally, they went home and enjoyed themselves.

XIX.

MUCHIE LAL.

ONCE upon a time there was a Rajah and Ranee who had no children. Long had they wished and prayed that the gods would send them a son, but it was all in vain—their prayers were not granted. One day a number of fish were brought into the royal kitchen to be cooked for the Rajah's dinner, and amongst them was one little fish that was not dead, but all the rest were dead. One of the palace maid-servants seeing this, took the little fish and put him in a basin of water. Shortly afterward the Ranee saw him, and thinking him very pretty, kept him as a pet; and because she had no children she lavished all her affection on the fish and loved him as a son; and the people called him Muchie Rajah (the Fish Prince). In a little while Muchie Rajah had grown too long to live in the small basin, so they put him in a larger one, and then (when he grew too long for that) into a big tub. In time, however, Muchie Rajah became too large for even the big tub to hold him; so the Ranee had a tank made for him in which he lived very happily, and twice a day she fed him with boiled rice. Now, though the people fancied Muchie Rajah was only a fish, this was not the case. He was, in truth, a young Rajah who had angered the gods, and been by them turned into a fish and thrown into the river as a punishment.

One morning, when the Ranee brought him his daily meal of boiled rice, Muchie Rajah called out to her and said, "Queen Mother, Queen Mother, I am so lonely here all by myself! Cannot you get me a wife?" The Ranee promised to try, and sent messengers to all the people she knew, to ask if they would allow one of their children to marry her son, the Fish Prince. But they all answered, "We cannot give one of our dear little daughters to be devoured by a great fish, even though he is the Muchie Rajah and so high in your Majesty's favor."

At news of this the Ranee did not know what to do. She was so foolishly fond of Muchie Rajah, however, that she resolved to get him a wife at any cost. Again she sent out messengers, but this time she gave them a great bag containing a lac of gold mohurs,* and said to them, "Go into every land until you find a wife for my Muchie Rajah, and to whoever will give you a child to be the Muchie Ranee† you shall give this bag of gold mohurs." The messengers started on their search, but for some time they were unsuccessful: not even the beggars were to be tempted to sell their children, fearing the great fish would devour them. At last one day the messengers came to a village where there lived a Fakeer, who had lost his first wife and married again. His first wife had had one little daughter, and his second wife also had a daughter. As it happened, the Fakeer's second wife hated her little step-daughter, always gave her the hardest work to do and the least

* A lac of gold mohurs is equal to about $750,000.

† Fish Queen.

food to eat, and tried by every means in her power to get her out of the way, in order that the child might not rival her own daughter. When she heard of the errand on which the messengers had come, she sent for them when the Fakeer was out, and said to them, "Give me the bag of gold mohurs, and you shall take my little daughter to marry the Muchie Rajah." ("For," she thought to herself, "the great fish will certainly eat the girl, and she will thus trouble us no more.") Then, turning to her step-daughter, she said, "Go down to the river and wash your saree, that you may be fit to go with these people, who will take you to the Ranee's court." At these words the poor girl went down to the river very sorrowful, for she saw no hope of escape, as her father was from home. As she knelt by the river-side, washing her saree and crying bitterly, some of her tears fell into the hole of an old Seven-headed Cobra, who lived on the river-bank. This Cobra was a very wise animal, and seeing the maiden, he put his head out of his hole, and said to her, "Little girl, why do you cry?" "Oh, sir," she answered, "I am very unhappy, for my father is from home, and my step-mother has sold me to the Ranee's people to be the wife of the Muchie Rajah, that great fish, and I know he will eat me up." "Do not be afraid, my daughter," said the Cobra; "but take with you these three stones and tie them up in the corner of your saree;" and so saying, he gave her three little round pebbles. "The Muchie Rajah, whose wife you are to be, is not really a fish, but a Rajah who has been enchanted. Your home will be a little room which the Ranee has had built in the tank wall. When you are taken there, wait and be sure you don't go to sleep, or the Muchie Rajah will certainly come and eat you up. But as you hear him coming rushing through the water, be prepared, and as soon as you see him throw this first stone at him; he will then sink to the bottom of the tank. The second time he comes, throw the second stone, when the same thing will happen. The third time he comes, throw this third stone, and he will immediately resume his human shape." So saying, the old Cobra dived down again into his hole. The Fakeer's daughter took the stones and determined to do as the Cobra had told her, though she hardly believed it would have the desired effect.

When she reached the palace the Ranee spoke kindly to her, and said to the messengers, "You have done your errand well; this is a dear little girl." Then she ordered that she should be let down the side of the tank in a basket to a little room which had been prepared for her. When the Fakeer's daughter got there, she thought she had never seen such a pretty place in her life (for the Ranee had caused the little room to be very nicely decorated for the wife of her favorite); and she would have felt very happy away from her cruel step-mother and all the hard work she had been made to do, had it not been for the dark water that lay black and unfathomable below the door, and the fear of the terrible Muchie Rajah.

After waiting some time she heard a rushing sound, and little waves came dashing against the threshold; faster they came and faster, and the noise got louder and louder, until she saw a great fish's head above the water—Muchie Rajah was coming toward her open-mouthed. The Fakeer's daughter seized one of the stones that the Cobra had given her and threw it at him, and down he sank to the bottom of the tank; a second time he rose and came toward her, and she threw the second stone at him, and he again sank down; a third time he came more fiercely than before, when, seizing a third stone, she threw it with all her force. No sooner did it touch him than the spell was broken, and there, instead of a fish, stood a handsome young Prince. The poor little Fakeer's daughter was so startled that she began so cry. But the Prince said to her, "Pretty maiden, do not be frightened. You have rescued me from a horrible thraldom, and I can never thank you enough; but if you will be the Muchie Ranee, we will be married to morrow." Then he sat down on the door-step, thinking over his strange fate and watching for the dawn.

Next morning early several inquisitive people came to see if the Muchie Rajah had eaten up his poor little wife, as they feared he would; what was their astonishment, on looking over the tank wall, to see, not the Muchie Rajah, but a magnificent Prince! The news soon spread to the palace. Down came the Rajah, down came the Ranee, down came all their attendants and dragged Muchie Rajah and the Fakeer's daughter up the side of the tank in a basket; and when they heard their story there were great and unparalleled rejoicings. The Ranee said, "So I have indeed found a son at last!" And the people were so delighted, so happy and so proud of the new Prince and Princess that they covered all their path with damask from the tank to the palace, and cried to their fellows, "Come and see our new Prince and Princess. Were ever any so divinely beautiful? Come see a right royal couple—a pair of mortals like the gods!" And when they reached the palace the Prince was married to the Fakeer's daughter.

There they lived very happily for some time. The Muchie Ranee's step-mother, hearing what had happened, came often to see her step-daughter, and pretended to be delighted at her good fortune; and the Ranee was so good that she quite forgave all her step-mother's former cruelty, and always received her very kindly. At last, one day, the Muchie Ranee said to her husband, "It is a weary while since I saw my father. If you will give me leave, I should much like to visit my native village and see him again." "Very well," he replied, "you may go. But do not stay away long; for there can be no happiness for me till you return." So she went, and her father was delighted to see her; but her step-mother, though she pretended to be very kind, was, in reality, only glad to think she had got the Ranee into her power, and determined, if possible, never to allow her to return to the palace again. One day, therefore, she said to her own daughter, "It is hard that your step-sister should have become Ranee of all the land instead of being eaten up by the great fish, while we gained no more than a lac of gold mohurs. Do now as I bid you, that you may become Ranee in her stead." She then went on to instruct her how that she must invite the Ranee down to the river-bank, and there beg her to let her try on her jewels, and whilst putting them on give her a push and drown her in the river.

The girl consented, and standing by the river-bank, said to her step-sister, "Sister, may I try on your jewels?—how pretty they are!" "Yes," said the Ranee, "and we shall be able to see in the river how they look." So, undoing her necklaces, she clasped them round the other's neck. But whilst she was doing so her step-sister gave her a push, and she fell backward into the water. The girl watched to see that the body did not rise, and then, running back, said to her mother, "Mother, here are all the jewels, and she will trouble us no more." But it happened that just when her step-sister pushed the Ranee into the river her old friend the Seven-headed Cobra chanced to be swimming across it, and seeing the little Ranee like to be drowned, he carried her on his back until he reached his hole, into which he took her safely. Now this hole, in which the Cobra and his wife and all his little ones lived, had two entrances—the one under the water and leading to the river, and the other above water, leading out into the open fields. To this upper end of his hole the Cobra took the Muchie Ranee, where he and his wife took care of her; and there she lived with them for some time. Meanwhile, the wicked Fakeer's wife, having dressed up her own daughter in all the Ranee's jewels, took her to the palace, and said to the Muchie Rajah, "See, I have brought your wife, my dear daughter, back safe and well." The Rajah looked at her, and thought, "This does not look like my wife." However, the room was dark and the girl was cleverly disguised, and he thought he might be mistaken. Next day he said again, "My wife must be sadly changed or this cannot be she, for she was always bright and cheerful. She had pretty loving ways and merry words, while this woman never opens her lips." Still, he did not like to seem to mistrust his wife, and comforted himself by saying, "Perhaps she is tired with the long journey." On the third day, however, he could bear the uncertainty no longer, and tearing off her jewels, saw, not the face of his own little wife, but another woman. Then he was very angry and turned her out of doors, saying, "Begone; since you are but the wretched tool of others, I spare your life." But of the Fakeer's wife he said to his guards, "Fetch that woman here instantly; for unless she can tell me where my wife is, I will have her hanged." It chanced, however, that the Fakeer's wife had heard of the Muchie Rajah having turned her daughter out of doors; so, fearing his anger, she hid herself, and was not to be found.

Meantime, the Muchie Ranee, not knowing how to get home, continued to live in the great Seven-headed Cobra's hole, and he and his wife and all his family were very kind to her, and loved her as if she had been one of them; and there her little son was born, and she called him Muchie Lal,* after the Muchie Rajah, his father. Muchie Lal was a lovely child, merry and brave, and his playmates all day long were the young Cobras.† When he was about three years old a bangle-seller came by that way, and the Muchie Ranee bought some bangles from him and put them on her boy's wrists and ankles; but by next day, in playing, he had broken them all. Then, seeing the bangle-seller, the Ranee called him again and bought some more, and so on every day until the bangle-seller got quite rich from selling so many bangles for the Muchie Lal, for the Cobra's hole was full of treasure, and he gave the Muchie Ranee as much money to spend every day as she liked. There was nothing she wished for he did not give her, only he would not let her try to get home to her husband, which she wished more than all. When she asked him he would say, "No, I will

* Little Ruby Fish. † See Notes at the end.

not let you go. If your husband comes here and fetches you, it is well; but I will not allow you to wander in search of him through the land alone."

And so she was obliged to stay where she was.

All this time the poor Muchie Rajah was hunting in every part of the country for his wife, but he could learn no tidings of her. For grief and sorrow at losing her he had gone well-nigh distracted, and did nothing but wander from place to place, crying, "She is gone! she is gone!" Then, when he had long inquired without avail of all the people in her native village about her, he one day met a bangle-seller and said to him, "Whence do you come?" The bangle-seller answered, "I have just been selling bangles to some people who live in a Cobra's hole in the river-bank." "People! What people?" asked the Rajah. "Why," answered the bangle-seller, "a woman and a child: the child is the most beautiful I ever saw. He is about three years old, and of course, running about, is always breaking his bangles, and his mother buys him new ones every day." "Do you know what the child's name is?" said the Rajah. "Yes," answered the bangle-seller, carelessly, "for the lady always calls him her Muchie Lal." "Ah," thought the Muchie Rajah, "this must be my wife." Then he said to him again, "Good bangle-seller, I would see these strange people of whom you speak; cannot you take me there?" "Not to-night," replied the bangle-seller; "daylight has gone, and we should only frighten them; but I shall be going there again to-morrow, and then you may come too. Meanwhile, come and rest at my house for the night, for you look faint and weary." The Rajah consented. Next morning, however, very early, he woke the bangle-seller, saying, "Pray let us go now and see the people you spoke about yesterday." "Stay," said the bangle-seller; "it is much too early. I never go till after breakfast." So the Rajah had to wait till the bangle-seller was ready to go. At last they started off, and when they reached the Cobra's hole the first thing the Rajah saw was a fine little boy playing with the young Cobras.

As the bangle-seller came along, jingling his bangles, a gentle voice from inside the hole called out, "Come here, my Muchie Lal, and try on your bangles." Then the Muchie Rajah, kneeling down at the mouth of the hole, said, "Oh, lady, show your beautiful face to me." At the sound of his voice the Ranee ran out, crying, "Husband, husband! have you found me again." And she told him how her sister had tried to drown her, and how the good Cobra had saved her life and taken care of her and her child. Then he said, "And will you now come home with me?" And she told him how the Cobra would never let her go, and said, "I will first tell him of your coming; for he has been as a father to me." So she called out, "Father Cobra, father Cobra, my husband has come to fetch me; will you let me go?" "Yes," he said, "if your husband has come to fetch you, you may go." And his wife said, "Farewell, dear lady, we are loth to lose you, for we have loved you as a daughter." And all the little Cobras were very sorrowful to think that they must lose their playfellow, the young Prince. Then the Cobra gave the Muchie Rajah and the Muchie Ranee and Muchie Lal all the most costly gifts he could find in his treasure-house; and so they went home, where they lived very happy ever after.

XX.

CHUNDUN RAJAH.

ONCE upon a time, a Rajah and Ranee died, leaving seven sons and one daughter. All these seven sons were married, and the wives of the six eldest used to be very unkind to their poor little sister-in-law; but the wife of the seventh brother loved her dearly, and always took her part against the others. She would say, "Poor little thing! her life is sad. Her mother wished so long for a daughter, and then the girl was born and the mother died, and never saw her poor child, or was able to ask any one to take care of her." At which the wives of the six elder brothers would answer, "You only take such notice of the girl in order to vex us." Then, while their husbands were away, they made up wicked stories against their sister-in-law, which they told them on their return home; and their husbands believed them rather than her, and were very angry with her and ordered her to be turned out of the house. But the wife of the seventh brother did not believe what the six others said, and was very kind to the little Princess, and sent her secretly as much food as she could spare from her own dinner. But as they drove her from their door, the six wives of the elder brothers cried out, "Go away, wicked girl, go away, and never let us see your face again until you marry Chundun Rajah!* When you invite us to the wedding, and give us, the six eldest, six common wooden stools to sit on, but the seventh sister (who always takes your part) a fine emerald chair, we will believe you innocent of all the evil deeds of which you are accused, but not till then!" This they said scornfully, railing at her; for Chundun Rajah, of whom they spoke (who was the great Rajah of a neighboring country), had been dead many months.

So, sad at heart, the Princess wandered forth into the jungle; and when she had gone through it, she came upon another, still denser than the first. The trees grew so thickly overhead that she could scarcely see the sky, and there was no village or house of living creature near. The food her youngest sister-in-law had given her was nearly exhausted, and she did not know where to get more. At last, however, after journeying on for many days, she came upon a large tank, beside which was a fine house that belonged to a Rakshas. Being very tired, she sat down on the edge of the tank to eat some of the parched rice that remained of her store of provisions; and as she did so she thought, "This house belongs doubtless to a Rakshas, who perhaps will see me and kill and eat me; but since no one cares for me, and I have neither home nor friends, I hold life cheap enough." It happened, however, that the Rakshas was then out, and there was no one in his house but a little cat and dog, who were his servants.

The dog's duty was to take care of the saffron with which the Rakshas colored his face on highdays and holidays, and the cat had charge of the antimony with

* King Sandlewood.

which he blackened his eyelids. Before the Princess had been long by the tank, the little cat spied her out, and running to her, said, "Oh, sister, sister, I am so hungry, pray give me some of your dinner." The Princess answered, "I have very little rice left; when it is all gone I shall starve. If I give you some, what have you to give me in exchange?" The cat said, "I have charge of the antimony with which my Rakshas blackens his eyelids—I will give you some of it;" and running to the house she fetched a nice little potful of antimony, which she gave to the Princess in exchange for the rice. When the little dog saw this, he also ran down to the tank, and said, "Lady, lady, give me some rice, I pray you, for I, too, am very hungry." But she answered, "I have very little rice left, and when it is all gone I shall starve. If I give you some of my dinner, what will you give me in exchange?" The dog said, "I have charge of my Rákshas' saffron, with which he colors his face. I will give you some of it." So he ran to the house and fetched a quantity of saffron and gave it to the Princess, and she gave him also some of the rice. Then, tying the antimony and saffron up in her saree, she said good-bye to the dog and cat and went on her way.

Three or four days after this, she found she had nearly reached the other side of the jungle. The wood was not so thick, and in the distance she saw a large building that looked like a great tomb. The Princess determined to go and see what it was, and whether she could find any one there to give her any food, for she had eaten all the rice and felt very hungry, and it was getting toward night.

Now the place toward which the Princess went was

the tomb of the Chundun Rajah, but this she did not know.

Chundun Rajah had died many months before, and his father and mother and sisters, who loved him veiy dearly, could not bear the idea of his being buried under the cold ground; so they had built a beautiful tomb, and inside it they had placed the body on a bed under a canopy, and it had never decayed, but continued as fair and perfect as when first put there. Every day Chundun Rajah's mother and sister would come to the place to weep and lament from sunrise to sunset, but each evening they returned to their own homes. Hard by was a shrine and small hut where a Brahmin lived, who had charge of the place; and from far and near people used to come to visit the tomb of their lost Rajah and see the great miracle, how the body of him who had been dead so many months remained perfect and undecayed; but none knew why this was. When the Princess got near the place a violent storm came on. The rain beat upon her and wetted her, and it grew so dark she could hardly see where she was going. She would have been afraid to go into the tomb had she known about Chundun Rajah; but as it was, the storm being so violent and night approaching, she ran in there for shelter as fast as she could, and sat down shivering in one-corner. By the light of an oil lamp that burnt dimly in a niche in the wall, she saw in front of her the body of the Rajah lying under the canopy, with the heavy jeweled coverlid over him and the rich hangings all round. He looked as if he were only asleep, and she did not feel frightened. But at twelve o'clock, to her great surprise, as she was watching and waiting, the Rajah came to life; and when he saw her sitting shivering in the corner, he fetched a light and came toward her and said, "Who are you?" She answered, "I am a poor lonely girl. I only came here for shelter from the storm. I am dying of cold and hunger." And then she told him all her story—how that her sisters-in-law had falsely accused her, and driven her from among them into the jungle, bidding her see their faces no more until she married the Chundun Rajah, who had been dead so many months; and how the youngest had been kind to her and sent her food, which had prevented her from starving by the way.

The Rajah listened to the Princess' words, and was certain that they were true and she no common beggar from the jungles. For, for all her ragged clothes, she looked a royal lady, and shone like a star in the darkness. Moreover, her eyelids were darkened with antimony and her beautiful face painted with saffron, like the face of a Princess. Then he felt a great pity for her, and said, "Lady, have no fear, for I will take care of you," and dragging the rich coverlid off his bed he threw it over her to keep her warm, and going to the Brahmin's house, which was close by, fetched some rice, which he gave her to eat. Then he said, "I am the Chundun Rajah, of whom you have heard. I die every day, but every night I come to life for a little while." She cried, "Do none of your family know of this? and if so, why do you stay here in a dismal tomb?" He answered, "None know it but the Brahmin who has charge of this place. Since my life is thus maimed, what would it avail to tell my family? It would but grieve them more than to think me dead. Therefore, I have forbidden him to let them know;

and since my parents only come here by day, they have never found it out. Maybe I shall some time wholly recover, and till then I will be silent about my existence." Then he called the Brahmin who had charge of the tomb and the shrine (and who daily placed an offering of food upon it for the Rajah to eat when he came to life), and said to him, "Henceforth, place a double quantity of food upon the shrine, and take care of this lady. If I ever recover she shall be my Ranee." And having said these words he died again. Then the Brahmin took the Princess to his little hut, and bade his wife see that she wanted for nothing, and all the next day she rested in that place. Very early in the morning Chundun Rajah's mother and sisters came to visit the tomb, but they did not see the Princess; and in the evening, when the sun was setting, they went away. That night, when the Chundun Rajah came to life, he called the Brahmin, and said to him, "Is the Princess still here?" "Yes," he answered; "for she is weary with her journey, and she has no home to go to." The Rajah said, "Since she has neither home nor friends, if she be willing, you shall marry me to her, and she shall wander no further in search of shelter." So the Brahmin fetched his shastra* and called all his family as witnesses, and married the Rajah to the little Princess, reading prayers over them and scattering rice and flowers upon their heads. And there the Chundun Ranee lived for some time. She was very happy; she wanted nothing, and the Brahmin and his wife took as much care of her as if she had been their daughter. Every day she would wait outside the tomb, but at sunset she always returned to it

* Sacred books.

and watched for her husband to come to life. One night she said to him, "Husband, I am happier to be your wife, and hold your hand and talk to you for two or three hours every evening, than were I married to some great living Rajah for a hundred years. But oh what joy it would be if you could come wholly to life again! Do you know what is the cause of your daily death? and what it is that brings you to life each night at twelve o'clock?"

"Yes," he said, "it is because I have lost my Chundun Har,* the sacred necklace that held my soul. A Peri stole it. I was in the palace garden one day, when many of those winged ladies flew over my head, and one of them, when she saw me, loved me and asked me to marry her. But I said no, I would not; and at that she was angry, and tore the Chundun Har off my neck and flew away with it. That instant I fell down dead, and my father and mother caused me to be placed in this tomb; but every night the Peri comes here and takes my necklace off her neck, and when she takes it off I come to life again, and she asks me to come away with her and marry her, and she does not put on the necklace again for two or three hours, waiting to see if I will consent. During that time I live. But when she finds I will not, she puts on the necklace again and flies away, and as soon as she puts it on, I die."†

"Cannot the Peri be caught?" asked the Chundun Ranee. Her husband answered, "No, I have often tried to seize back my necklace, for if I could regain it I should come wholly to life again; but the Peri can at will render herself invisible and fly away

* Sandlewood necklace. † See Notes at the end.

with it, so that it is impossible for any mortal man to get it." At this news the Chundun Ranee was sad at heart, for she saw no hope of the Rajah's being restored to life; and grieving over this she became so ill and unhappy that even when she had a little baby boy born, it did not much cheer her, for she did nothing but think, "This poor child will grow up in this desolate place, and have no kind father day by day to teach him and help him as other children have, but only see him for a little while by night; and we are all at the mercy of the Peri, who may any day fly quite away with the necklace and not return." The Brahmin, seeing how ill she was, said to the Chundun Rajah, "The Ranee will die unless she can be somewhere where much care will be taken of her, for in my poor home my wife and I can do but little for her comfort. Your mother and sister are good and charitable; let her go to the palace, where they will only need to see she is ill to take care of her." Now it happened that in the palace courtyard there was a great slab of white marble, on which the Chundun Rajah would often rest on the hot summer days; and because he used to be so fond of it, when he died his father and mother ordered that it should be taken great care of, and no one was allowed to so much as touch it. Knowing this, Chundun Rajah said to his wife, "You are ill; I should like you to go to the palace, where my mother and sisters will take the greatest care of you. Do this, therefore: take our child and sit down with him upon the great slab of marble in the palace courtyard. I used to be very fond of it; and so now for my sake it is kept with the greatest care, and no one is allowed to so much as touch it. They will most likely see you there and order you to go away; but if you then tell them you are ill, they will, I know, have pity on you and befriend you." The Chundun Ranee did as her husband told her, placing her little boy on the great slab of white marble in the palace courtyard and sitting down herself beside him. Chundun Rajah's sister, who was looking out of the window, saw her and cried, "Mother, there are a woman and her child resting on my brother's marble slab; let us tell them to go away." So she ran down to the place, but when she saw Chundun Ranee and the little boy she was quite astonished, the Chundun Ranee was so fair and lovable-looking, and the baby was the image of her dead brother. Then returning to her mother, she said, "Mother, she who sits upon the marble stone is the prettiest little lady I ever saw; and do not let us blame the poor thing; she says she is ill and weary, and the baby (I know not if it is fancy, or the seeing him on that stone) seems to me the image of my lost brother."

At this the old Ranee and the rest of the family went out, and when they saw the Chundun Ranee, they all took such a fancy to her and to the child that they brought her into the palace, and were very kind to her, and took great care of her; so that in a while she got well and strong again, and much less unhappy; and they all made a great pet of the little boy, for they were struck with his strange likeness to the dead Rajah; and after a time they gave his mother a small house to live in, close to the palace, where they often used to go and visit her. There also the Chundun Rajah would go each night when he came to life, to laugh and talk with his wife and play with his boy, although he still refused to tell his father and mother of his existence. One day

CHUNDUN-RANEE.—p. 276.

it happened, however, that the little child told one of the Princesses (Chundun Rajah's sister) how every evening some one who came to the house used to laugh and talk with his mother and play with him, and then go away. The Princess also heard the sound of voices in Chundun Ranee's house, and saw lights flickering about there when they were supposed to be fast asleep. Of this she told her mother, saying, "Let us go down to-morrow night and see what this means; perhaps the woman we thought so poor and befriended thus is nothing but a cheat, and entertains all her friends every night at our expense."

So the next evening they went down softly, softly to the place, when they saw, not the strangers they had expected, but their long-lost Chundun Rajah. Then, since he could not escape, he told them all—how that every night for an hour or two he came to life, but was dead all day. And they rejoiced greatly to see him again, and reproached him for not letting them know he ever lived, though for so short a time. He then told them how he had married the Chundun Ranee, and thanked them for all their loving care of her.

After this he used to come every night and sit and talk with them; but still each day, to their great sorrow, he died; nor could they divine any means for getting back his Chundun Har, which the Peri wore round her neck.

At last one evening, when they were all laughing and chatting together, seven Peris flew into the room unobserved by them, and one of the seven was the very Peri who had stolen Chundun Rajah's necklace, and she held it in her hand.

All the young Peris were very fond of the Chundun

Rajah and Chundun Ranee's boy, and used often to come and play with him, for he was the image of his father's and mother's loveliness, and as fair as the morning; and he used to laugh and clap his little hands when he saw them coming; for though men and women cannot see Peris, little children can.

Chundun Rajah was tossing the child up in the air when the Peris flew into the room, and the little boy was laughing merrily. The winged ladies fluttered round the Rajah and the child, and she that had the necklace hovered over his head. Then the boy, seeing the glittering necklace which the Peri held, stretched out his little arms and caught hold of it, and as he seized it the string broke, and all the beads fell upon the floor. At this the seven Peris were frightened and flew away, and the Chundun Ranee, collecting the beads, strung them and hung them round the Rajah's neck; and there was great joy amongst those that loved him, because he had recovered the sacred necklace, and that the spell which doomed him to death was broken.

The glad news was soon known throughout the kingdom, and all the people were happy and proud to hear it, crying, "We have lost our young Rajah for such a long, long time, and now one little child has brought him back to life." And the old Rajah and Ranee (Chundun Rajah's father and mother) determined that he should be married again to the Chundun Ranee with great pomp and splendor, and they sent letters into all the kingdoms of the world, saying, "Our son the Chundun Rajah has come to life again, and we pray you come to his wedding."

Then, among those who accepted the invitation, were the Chundun Ranee's seven brothers and their seven wives; and for her six sisters-in-law, who had been so cruel to her and caused her to be driven out into the jungle, the Chundun Ranee prepared six common wooden stools; but for the seventh, who had been kind to her, she made ready an emerald throne and a foot-stool adorned with emeralds.

When all the Ranees were taken to their places, the six eldest complained, saying, "How is this? Six of us are given only common wooden stools to sit upon, but the seventh has an emerald chair?" Then the Chundun Ranee stood up, and before the assembled guests told them her story, reminding her six elder sisters-in-law of their former taunts, and how they had forbidden her to see them again until the day of her marriage with the Chundun Rajah, and she explained how unjustly they had accused her to her brothers. When the Ranees heard this they were struck dumb with fear and shame, and were unable to answer a word; and all their husbands, being much enraged to learn how they had conspired to kill their sister-in-law, commanded that these wicked woman should be instantly hanged, which was accordingly done. Then, on the same day that the Chundun Rajah remarried their sister, the six elder brothers were married to six beautiful ladies of the court amid great and unheard-of rejoicings, and from that day they all lived together in perfect peace and harmony until their lives' end.

XXI.

SODEWA BAI.

ONCE upon a time there lived a Rajah and Ranee, who had one only daughter, and she was the most beautiful Princess in the world. Her face was as fair and delicate as the clear moonlight, and they called her Sodewa Bai.* At her birth her father and mother had sent for all the wise men in the kingdom to tell her fortune, and they predicted that she would grow up richer and more fortunate than any other lady; and so it was, for from her earliest youth she was good and lovely, and whenever she opened her lips to speak pearls and precious stones fell upon the ground, and as she walked along they would scatter on either side of her path, insomuch that her father soon became the richest Rajah in all that country, for his daughter could not go across the room without shaking down jewels worth a dowry. Moreover, Sodewa Bai was born with a golden necklace about her neck, concerning which also her parents consulted astrologers, who said, "This is no common child; the necklace of gold about her neck contains your daughter's soul: let it therefore be guarded with the utmost care, for if it were taken off and worn by another person she would die." So the Ranee, her mother, caused it to be firmly fastened

* The Lady Good Fortune.

round the child's neck, and as soon as she was old enough to understand, instructed her concerning its value, and bade her on no account ever to allow it to be taken off.

At the time my story begins this Princess was fourteen years old, but she was not married, for her father and mother had promised that she should not do so until it pleased herself; and although many great rajahs and nobles sought her hand, she constantly refused them all.

Now Sodewa Bai's father, on one of her birth-days, gave her a lovely pair of slippers made of gold and jewels. Each slipper was worth a hundred thousand gold mohurs. There were none like them in all the earth. Sodewa Bai prized these slippers very much, and always wore them when she went out walking, to protect her tender feet from the stones; but one day, as she was wandering with her ladies upon the side of the mountain on which the palace was built, playing and picking the wild flowers, her foot slipped and one of the golden slippers fell down, down, down the steep hill-slope, over rocks and stones, into the jungle below. Sodewa Bai sent attendants to search for it, and the Rajah caused criers to go throughout the town and proclaim that whoever discovered the Princess' slipper should receive a great reward; but though it was hunted for far and near, high and low, it could not be found.

It chanced, however, that not very long after this a young Prince, the eldest son of a Rajah who lived in the plains, was out hunting, and in the jungle he picked up the very little golden slipper which Sodewa Bai had lost, and which had tumbled all the way from the mountain-side into the depths of the forest. He took it home with him, and showed it to his mother, saying, "What a fairy foot must have worn this tiny slipper!" "Ah, my boy," she said, "this must have belonged to a lovely Princess, in truth (if she is but as beautiful as her slipper); would that you could find such a one to be your wife!" Then they sent into all the towns of the kingdom to inquire for the owner of the lost slipper, but she could not be found. At last, when many months had gone by, it happened that news was brought by travelers to the Rajah's capital, of how, in a far distant land, very high among the mountains, there lived a beautiful Princess who had lost her slipper, and whose father had offered a great reward to whoever should restore it; and from the description they gave all were assured it was the one that the Prince had found.

Then his mother said to him, "My son, it is certain that the slipper you found belongs to none other than the great Mountain Rajah's daughter; therefore take it to his palace, and when he offers you the promised reward, say that you wish for neither silver nor gold, but ask him to give you his daughter in marriage. Thus you may gain her for your wife."

The Prince did as his mother advised; and when, after a long, long journey, he reached the court of Sodewa Bai's father, he presented the slipper to him, saying, "I have found your daughter's slipper, and for restoring it I claim a great reward." "What will you have?" said the Rajah. "Shall I pay you in horses? or in silver? or in gold?" "No," answered the Prince, "I will have none of these things. I am the son of a Rajah who lives in the plains, and I found this slipper in the jungle where I was hunting, and have traveled for many weary days to bring it you; but the only payment I care for is the hand of your beautiful daughter; if it pleases you, let me become your son-in-law." The Rajah replied, "This only I cannot promise you; for I have vowed I will not oblige my daughter to marry against her will. This matter depends upon her alone. If she is willing to be your wife, I also am willing; but it rests with her free choice." Now it happened that Sodewa Bai had from her window seen the Prince coming up to the palace gate, and when she heard his errand, she said to her father, "I saw that Prince, and I am willing to marry him." So they were married with great pomp and splendor. When all the other Rajah's, Sodewa Bai's suitors, heard of this, they were, however much astonished as well as vexed, and said, "What can have made Sodewa Bai take a fancy to that young Prince? He is not so wonderfully handsome, and he is very poor. This is a most foolish marriage." But they all came to it, and were entertained at the palace, where the wedding festivities lasted many days. After Sodewa Bai and her husband had lived there for some little time, he one day said to his father-in-law, "I have a great desire to see my own people again and to return to my own country. Let me take my wife home with me."

The Rajah said, "Very well. I am willing that you should go. Take care of your wife; guard her as the apple of your eye; and be sure you never permit the golden necklace to be taken from her neck and given to any one else, for in that case she would die." The Prince promised, and he returned with Sodewa Bai to his father's kingdom. At their departure the

Rajah of the Mountain gave them many elephants, horses, camels and attendants, besides jewels innumerable and much money, and many rich hangings, robes and carpets. The old Rajah and Ranee of the Plain were delighted to welcome home their son and his beautiful bride; and there they might all have lived their lives long in uninterrupted peace and happiness, had it not been for one unfortunate circumstance. Rowjee (for that was the Prince's name) had another wife, to whom he had been married when a child, long before he had found Sodewa Bai's golden slipper; she therefore was the first Ranee, though Sodewa Bai was the one he loved the best (for the first Ranee was of a sullen, morose and jealous disposition.) His father also, and his mother, preferred Sodewa Bai to their other daughter-in-law. The first Ranee could not bear to think of any one being Ranee beside herself; and more especially of another not only in the same position, but better loved by all around than she; and therefore in her wicked heart she hated Sodewa Bai and longed for her destruction, though outwardly she pretended to be very fond of her. The old Rajah and Ranee, knowing of the first Rance's jealous and envious disposition, never liked Sodewa Bai to be much with her; but as they had only a vague fear, and no certain ground for alarm, they could do no more than watch both carefully; and Sodewa Bai, who was guileless and unsuspicious, would remonstrate with them when they warned her not to be so intimate with Rowjee Rajah's other wife, saying, "I have no fear. I think she loves me as I love her. Why should we disagree? Are we not sisters?" One day, Rowjee Rajah was obliged to go on a journey to a distant part of his father's kingdom, and, being unable to take Sodewa Bai with him, he left her in his parents' charge, promising to return soon, and begging them to watch over her, and to go every morning and see that she was well; which they agreed to do.

A little while after their husband had gone, the first Ranee went to Sodewa Bai's room and said to her, "It is lonely for us both, now Rowjee is away; but you must come often to see me, and I will come often to see you and talk to you, and so we will amuse ourselves as well as we can." To this Sodewa Bai agreed, and to amuse the first Ranee she took out all her jewels and pretty things to show her. As they were looking over them, the first Ranee said, "I notice you always wear that row of golden beads round your neck. Why do you? Have you any reason for always wearing the same ones?" "Oh, yes," answered Sodewa Bai, thoughtlessly. "I was born with these beads round my neck, and the wise men told my father and mother that they contain my soul, and that if any one else wore them I should die. Therefore I always wear them. I have never once taken them off." When the first Ranee heard this news she was very much pleased; yet she feared to steal the beads herself, both because she was afraid she might be found out, and because she did not like with her own hands to commit the crime. So, returning to her house, she called her most confidential servant, a negress, whom she knew to be trustworthy, and said to her, "Go this evening to Sodewa Bai's room when she is asleep, and take from her neck the string of golden beads, and fasten them round your own neck, and return to me. Those beads contain her soul, and as soon as you put them on she will cease to live." The negress agreed to do as she was told; for she had long known that her mistress hated Sodewa Bai and desired nothing so much as her death. So that night, going softly into the sleeping Ranee's room, she stole the golden necklace, and fastening it round her own neck, crept away without any one knowing what was done; and when the negress put on the necklace, Sodewa Bai's spirit fled.

Next morning the old Rajah and Ranee went as usual to see their daughter-in-law, and knocked at the door of her room. No one answered. They knocked again and again; still no reply. They then went in, and found her lying there, cold as marble and quite dead, though she seemed very well when they had seen her before. They asked her attendants, who slept just outside her door, whether she had been ill that night, or if any one had gone into her room? But they declared they had heard no sound, and were sure no one had been near the place. In vain the Rajah and Ranee sent for the most learned doctors in the kingdom, to see if there was still any spark of life remaining; all said that the young Ranee was dead, beyond reach of hope or help.

Then the Rajah and Ranee were very much grieved, and mourned bitterly; and because they desired that, if possible, Rowjee Rajah should see his wife once again, instead of burying her underground, they placed her beneath a canopy in a beautiful tomb near a little tank, and would go daily to visit the place and look at her. Then did a wonder take place, such as had never been known throughout the land before! Sodewa Bai's body did not decay nor the color of her face change; and a month afterward, when her husband returned home, she looked as fair and lovely as on the night on which she died. There was a fresh color in her cheeks and on her lips; she seemed to be only asleep. When poor Rowjee Rajah heard of her death he was so broken-hearted they thought he also would die. He cursed the evil fate that had obliged him to go away and deprive him of hearing her last words, or bidding her farewell, if he could not save her life; and from morning to evening he would go to her tomb, and rend the air with his passionate lamentations, and looking through the grating to where she lay calm and still under the canopy, say, before he went away, "I will take one last look at that fair face. To-morrow Death may have set his seal upon it. Oh, loveliness, too bright for earth! Oh, lost, lost wife!"

The Rajah and Ranee feared that he would die or go mad, and they tried to prevent his going to the tomb; but all was of no avail; it seemed to be the only thing he cared for in life.

Now the negress who had stolen Sodewa Bai's necklace used to wear it all day long, but late each night, on going to bed, she would take it off and put it by till next morning, and whenever she took it off Sodewa Bai's spirit returned to her again, and she lived till day dawned and the negress put on the necklace, when she again died. But as the tomb was far from any houses, and the old Rajah and Ranee and Rowjee Rajah only went there by day, nobody found this out. When Sodewa Bai first came to life in this way, she felt very much frightened to find herself there all alone in the dark, and thought she was in prison; but afterward she got more accustomed to it, and determined when morning came to look about the place and find her way back to the palace, and recover the necklace she found she had lost (for it would have been dangerous to go at night through the jungles that surrounded the tomb, where she could hear the wild beasts roaring all night long); but morning never came, for whenever the negress awoke and put on the golden beads Sodewa Bai died. However, each night, when the Ranee came to life, she would walk to the little tank by the tomb and drink some of the cool water, and return; but food she had none. Now, no pearls or precious stones fell from her lips, because she had no one to talk to; but each time she walked down to the tank she scattered jewels on either side of her path; and one day, when Rowjee Rajah went to the tomb, he noticed all these jewels, and thinking it very strange (though he never dreamed that his wife could come to life), determined to watch and see whence they came. But although he watched and waited long, he could not find out the cause, because all day long Sodewa Bai lay still and dead, and only came to life at night. It was just at this time, two whole months after she had been buried, and the night after the very day that Rowjee Rajah had spent in watching by the tomb, that Sodewa Bai had a little son; but directly after he was born day dawned, and the mother died. The little lonely baby began to cry, but no one was there to hear him; and, as it chanced, the Rajah did not go the tomb that day, for he thought, "All yesterday I watched by the tomb and saw nothing; instead, therefore, of going to-day, I will wait till the evening, and then see again if I cannot find out how the jewels came there."

So at night he went to the place. When he got there he heard a faint cry from inside the tomb, but what it was he knew not; perhaps it might be a Peri or an evil spirit. As he was wondering the door opened and Sodewa Bai crossed the courtyard to the tank with a child in her arms, and as she walked showers of jewels fell on both sides of her path. Rowjee Rajah thought he must be in a dream; but when he saw the Ranee drink some water from the tank and return toward the tomb, he sprang up and hurried after her. Sodewa Bai, hearing footsteps follow her, was frightened, and running into the tomb, fastened the door. Then the Rajah knocked at it, saying, "Let me in; let me in." She answered, "Who are you? Are you a Rakshas or a spirit?" (For she thought, "Perhaps this is some cruel creature who will kill me and the child.") "No, no," cried the Rajah, "I am no Rakshas, but your husband. Let me in, Sodewa Bai, if you are indeed alive." No sooner did he name her name than Sodewa Bai knew his voice, and unbolted the door and let him in. Then, when he saw her sitting on the tomb with the baby on her lap, he fell down on his knees before her, saying, "Tell me, little wife, that this is not a dream." "No," she answered, "I am indeed alive, and this our child was born last night; but every day I die, for while you were away some one stole my golden necklace."

Then for the first time Rowjee Rajah noticed that the beads were no longer round her neck. So he bade her fear nothing, for that he would assuredly recover them and return; and going back to the palace, which he reached in the early morning, he summoned before him the whole household.

Then, upon the neck of the negress, servant to the first Ranee, he saw Sodewa Bai's missing necklace, and seizing it, ordered the guards to take the woman to prison. The negress, frightened, confessed all she had done by order of the first Ranee, and how, at her command, she had stolen the necklace. And when the Rajah learnt this he ordered that the first Ranee also should be imprisoned for life, and he and his father and mother all went together to the tomb, and placing the lost beads round Sodewa Bai's neck, brought her and the child back in triumph with them to the palace. Then, at news of how the young Ranee had been restored to life, there was great joy throughout all that country, and many days were spent in rejoicings in honor of that happy event; and for the rest of their lives the old Rajah and Ranee, and Rowjee Rajah and Sodewa Bai, and all the family, lived in health and happiness.

XXII.

CHANDRA'S VENGEANCE.

THERE was once a Sowkar's* wife who had no children; one day she went crying to her husband and saying, "What an unhappy woman I am to have no children! If I had any children to amuse me I should be quite happy." He answered, "Why should you be miserable on that account; though you have no children, your sister has eight or nine; why not adopt one of hers?" The Sowkar's wife agreed, and, adopting one of her sister's little boys, who was only six months old, brought him up as her own son. Some time afterward, when the child was one day returning from school, he and one of his schoolfellows quarreled and began to fight, and the other boy (being much the older and stronger of the two) gave him a great blow on the head and knocked him down, and hurt him very much. The boy ran crying home, and the Sowkar's wife bathed his head and bandaged it up, but she did not send and punish the boy who hurt him, for she thought, "One can't keep children shut up always in the house, and they will be fighting together sometimes and hurting themselves." Then the child grumbled to himself, saying, "This is only my aunt; that is why

* Merchant's.

she did not punish the other boy. If she had been my mother, she would certainly have given him a great knock on his head to punish him for knocking mine, but because she is only my aunt, I suppose she doesn't care." The Sowkar's wife overheard him, and felt very much grieved, saying, "This little child, whom I have watched over from his babyhood, does not love me as if I were his mother. It is of no use; he is not my own, and he will never care for me as such." So she took him home to his own mother, saying, "Sister, I have brought you back your child." "How is this?" asked her sister. "You adopted him as yours for all his life. Why do you now bring him back?" The Sowkar's wife did not tell her sister what she had heard the boy say, but she answered, "Very well; let him be yours and mine: he shall live a while with you, and then come and visit me; we will both take care of him." And returning to her husband, she told him what she had done, saying "All my pains are useless; you know how kind I have been to my sister's boy, yet, after all I have done for him, at the end of seven years he does not love me as well as he does his mother, whom he had scarcely seen. Now, therefore, I will never rest until I have seen Mahdeo* and asked him to grant that I may have a child of my own."†

"What a foolish woman you are!" answered her husband; "why not be content with your lot? How do you think you will find Mahdeo? Do you know the road to heaven?" "Nay," she replied, "but I will seek for it until I find it out, and if I never find it, it cannot be helped, but I will return home no more unless my prayer is answered." So she left the house,

* The Creator. † See Notes at the end.

and wandered into the jungle, and after she had traveled through it for many, many days, and left her own land very far behind, she came to the borders of another country, even the Madura Tinivelly* country, where a great river rolled down toward the sea. On the river-bank sat two women—a Ranee named Coplinghee Ranee and a Nautch woman.

Now, neither the Ranee, the Nautch woman nor the Sowkar's wife had ever seen each other before they met at the river-side. Then, as she sat down to rest and drink some of the water, the Ranee turned to the Sowkar's wife and said to her, "Who are you, and where are you going?" She answered, "I am a Sowkar's wife from a far country, and because I was very unhappy at having no children, I am going to find Mahdeo and ask him to grant that I may have a child of my own."

Then, in her turn, she said to the Ranee, "And pray who are you, and where are you going?" The Ranee answered, "I am Coplinghee Ranee, queen of all this country, but neither money nor riches can give me joy, for I have no children ; I therefore am going to seek Mahdeo and ask him to grant that I may have a child." Then Coplinghee Ranee asked the Nautch woman the same question, saying, "And who may you be, and where are you going?" The Nautch woman answered, "I am a dancing woman and I also have no children, and am going to seek Mahdeo and pray to him for a child." At hearing this, the Sowkar's wife said, "Since we are all journeying on the same errand, why should we not go together?" To this Coplinghee Ranee and the Dancing woman agreed, so

* Two provinces of the Madras Presidency, on the mainland opposite Ceylon. They are famous in Hindoo mythology.

they all three continued their journey together through the jungle.

On, on, on they went, every day further and further; they never stayed to rest nor saw another human being. Their feet ached dreadfully and their clothes wore out, and they had nothing to live on but the jungle plants, wild berries and seeds. So weary and worn did they become that they looked like three poor old beggar women. Never had they by night-time sleep nor by day-time rest; and so, hour after hour, month after month, year after year, they traveled on.

At last one day they came to where, in the midst of the jungle, there rolled a great river of fire. It was the biggest river they had ever seen, and made of flames instead of water. There was no one on this side and no one on that—no way of getting across but by walking through the fire.

When Coplinghee Ranee and the Nautch woman saw this, they said, "Alas! here is the end of all our pains and trouble. All hope is over, for we can go no farther." But the Sowkar's wife answered, "Shall we be deterred by this after having come so far? Nay, rather seek a way across the fire." And so saying, she stepped into the fire waves; the others, however, were afraid, and would not go. When the Sowkar's wife had half crossed the river of fire, she turned, and waving her hands toward them, said, "Come on, come on, do not be afraid. The fire does not burn me. I go to find Mahdeo; perhaps he is on the other side."* But they still refused, saying, "We cannot come, but we will wait here until your return; and if you find Mahdeo, pray for us also, that we may have children."

* See Notes at the end.

So the Sowkar's wife went on her way, and the fire-waves lapped round her feet as if they had been water, but they did not hurt her.

When she reached the other side of the river she came upon a great wilderness, full of wild elephants, and bison, and lions, and tigers, and bears, that roared and growled on every side. But she did not turn back for fear of them, for she said to herself, "I can but die once, and it is better that they should kill me than that I should return without finding Mahdeo." And all the wild beasts allowed her to pass through the midst of them and did her no harm.

Now it came to pass that Mahdeo looked down from heaven and saw her, and when he saw her he pitied her greatly, for she had been twelve years wandering upon the face of the earth to find him. Then he caused a beautiful mango tree, beside a fair well, to spring up in the desert to give her rest and refreshment, and he himself, in the disguise of a Gosain Fakeer, came and stood by the tree. But the Sowkar's wife would not stay to gather the fruit or drink the water; she did not so much as notice the Fakeer, but walked straight on in her weary search for Mahdeo. Then he called after her, "Bai, Bai, where are you going? Come here." She answered, scarcely looking at him, "It matters not to you, Fakeer, where I am going. You tell your prayer-beads and leave me alone." "Come here," he cried; "come here." But she would not, so Mahdeo went and stood in front of her, no longer disguised as a Fakeer, but shining brightly, the Lord of Kylas* in all his beauty, and at the sight of him the poor Sowkar's wife fell down on the ground and kissed his feet, and

* The Hindoo heaven.

he said to her, "Tell me, Bai, where are you going?" She answered, "Sir, I seek Mahdeo, to pray him to grant that I may have a child, but for twelve years I have looked for him in vain." He said, "Seek no further, for I am Mahdeo; take this mango," and he gathered one off the tree that grew by the well, "and eat it, and it shall come to pass that when you return home you shall have a child." Then she said, "Sir, three women came seeking you, but two stayed by the river of fire, for they were afraid; may not they also have children?"

"If you will," he answered, "you may give them some of your mango, and then they also will each have a child."

So saying, he faded from her sight, and the Sowkar's wife returned glad and joyful, through the wilderness and the river of fire, to where the Ranee and the Dancing woman were waiting for her on the other side. When they saw her, they said, "Well, Sowkar's wife, what news?" She answered, "I have found Mahdeo, and he has given me this mango, of which if we eat we shall each have a child." And she took the mango, and squeezing it gave the juice to the Ranee, and the skin she gave to the Nautch woman, and the pulp and the stone she ate herself.

Then these three women returned to their own homes; Coplinghee Ranee and the Dancing woman to the Madura Tinivelly country, and the Sowkar's wife to very, very far beyond that, even the land where her husband lived, and whence she had first started on her journey.

But on their return all their friends only laughed at them, and the Sowkar said to his wife, "I cannot see much good in your mad twelve-years' journey; you only come back looking like a beggar, and all the world laughs at you."

"I don't care," she answered; "I have seen Mahdeo and eaten of the mango, and I shall have a child."

And within a little while it came to pass that there was born to the Sowkar and his wife a little son, and on the very same day Coplinghee Ranee had a daughter and the Nautch woman had a daughter.

Then were they all very happy, and sent everywhere to tell their friends the good news; and each gave, according to her power, a great feast to the poor as a thank-offering to Mahdeo, who had been merciful to them. And the Sowkar's wife called her son "Koila,"* in memory of the mango stone; and the Nautch woman called her daughter "Moulee;"† and the little Princess was named Chandra Bai,‡ for she was as fair and beautiful as the white moon.

Chandra Ranee was very beautiful, the most beautiful child in all that country, so pretty and delicately made that everybody, when they saw her, loved her. She was born, moreover, with, on her ankles, two of the most costly anklets that ever were seen. They were made of gold and very precious stones, dazzling to look at, like the sun. No one had ever seen any like them before. Every day, as the baby grew, these bangles grew, and round them were little bells, which tinkled when any one came near. Chandra's parents were very happy and proud, and sent for all the wise men in the kingdom to tell her fortune. But the most learned Brahmin of them all, when he saw her, said, "This child must be sent out of the country at once, for if she

* He of the mango stone. † From the sweet mango pulp.

‡ The Moon Lady.

stays in it she will destroy all the land with fire, and burn it utterly."

The Rajah, at hearing these words, was very angry, and said to the Brahmin, "I will cut off your head, for you tell lies and not the truth." The Brahmin answered, "Cut off my head if you will, but it is the truth I speak, and no lie. If you do not believe me, let a little wool be fetched, and put it upon the child, that you may know my words are true."

So they fetched some wool and laid it upon the baby, and no sooner had they done so than it all blazed up and burnt till not a bit was left, and it scorched the hands of the attendants.

Then the Brahmin said, "As this fire has burnt the wool, so will this Princess one day, if she comes here, burn this whole land." And they were all very much frightened, and the Rajah said to the Ranee, "This being so, the child must be sent out of the country instantly." The poor Ranee thereat was very sad, and she did all in her power to save her little baby, but the Rajah would not hear of it, and commanded that the Princess should be placed in a large box, and taken to the borders of his land, where a great river rolled down to the sea, and there thrown into the stream, that it might carry her far, far away, each minute farther from her native land.* Then the Ranee caused a beautiful golden box to be made, and put her little baby in it with many tears (since all her efforts to save it were of no avail), and it was taken away and thrown into the river.

The box floated on, and on, and on, until at last it reached the country where the Sowkar and the Sowkar's wife lived. Now it chanced that, just as the box

* See Notes at the end.

was floating by, the Sowkar, who had gone down to the river to wash his face, caught sight of it, and seeing a Fisherman not far off prepared to throw his net into the water, he cried, "Run, Fisherman, run, run; do not stop to fish, but cast your net over that glittering box and bring it here to me."

"I will not, unless you promise me that the box shall be mine," said the Fisherman. "Very well," answered the Sowkar, "the box shall be yours, and whatever it contains shall belong to me."

So the Fisherman cast his net in that part of the river and dragged the box ashore.

I don't know which was most astonished—the Merchant or the Fisherman—when they saw what a prize they had found. For the box was composed entirely of gold and precious stones, and within it lay the most lovely little child that ever was seen.

She seemed a little Princess, for her dress was all made of cloth of gold, and on her feet were two anklets that shone like the sun.

When the Sowkar opened the box, she smiled; and stretched out her little arms toward him. Then he was pleased, and said, "Fisherman, the box is yours, but this child must belong to me." The Fisherman was content that it should be so, for he had many children of his own at home, and wanted no more, but was glad to have the golden box; while the Sowkar, who had only his one little son and was rich, did not care for the box, but was well pleased to have the baby.

He took her home to his wife, and said, "See, wife, here is a pretty little daughter-in-law for us. Here is a wife for your little son." And when the Sowkar's wife saw the child looking so beautiful and smiling so sweetly, her heart was glad and she loved her, and from that day took the greatest care of her, just as if the baby girl had been her own daughter. And when Chandra Ranee was a year old they married her to their son, Koila.

Years wore on, and the Sowkar and his wife were in a good old age gathered to their fathers. Meantime, Koila and Chandra had grown up the handsomest couple in all the country: Koila tall and straight, with a face like a young lion, and Chandra as lithe and graceful as a palm tree, with a face calm and beautiful like the silver moonlight.

Meantime Moulee, the Nautch woman's daughter (and third of the mango children), had likewise grown up in the Madura Tinivelly country, and was also very fair—fairer than any one in all the land around. Moreover, she danced and sang more beautifully than any of the other Nautch girls. Her voice was clear as the voice of a quail, and it rang through the air with such power that the sound could be heard a twelve-days' journey off. The Nautch people used to travel about from place to place, staying one day in one town and the next in another, and so it happened that in their wanderings they reached the borders of the land where Koila and Chandra lived.

One morning Koila heard the sound of singing in the distance, and it pleased him so well that he determined to try and discover who it was that possessed such an exquisite voice. For twelve days he journeyed on through the jungle, each day hearing the singing repeated louder and louder, yet still without reaching the place whence it came. At last, on the twelfth day, he got close to the Nautch people's encampment, not far from a large town, and there saw the singer (who was none other than Moulee), singing and dancing in the midst of a great crowd of people who had collected around her. In her hand she held a garland of flowers, which she waved over her head as she danced.

Koila was so charmed with the sound of her voice that he felt spell-bound, and stood where he was, far off on the outskirts of the jungle, listening, without going any nearer.

When the entertainment was over, all the people crowded round Moulee, saying, "Why should you, who have such a beautiful voice, go away and leave our city? Marry one of us, and then you will stay here always." Then, the number of her suitors being so great that she did not know whom to choose, she said, "Very well; he on whose neck this garland falls shall be my husband." And waving the flowers she held two or three times round her head, she threw them from her with her utmost force.

The impetus given to the garland was so great that it swung through the air beyond the crowd and fell upon the neck of Koila as he stood by the borders of the jungle. And the people ran to see who was the fortunate possessor, and when they saw Koila they were astonished, for he looked more beautiful than any of the sons of men: it was as if an immortal had suddenly come among them. And the Nautch people dragged him back to their camp, crying, "You have won the garland; you must be Moulee's husband." He answered, "I only came here to look on; I cannot stay. This is not my country; I have a wife of my own at home." "That is nothing to us," they said; "it is your destiny to marry Moulee—Moulee the beautiful one—Moulee, whose voice you heard and who dances so well. You must marry her, for the garland fell on you."

Now so it was, that though Koila was very kind to his wife, he did not love her as well as she loved him (perhaps it was that, having been accustomed to her from a child, Chandra's goodness and beauty struck him less than it did other people); and instead of thinking how unhappy she would be if he did not return, and going back at once, he stopped and hesitated and debated what to do. And the Nautch people gave him a drink that was a very powerful spell, insomuch that he soon totally forgot about his own home, and was married to Moulee, the Nautch girl, and lived among the Nautch people for many months. At last, one day, Moulee's mother (the very Nautch woman who had gone with Coplinghee Ranee and the Sowkar's wife to find Mahdeo) said to Koila, "Son-in-law, you are a lazy fellow; you have been here now for a long time, but you do nothing for your support; it is we who have to pay for your food, we who have to provide your clothes. Go now and fetch us some money, or I will turn you out of the house, and you shall never see your wife Moulee again." Koila had no money to give his mother-in-law: then, for the first time he bethought him of his own country and of Chandra, and he said "My first wife, who lives in my own country, has on her feet two bangles of very great value; let me return home and fetch one of them to sell, which will more than pay whatever I owe you." The Nautch people consented. So Koila returned to his own home, and told Chandra what he wanted the money for, and asked her to let him have one of her bangles; but she refused, saying, "You have been away a long, long time, and left me all alone, and chosen for your second wife one of the Nautch people, and become one of them; and now you want to take one of my bangles—the bangles that I had when a little child, that have grown with my growth, and never been taken off—and to give it to your other wife. This shall not be; go back, if you will, to your new friends, but I will not give you my bangle."

He answered, "They gave me an enchanted drink which made me forget you for a time, but I am weary of them all; let me but go and pay my mother-in-law the money I owe her for food and clothes, and I will return and live in my own land, for you are my first wife."

"Very well," she said, "you may take the bangle and sell it, and give the money to your second wife's mother, but take me also with you when you go; do not leave me here all alone again." Koila agreed, and they both set off together toward the Madura Tinivelly country.

As they journeyed, Krishnaswami,* who was playing at cards with his three wives, saw them, and when he saw them he laughed. Then his wives said to him, "Why do you laugh? You have not laughed for such a long time: what amuses you so much now?" He answered, "I am laughing to see Koila and his wife Chandra Ranee journeying toward the Madura Tinivelly country. He is going to sell his wife's bangle, and he will only be killed, and then she in anger will burn up all the country. O foolish people!" The goddesses answered, "This is a very dreadful thing; let us go in disguise and warn him not to enter the country."

* The Hindoo god Krishna, an incarnation of Vishnu.

"It would be useless," said Krishnaswami; "if you do, he will only laugh at you and get angry with you." But the goddesses determined to do their best to avert the threatened calamity. So they disguised themselves as old fortune-tellers, and went out with little lamps and their sacred books to meet Koila as he came along the road, followed by his wife. Then they said to him, "Come not into the Madura Tinivelly country, for if you come you will be killed, and your wife in her fury will burn all the land with fire." At first, Koila would not listen to them; then he bade them go away; and lastly, when they continued warning him, got angry and beat them out of his path, saying, "Do you think I am to be frightened out of the country by a parcel of old crones like you?"

Then Krishnaswami's three wives returned to him, much enraged at the treatment they had received; but he only said to them, "Did not I tell you not to go, warning you that it would be useless?"

On getting near the Rajah's capital, Koila and Chandra came to the house of an old milk-seller, who was very kind to them and gave them food and shelter for the night. Next morning Koila said to his wife, "You had better stay here; this good old woman will take care of you while I go into the town to sell your bangle." Chandra agreed, and remained at the old woman's house while her husband went into the town. Of course he did not know that the Rajah and his wife (the Coplinghee Ranee) were Chandra's father and mother, any more than they, or Chandra herself, knew it, or than the three mango children knew the story of their mothers' journey in search of Mahdeo.

Now a short time before Koila and Chandra reached

the Madura Tinivelly country, Coplinghee Ranee had sent a very handsome pair of bangles to a Jeweler in the town to be cleaned. It chanced that in a high tree close to the Jeweler's house two eagles had built their nest, and the young eagles, who were very noisy birds, used to scream all day long and greatly disturb the Jeweler's family. So one day, when the old birds were away, the Jeweler's son climbed up the tree and pulled down the nest, and put the young eagles to death. When the old birds returned home and saw what was done, it grieved them very much, and they said, "These cruel people have killed our children; let us punish them." And seeing in the porch one of Coplinghee Ranee's beautiful bangles, which the Jeweler had just been cleaning, they swooped down and flew away with it.*

The Jeweler did not know what to do: he said to his wife, "To buy such a bangle as that would cost more than all our fortune, and to make one like it would take many, many years; I dare not say I have lost it, or they would think I had stolen it and put me to death. The only thing I can do is to delay returning the other as long as possible, and try somehow to get one like it." So next day, when the Ranee sent to inquire if her bangles were ready, he answered, "They are not ready yet; they will be ready to-morrow." And the next day and the next he said the same thing. At last the Ranee's messengers got very angry at the continued delays; then, seeing he could no longer make excuses, the Jeweler sent the one bangle by them to the palace, beautifully cleaned, with a message that the other also would shortly be ready; but all this time he was hunting for a bangle

* See Notes at the end.

costly enough to take the Ranee as a substitute for the one the eagles had carried away. Such a bangle, however, he could not find.

When Koila reached the town, he spread out a sheet in the corner of a street near the market-place, and, placing the bangle upon it, sat down close by, waiting for customers. Now he was very, very handsome. Although dressed so plainly, he looked like a Prince, and the bangle he had to sell flashed in the morning light like seven suns. Such a handsome youth and such a beautiful bangle the people had never seen before; and many passers-by, with chattees on their heads, for watching him, let the chattees tumble down and break, they were so much astonished; and several men and women, who were looking out of the windows of their houses, leant too far forward and fell into the street, so giddy did they become from wonder and amazement!

But no one could be found to buy the bangle, for they all said, "We could not afford to buy such jewels; this bangle is fit only for a Ranee to wear." At last, when the day had nearly gone, who should come by but the Jeweler who had been employed to clean Coplinghee Ranee's bangles, and was in search of one to replace that which the eagles had stolen. No sooner did he see the one belonging to Chandra, which Koila was trying to sell, than he said to himself, "That is the very thing I want, if I can only get it." So he called his wife, and said to her, "Go to that bangle-seller and speak kindly to him; say that the day is nearly gone, and invite him to come and lodge at our house for the night. For if we can make friends with him and get him to trust us, I shall be able to take the bangle from him and say he stole it from me. And as he is a stranger here, every one will believe my word rather than his. This bangle is exactly the very thing for me to take Coplinghee Ranee, for it is very like her own, only more beautiful.

The Jeweler's wife did as she was told, and then the Jeweler himself went up to Koila and said to him, "You are a bangle-seller, and I am a bangle-seller; therefore I look upon you as a brother. Come home, I pray you, with us, as my wife begs you to do, and we will give you food and shelter for the night, since you are a stranger in this country." So these cunning people coaxed Koila to go home with them to their home, and pretended to be very kind to him, and gave him supper, and a bed to rest on for the night; but next morning early the Jeweler raised a hue and cry and sent for the police, and bade them take Koila before the Rajah instantly, since he had stolen and tried to sell one of Coplinghee Ranee's bangles, which he (the Jeweler) had been given to clean. It was in vain that Koila protested his innocence, and declared that the bangle he had belonged to his wife; he was a stranger—nobody would believe him. They dragged him to the palace, and the Jeweler accused him to the Rajah, saying, "This man tried to steal the Ranee's bangle (which I had been given to clean) and to sell it. If he had done so, you would have thought I had stolen it, and killed me; I demand, therefore, that he in punishment shall be put to death."

Then they sent for the Ranee to show her the bangle, but as soon as she saw it she recognized it as one of the bangles which had belonged to Chandra, and burst into tears, crying, "This is not my bangle. Oh, my lord, no jeweler on earth made this bangle! See, it is different to mine; and when any one comes near it, it tinkles and all the little bells begin to ring. Have you forgotten it? This was my beauty's bangle! My diamond's! My little darling's! My lost child's! Where did it come from? How did it come here? How into this land, and into this town and bazaar, among these wicked people? For this Jeweler must have kept my bangle and brought this one in its place. No human goldsmith's hands made this, for it is none other than Chandra's." Then she begged the Rajah to inquire further about it.

But they all thought her mad; and the Jeweler said, "It is the Ranee's fancy, for this is the same bangle she gave me to clean." The other people also agreed that both the bangles were almost exactly alike, and must be a pair; and it being certain that Koila had had the bangle when he was seized by the police, the Rajah ordered him to be instantly executed. But the Ranee took Chandra's bangle and locked it away in a strong cupboard, apart from all her other jewels.

Then they took Koila out into the jungle and would have cut off his head, but he said to his guards, "If I must die, let me die by my own hands," and drawing his sword he fell upon it, and as the sword was very sharp it cut his body in two—one half fell on one side of the sword, and the other half on the other side—and they left his body where it fell.

When the news of what had taken place came to the town, many people who had seen Koila selling his bangle the day before began to murmur, saying, "There must be some injustice here—the Rajah has been overhasty. Most likely the poor man did not steal the bangle. It is not likely that he would have tried to sell it openly before us all in the bazaar if it had been stolen property. How cruel of the Rajah to put such a handsome, gentle, noble-looking youth to death!—and he was a stranger, too!" And many wept at thought of his hard fate. When the Rajah heard of this he was very angry, and sent and commanded that the matter should be no further discussed in the town, saying, "If any one speaks another word of what has been done, or laments or sheds tears for the dead, he shall be instantly hanged." Then the people all felt very frightened, and not a soul dared to speak of Koila, though every one thought about him much.

Early the very morning that this happened the old milk-seller (at whose house, which was a little out of the town, Chandra had been sleeping) took her guest a bowl full of milk to drink; but no sooner had Chandra tasted it than she began to cry, saying, "Good mother, what have you done? my mouth is full of blood!" "No, no, my daughter," answered the old woman; "you must have been dreaming some bad dream. See, this is pure, fresh, warm milk I have brought you; drink again." But when Chandra tasted it for the second time, she answered, "Oh no! oh no! it is not milk that I taste, but blood. All last night I had a dreadful dream, and this morning when I woke I found that my marriage necklace had snapped in two; and now this milk tastes to me as blood. Let me go! let me go! for I know my husband is dead."

The old woman tried to comfort her, saying, "Why should you fancy he is dead? he was quite well yesterday, when he went to sell your bangle; and he said he would come back to you soon; in a little while, very likely, he will be here." But she answered, "No, no; I feel sure that he is dead! Oh, let me go! for I must find him before I die." Then the old woman said, "You must not go; you are too beautiful to run about through the streets of this strange town alone, and your husband would be very angry if he saw you doing so; and who knows but that you might lose your way, and get carried off as a slave; remember, he told you to stay here till he returned. Be patient; remain where you are, and I will go quickly into the town and seek your husband. If he is alive, I will bring him back to you, and if he is dead I will bring you word." So, taking a chattee full of milk on her head, as if to sell, she went to the town to find Koila, while every minute seemed an hour to Chandra until her return.

When the old milk-seller reached the town, she went up and down all the streets looking for Koila, or expecting to hear some one mention the handsome stranger who had gone to sell such a wonderful bangle the day before. But she could not find him, nor did she hear him spoken of, for all were afraid to say a word about him on account of the Rajah's decree. Being unable to trace him, the old woman got suspicious, and began to search, more carefully than before, down all the streets near the market-place, where she thought he was most likely to have gone; but, lest people should wonder at her errand, she called out each time as if she had some different thing to sell. First, "Buy some milk—who'll buy milk—who'll buy?" Then, on going for a second time down the same street, "Buy butter—butter! very fine butter!" and so on. At last one woman, who had been watch ing her with some curiosity, said, "Old woman, what nonsense you talk! you have been half-a-dozen times up and down this same street, as if you had half-a-dozen different things to sell in that one chattee. Any one would think you had as little sense as that pretty young bangle-seller yesterday, who spent all the day trying to sell a bangle, and got put to death for his pains."

"Of whom do you speak?" asked the old woman. "Oh," said the other, "I suppose, as you're a milk-seller from the country, you know nothing about it. But that's not to be talked about, for the Rajah has said that whoever speaks of him or mourns him shall be instantly hanged. Ah! he was very handsome."

"Where is he now?" whispered the old woman. "There," answered the other; "you can see the place where that crowd of people has collected. The Rajah's Jeweler accused him of having stolen the bangle; so he was executed, many thought unjustly; but do not say I said it." And so saying, she pointed toward the jungle some way off. The old woman ran to the place, but when she there saw two halves of Koila's body lying side by side, stiff and cold, she threw her earthen chattee down on the ground and fell on her knees, crying bitterly. The noise attracted the attention of the Rajah's guards, some of whom immediately seized her, saying, "Old woman, it is against the law to lament that dead man or murmur at the Rajah's decree; you deserve to be put to death." But she answered quickly, "The dead man! I do not cry for the dead man: can you not see that my chattee is broken and all the milk spilt? Is it not enough to make one weep?" And she began to cry again.

"Hush! hush!" they answered; "don't cry; come, the chattee wasn't worth much; it was only an earthen thing. Stop your tears, and maybe we'll give you a chattee of gold."

"I neither care for your golden chattees nor for silver," she said, angrily. "Go away; go away! my earthen chattee was worth them all. My grandfather's grandfather and my grandmother's grandmother used this chattee; and to think that it should now be broken and all the milk spilt!" And picking up the broken pieces, she went home sobbing, as if the loss of her chattee was all her grief. But when she got to her own house, she ran into where Chandra was, crying, "Alas! my pretty child! alas, my daughter! your fears are true!" and as gently as she could she told her what had happened.

No sooner did Chandra hear it than she ran away straight to the Rajah's palace in the midst of the town, and rushing into the room where he was, said, "How did you dare to kill my husband?"

Now, at the sound of her voice, her bangle, which the Ranee had locked up in the cupboard, broke through all the intervening doors and rolled to Chandra's feet.

The Rajah was unable to answer her a word. Then she fell on her knees and rent her clothes and tore her hair; and when she tore it all the land began to burn and all her hair burned too.

Then the old milk-seller, who had followed her, ran and put a lump of butter on her head, thinking to cool it; and two other woman, who were by, fetched water to pour upon her hair, but by this time nineteen lines of houses were in flames. Then the old woman cried,

"Oh! spare the Purwari* lines; don't burn them down, for I did all I could for you." So Chandra did not burn that part of the town near which the old woman and her friends lived. But the fire burnt on and on in the other direction; and it killed the Rajah and the Ranee and all the people in the palace, and the wicked Jeweler and his wife; and as he was dying Chandra tore out his heart and gave it to the eagles who hovered overhead, saying, "Here is vengeance for the death of your little ones." And the Nautch girl, Moulee, and her mother, who were watching the fire from far off, were smothered in the flames.†

Then Chandra went to where Koila's dead body lay and wept over it bitterly; and as she was weeping, there fell down to her from heaven a needle and thread; and she took them, saying, "Oh, that I could by any means restore you!" and, placing the two halves of his body side by side, she sewed them together.

And when she had done this, she cried to Mahdeo, saying, "Sire, I have done the best I can; I have joined the body; give it life." And as she said these words Mahdeo had pity on her, and he sent Koila's spirit back and it returned to his body again. Then Chandra was glad, and they returned and lived in their own land.

But to this day in the Madura Tinivelly country you can trace where all the land was burnt.

* Or outcasts'; literally, "the extra-muralists'," *i.e.*, the houses of the lowest classes, not permited to live within the city walls.

† See Notes at the end.

XXIII.

HOW THE THREE CLEVER MEN OUTWITTED THE DEMONS.

THERE was once upon a time a very rich man who had a very beautiful wife, and this man's chief amusement used to be shooting with a bow and arrow, at which he was so clever that every morning he would shoot through one of the pearls in his wife's nose-ring without hurting her at all.* One fine day, that was a holiday, the Pearl-shooter's brother-in-law came to take his sister to their father and mother's house to pay her own family a little visit; and when he saw her, he said, "Why do you look so pale and thin and miserable? is your husband unkind to you, or what is the matter?" "No," she answered; "my husband is very kind to me, and I have plenty of money and jewels, and as nice a house as I could wish; my only grief is that every morning he amuses himself by shooting one of the pearls from my nose-ring, and that frightens me; for I think perhaps some day he may miss his aim and the arrow run into my face and kill me. So I am in constant terror of my life; yet I do not like to ask him not to do it, because it gives him so much pleasure; but if he left off of his own accord, I should be very glad." "What does he say to you himself about it?" asked

* See Notes at the end.

the brother. "Every day," she replied, "when he has shot the pearl, he comes to me quite happy and proud, and says, 'Was there ever a man as clever as I am?' and I answer him, 'No, I do not think there ever was any as clever as you.'" "Do not say so again," said the brother; "but next time he asks you the question, answer, 'Yes, there are many men in the world more clever than you.'" The Pearl-shooter's wife promised to take her brother's advice. So, next time her husband shot the pearl from her nose-ring, and said to her, "Was there ever a man as clever as I am?" she answered, "Yes, there are many men in the world more clever than you."

Then he said, "If so be that there are, I will not rest until I have found them." And he left her, and went a far journey into the jungle in order to find, if possible, a cleverer man than himself. On, on, on he journeyed a very long way, until at last he came to a large river, and on the river-bank sat a traveler eating his dinner. The Pearl-shooter sat down beside him and the two began conversing together. At last, the Pearl-shooter said to his friend, "What is the reason of your journey, and where are you going?" The stranger answered, "I am a Wrestler, and the strongest man in all this country; I can do many wonderful things in the way of wrestling and carrying heavy weights, and I began to think that in all this world there was no one so clever as I; but I have lately heard of a still more wonderful man who lives in a distant country, and who is so clever that every morning he shoots one of the pearls from his wife's nose-ring without hurting her. So I go to find him, and learn if this is true."

The Pearl-shooter answered, "Then you need travel no further, for I am that man of whom you heard." "Why are you traveling about, then, and where are you going?" asked the Wrestler. "I," replied the other, "am also traveling to see if in all the world I can find a cleverer man than myself; therefore, as we have both the same object in view, let us be as brothers and go about together; perhaps there is still in the world a better man than we." The Wrestler agreed; so they both started on their way together. They had not gone very far before they came to a place where three roads met, and there sat another man, whom neither of them had ever seen before. He accosted the Wrestler and the Pearl-shooter and said to them, "Who are you, friends, and where are you going?" "We," answered they, "are two clever men, who are traveling through the world to see if we can find a cleverer man than we; but who may you be, and where are you going?" "I," replied the third man, "am a Pundit,* a man of memory, renowned for my good head, a great thinker; and verily I thought there was not in the world a more wonderful man than I; but having heard of two men in distant lands of very great cleverness, the one of whom is a Wrestler, and the other a shooter of pearls from his wife's nose-ring, I go to find them and learn if the things I heard are true." "They are true," said the other; "for we, O Pundit, are the very two men of whom you speak."

At this news the Pundit was overjoyed, and cried, "Then let us be as brothers; since your homes are far distant, return with me to my house, which is close by; there you can rest a while, and each of us put our

* Wise man.

various powers to the proof." This proposal pleased the Wrestler and the Pearl-shooter, who accompanied the Pundit to his house.

Now, in the kitchen there was an enormous cauldron of iron, so heavy that five-and-twenty men could hardly move it; and in the dead of night the Wrestler, to prove his power, got up from the veranda where he was sleeping, and as quietly as possible lifted this great cauldron on his shoulders and carried it down to the river, where he waded with it into the deepest part of the water, and there buried it. After having accomplished this feat, he returned to the Pundit's house as quietly as he had left it, and, rolling himself up in his blanket, fell fast asleep. But though he had come never so softly, the Pundit's wife heard him, and waking her husband, she said, "I hear footsteps as of people creeping quietly about and not wishing to be heard, and but a little while ago I noticed the same thing; perhaps there are thieves in the house; let us go and see: it is strange they should choose such a bright moonlight night." And they both got up quickly and walked round the house. They found nothing, however, out of order, nor any signs of anything having been touched or disarranged, until they came to the kitchen. And, indeed, at first they thought all was as they left it there, when, just as they were going away, the Pundit's wife cried out to him, "Why, what has become of the great cauldron? I never thought of looking to see if that was safe; for it did not seem possible that it could have been moved." And they both looked inside the house and outside, but the cauldron was nowhere to be seen. At last, however, they discovered deep footprints in the sand close to the kitchen door, as of some one who had been carrying a very heavy weight, and these they traced down to the river-side.

Then the Pundit said, "Some one immensely strong has evidently done this, for here are the footprints of one man only; and he must have buried the cauldron in the water, for, see, there is no continuation of the footprints on the other side. I wonder who can have done it? Let us go and see that our two guests are asleep; perhaps the Wrestler played us this trick to prove his great strength." And with his wife he went into the veranda, where the Pearl-shooter and the Wrestler lay rolled up in their blankets, fast asleep. First, they looked at the Pearl-shooter; but on seeing him the Pundit shook his head, saying, "No, he certainly has not done this thing." They then looked at the Wrestler, and the cunning Pundit licked the skin of the sleeping man, and, turning his wife, whispered, "This is assuredly the man who stole the cauldron and put it in the river, for he must have been but lately up to his neck in fresh water, since there is no taste of salt on his skin from his foot even to his shoulders. To-morrow I will surprise him by showing him I know this." And so saying, the Pundit crept back into the house, followed by his wife.

Next morning early, as soon as it was light, the Pearl-shooter and the Wrestler were accosted by their host, who said to them, "Let us go down to the river and have a wash, for I cannot offer you a bath, since the great cauldron, in which we generally bathe, has been mysteriously carried away this very night." "Where can it have gone?" said the Wrestler. "Ah, where indeed?" answered the Pundit; and he led them down to where the cauldron had been put into the river by the Wrestler the night before, and wading about in the water until he found it, pointed it out to him, saying, "See, friend, how far this cauldron traveled!" The Wrestler was much surprised to find that the Pundit knew where the cauldron was hidden, and said, "Who can have put it there?" "I will tell you," answered the Pundit; "why, I think it was you!" And then he related how his wife had heard footsteps, and, being afraid of thieves, had awakened him the night before, and how they had discovered that the cauldron was missing, and traced it down to the riverside; and then how he had found out that the Wrestler had just before been into the water up to his neck. The Wrestler and the Pearl-shooter were both much astonished at the Pundit's wisdom in having found this out; and the Pearl-shooter said to himself, "Both these men are certainly more clever than I." Then the three clever men returned to the house, and were very happy and joyful, and amused themselves laughing and talking all the rest of the day; and when evening came, the Pundit said to the Wrestler, "Let us to night forego all meagre fare and have a royal feast; friend Strongman, pray you go and catch the fattest of those goats that we see upon the hills yonder, and we will cook it for our dinner." The Wrestler assented, and ran on and on until he reached the flock of goats browsing upon the hill-side. Now, just at that moment a wicked little Demon came by that way, and on seeing the Wrestler looking at the goats (to see which seemed the finest to take home to dinner), he thought to himself, "If I can make him choose me, and take me home with him for his dinner, I shall be able to play him and his friends some fine tricks." So, quick as thought, he changed himself into a very handsome goat, and when the Wrestler saw this one goat, so much taller and finer and fatter than all the rest, he ran and caught hold of him and tucked him under his arm, to carry him home for dinner. The goat kicked and kicked and jumped about, and tried to butt more fiercely than the Wrestler had ever known any mortal goat do before, but still he held him tight and brought him in triumph to the Pundit's door. The Pundit heard him coming and ran out to meet him; but when he saw the goat, he started back quite frightened, for the Wrestler was holding it so tight that its eyes were almost starting out of its head, and they were fiery and evil-looking and burning like two living coals, and the Pundit saw at once that it was a Demon, and no goat, that his friend held; then he thought quickly, "If I appear to be frightened, this cruel Demon will get into the house and devour us all; I must endeavor to intimidate him." So, in a bold voice, he cried, "O Wrestler! Wrestler! foolish friend! what have you done? We asked you to fetch a fat goat for our dinner, and here you have only brought one wretched little Demon. If you could not find goats, while you were about it you might as well have brought more Demons, for we are hungry people. My children are each accustomed to eat one Demon a day, and my wife eats three, and I myself eat twelve, and here you have only brought one between us all! What are we to do?" At hearing these reproaches, the Wrestler was so much astonished that he dropped the Demon-goat, who, for his part, was so frightened at the Pundit's words, that he came crawling along quite humbly upon his knees. saying, "Oh, sir, do not eat me, do not eat me, and I will give you anything you like in the world. Only let me go, and I will fetch you mountains of treasure, rubies and diamonds, and gold and precious stones beyond all count. Do not eat me; only let me go!" "No, no," said the Pundit; "I know what you'll do; you'll just go away and never return: we are very hungry; we do not want gold and precious stones, but we want a good dinner; we must certainly eat you." The Demon thought all that the Pundit said must be true, he spoke so fearlessly and naturally. So he only repeated more earnestly, "Only let me go; I promise you to return and bring you all the riches that you could desire."

The Pundit was too wise to seem glad; but he said sternly, "Very well, you may go; but unless you return quickly and bring the treasure you promise, be you in the uttermost part of the earth, we will find you and eat you, for we are more powerful than you and all your fellows."

The Demon, who had just experienced how much stronger the Wrestler was than ordinary men, and then heard from the Pundit's own lips of his love for eating Demons, thought himself exceedingly lucky to have escaped their clutches so easily; and returning to his own land, he fetched from the Demons' storehouse a vast amount of precious things, with which he was flying away with all speed (in order to pay his debt and avoid being afterward hunted and eaten), when several of his comrades caught hold of him, and in angry tones asked where he was carrying away so much of their treasure. The Demon answered, "I take it to save my life; for whilst wandering round the world I was caught by terrible creatures, more dreadful than the sons of men, and they threaten to eat me unless I bring the treasure."

"We should like to see these dreadful creatures," answered they, "for we never before heard of mortals who devoured Demons." To which he replied, "These are not ordinary mortals; I tell you they are the fiercest creatures I ever saw, and would devour our Rajah, himself, did they get the chance; one of them said that he daily ate twelve Demons, that his wife ate three, and each of his children one." At hearing this they consented to let him go for the time; but the Demon Rajah commanded him to return with all speed next day, that the matter might be further discussed in solemn council.

When, after three days' absence, the Demon returned to the Pundit's house with the treasure, the Pundit angrily said to him, "Why have you been so long away? You promised to return as soon as possible." He answered, "All my fellow-Demons detained me, and would hardly let me go, they were so angry at my bringing you so much treasure; and though I told them how great and powerful you are, they would not believe me, but will, as soon as I return, judge me in solemn council for serving you." "Where is your solemn council held?" asked the Pundit. "Oh, very far, far away," answered the Demon, "in the depths of the jungle, where our Rajah daily holds his court." "I and my friends should like to see that place, and your Rajah and all his court," said the Pundit; "you must take us with you when you go, for we have absolute mastery over all Demons, even over their Rajah himself, and unless you do as we command we shall be very angry." "Very well," answered the Demon, for he felt quite frightened at the Pundit's fierce words; "mount on my back and I'll take you there." So the Pundit, the Wrestler and the Pearl-shooter all mounted the Demon, and he flew away with them, on, on, on, as fast as wings could cut the air, till they reached the great jungle where the durbar* was to be held, and there he placed them all on the top of a high tree just over the Demon Rajah's throne. In a few minutes the Pearl-shooter, the Wrestler and the Pundit heard a rushing noise, and thousands and thousands of Demons filled the place, covering the ground as far as the eye could reach, and thronging chiefly round the Rajah's throne; but they did not notice the men in the tree above them. Then the Rajah ordered that the Demon who had taken of their treasure to give to mortals should be brought to judgment; and when they had dragged the culprit into the midst of them, they accused him, and having proved him guilty, would have punished him; but he defended himself stoutly, saying, "Noble Rajah, those who forced me to fetch them treasure were no ordinary mortals, but great and terrible; they said they ate many Demons; the man ate twelve a day, his wife ate three, and each of his children one. He said, moreover, that he and his friends were more powerful than us all, and ruled your majesty as absolutely as we are ruled by you." The Demon Rajah answered, "Let us see these great people of whom you speak, and we will believe you; but ——" At this moment the tree upon which the Pundit, the Pearl-shooter and the Wrestler were, broke, and down they all tumbled—first, the Wrestler, then the Pearl-shooter, and lastly the Pundit—upon the

* Council.

head of the Demon Rajah as he sat in judgment. They seemed to have come down from the sky, so suddenly did they appear, and, being very much alarmed at their awkward position determined to take the aggressive. So the Wrestler kicked and hugged and beat the Rajah with all his might and main, and the Pearl-shooter did likewise, while the Pundit, who was perched up a little higher than either of the others, cried, "So be it, so be it. We will eat him first for dinner, and afterward we will eat all the other Demons." The Demons hearing this, one and all flew away from the confusion and left their Rajah to his fate; while he cried, "Oh spare me! spare me! I see it is all true; only let me go, and I will give you as much treasure as you like." "No, no," said the Pundit; "don't listen to him, friends; we will eat him for dinner." And the Wrestler and the Pearl-shooter kicked and beat him harder than before. Then the Demon cried again, "Let me go! let me go!" "No, no," they answered; and they chastised him vigorously for the space of an hour, until, at last, fearing they should get tired, the Pundit said, "The treasure would be no use to us here in the jungle; but if you brought us a very great deal to our own house, we might give up eating you for dinner to-day; you must, however, give us great compensation, for we are all very hungry." To this the Demon Rajah gladly agreed, and, calling together his scattered subjects, ordered them to take the three valiant men home again and convey the treasure to the Pundit's house. The little Demons obeyed his orders with much fear and trembling, but they were very willing to do their best to get the Pundit, the Pearl-shooter and the Wrestler out of Demon-land,

and they, for their parts, were no less anxious to go. When they got home, the Pundit said, "You shall not go until the engagement is fulfilled." Instantly Demons without number filled the house with riches, and when they had accomplished their task, they all flew away, fearing greatly the terrible Pundit and his friends, who talked of eating Demons as men would eat almonds and raisins. So, by never showing that he was afraid, this brave Pundit saved his family from being eaten by these Demons, and also got a vast amount of treasure. Then he divided it into three equal portions: a third he gave to the Wrestler, a third he gave to the Pearl-shooter, and a third he kept himself; after which he sent his friends, with many kindly words, back to their own homes. So the Pearl-shooter returned to his house laden with gold and jewels of priceless worth; and when he got there, he called his wife and gave them to her, saying, "I have been a far journey and brought back all these treasures for you, and I have learnt that your words were true, since in the world there are cleverer men than I; for mine is a cleverness that profits not, and but for a Pundit and a Wrestler, I should not have gained these riches. I will shoot the pearl from your nose-ring no more." And he never did.

XXIV.

THE ALLIGATOR AND THE JACKAL

A HUNGRY JACKAL once went down to the river-side in search of little crabs, bits of fish and whatever else he could find for his dinner. Now it chanced that in this river there lived a great big Alligator, who, being also very hungry, would have been extremely glad to eat the Jackal.

The Jackal ran up and down, here and there, but for a long time could find nothing to eat. At last, close to where the Alligator was lying among some tall bulrushes under the clear, shallow water, he saw a little crab sidling along as fast as his legs could carry him. The Jackal was so hungry that when he saw this he poked his paw into the water to try and catch the crab, when snap! the old Alligator caught hold of him. "Oh dear!" thought the Jackal to himself, "what can I do? This great big Alligator has caught my paw in his mouth, and in another minute he will drag me down by it under the water and kill me. My only chance is to make him think he has made a mistake." So he called out in a cheerful voice, "Clever Alligator, clever Alligator, to catch hold of a bulrush root instead of my paw! I hope you find it very tender." The Alligator, who was so buried among the bulrushes that he could hardly see, thought, on hearing this, "Dear me, how tiresome! I fancied I had caught hold of the Jackal's paw; but there he is, calling out in a cheerful voice. I suppose I must have seized a bulrush root instead, as he says;" and he let the Jackal go.

The Jackal ran away as fast as he could, crying, "O wise Alligator, wise Alligator! So you let me go again!" Then the Alligator was very much vexed, but the Jackal had run away too far to be caught. Next day the Jackal returned to the river-side to get his dinner, as before; but because he was very much afraid of the Alligator he called out, "Whenever I go to look for my dinner, I see the nice little crabs peeping up through the mud; then I catch them and eat them. I wish I could see one now."

The Alligator, who was buried in the mud at the bottom of the river, heard every word. So he popped the little point of his snout above it, thinking, "If I do but just show the tip of my nose, the Jackal will take me for a crab and put in his paw to catch me, and as soon as ever he does I'll gobble him up."

But no sooner did the Jackal see the little tip of the Alligator's nose than he called out, "Aha, my friend! there you are. No dinner for me in this part of the river, then, I think." And so saying he ran farther on and fished for his dinner a long way from that place. The Alligator was very angry at missing his prey a second time, and determined not to let him escape again.

So on the following day, when his little tormentor returned to the water-side, the Alligator hid himself close to the bank, in order to catch him if he could. Now the Jackal was rather afraid going near the river, for he thought, "Perhaps this Alligator will catch me to-day." But yet, being hungry, he did not wish to go without his dinner; so to make all as safe as he could, he cried, "Where are all the little crabs gone? There is not one here and I am so hungry; and generally, even when they are under water, one can see them going bubble, bubble, bubble, and all the little bubbles go pop! pop! pop!" On hearing this the Alligator, who was buried in the mud under the river-bank, thought, "I will pretend to be a little crab." And he began to blow, "Puff, puff, puff! Bubble, bubble, bubble!" and all the great big bubbles rushed to the surface of the river and burst there, and the waters eddied round and round like a whirlpool; and there was such a commotion when the huge monster began to blow bubbles in this way that the Jackal saw very well who must be there, and he ran away as fast as he could, saying, "Thank you, kind Alligator, thank you; thank you! Indeed I would not have come here had I known you were so close."

This enraged the Alligator extremely; it made him quite cross to think of being so often deceived by a little Jackal, and he said to himself, "I will be taken in no more. Next time I will be very cunning." So for a long time he waited and waited for the Jackal to return to the river-side; but the Jackal did not come, for he had thought to himself, "If matters go on in this way, I shall some day be caught and eaten by the wicked old Alligator. I had better content myself with living on wild figs," and he went no more near the river, but stayed in the jungles and ate wild figs, and roots which he dug up with his paws.

When the Alligator found this out, he determined to try and catch the Jackal on land; so, going under the largest of wild fig trees, where the ground was covered with the fallen fruit, he collected a quantity of it together, and, burying himself under the great heap, waited for the Jackal to appear. But no sooner did the cunning little animal see this great heap of wild figs all collected together, than he thought, "That looks very like my friend the Alligator." And to discover if it was so or not, he called out, "The juicy little wild figs I love to eat always tumble down from the tree, and roll here and there as the wind drives them; but this great heap of figs is quite still; these cannot be good figs; I will not eat any of them." "Ho, ho!" thought the Alligator, "is that all? How suspicious this Jackal is! I will make the figs roll about a little then, and when he sees that he will doubtless come and eat them."

So the great beast shook himself, and all the heap of little figs went roll, roll, roll—some a mile this way, some a mile that, farther than they had ever rolled before or than the most blustering wind could have driven them.

Seeing this, the Jackal scampered away, saying, "I am so much obliged to you, Alligator, for letting me know you are there, for indeed I should hardly have guessed it. You were so buried under that heap of figs." The Alligator, hearing this, was so angry that he ran after the Jackal, but the latter ran very, very fast away, too quickly to be caught.

Then the Alligator said to himself, "I will not allow that little wretch to make fun of me another time and then run away out of reach; I will show him that I can be more cunning than he fancies." And early the next morning he crawled as fast as he could to the

Jackal's den (which was a hole in the side of a hill) and crept into it, and hid himself, waiting for the Jackal, who was out, to return home. But when the Jackal got near the place, he looked about him and thought, "Dear me! the ground looks as if some heavy creature had been walking over it, and here are great clods of earth knocked down from each side of the door of my den, as if a very big animal had been trying to squeeze himself through it. I certainly will not go inside until I know that all is safe there." So he called out, "Little house, pretty house, my sweet little house, why do you not give an answer when I call? If I come, and all is safe and right, you always call out to me. Is anything wrong, that you do not speak?"

Then the Alligator, who was inside, thought, "If that is the case I had better call out, that he may fancy all is right in his house." And in as gentle a voice as he could, he said, "Sweet little Jackal."

At hearing these words the Jackal felt quite frightened, and thought to himself, "So the dreadful old Alligator is there. I must try to kill him if I can, for if I do not he will certainly catch and kill me some day." He therefore answered, "Thank you, my dear little house. I like to hear your pretty voice. I am coming in in a minute, but first I must collect firewood to cook my dinner." And he ran as fast as he could, and dragged all the dry branches and bits of stick he could find close up to the mouth of the den. Meantime, the Alligator inside kept as quiet as a mouse, but he could not help laughing a little to himself, as he thought, "So I have deceived this tiresome little Jackal at last. In a few minutes he will run in here, and then won't I snap him up!" When the Jackal had gathered together all the sticks he could find and put them round the mouth of his den, he set them on fire and pushed them as far into it as possible. There was such a quantity of them that they soon blazed up into a great fire, and the smoke and flames filled the den and smothered the wicked old Alligator and burnt him to death, while the little Jackal ran up and down outside, dancing for joy and singing—

"How do you like my house, my friend? Is it nice and warm? Ding-dong! ding-dong! The Alligator is dying! ding-dong, ding-dong! He will trouble me no more. I have defeated my enemy! Ring-a-ting! ding-a-ting! ding-ding-dong!"

NOTES ON THE NARRATOR'S NARRATIVE.

NOTE A.

THE battle of Kirkee was the turning-point in the last Mahratta war, which sealed the fate of the Peishwa's dynasty and transferred the Deccan to British rule, and is naturally, in that part of India, still regarded, by all whose recollections go back to those days, as the one great event of modern history.

When the collector of these tales was in India, the house temporarily occupied by the Governor of Bombay overlooked the field of battle, and among those who came to see the Governor on business or pleasure were some—natives as well as Europeans—to whom the events of half a century ago were matters of living memory.

Old soldiers would tell how the fidelity of the native Sepoys resisted all the bribes and threats of Bajee Row Peishwa, the absolute Brahmin ruler of Poona, and thus, while the Peishwa hoped to effect his purpose by treachery, enabled Mr. Mountstuart Elphinstone to defer open hostilities—a matter of vital importance to the operations of Lord Hastings on the other side of India, in preparing for his great campaign against the Pindarees.

The veterans would recount all the romantic incidents of the struggle which followed—how the "old Toughs" (now H. M.'s 103d Regiment), the only European corps within reach, when at last slipped from the leash at Panwell, marched seventy-two miles straight up over the ghauts to Poona, with only a single three-hours' halt en route; how they closed up their ranks of travel-soiled warriors and entered the British lines with band playing and colors flying; and how not a straggler dropped behind, "for all knew that there must be a battle soon." Their arrival was the signal for the Peishwa to throw off the mask, and, as the British Residency was untenable, the English troops moved out to take up a safer position at Kirkee, about three miles from the city of Poona; and as they marched they saw all the houses of the Resident and his suite fired by the enemy, who swarmed out of the city. As they formed in line of battle, they anxiously watched the native regiments coming up on their flank from Dapoorie, for that was the moment for successful treachery if the native soldiers were untrue! Not a Sepoy, however, in the British ranks wavered, though before the junction was complete a cloud of Mahratta cavalry poured down upon them, dashed through the opening left between the two lines, enveloped either flank of the little army, and attacked the European regiment in the rear. Then, as a last resource, the European regiment faced about their second rank, and kept up such a steady rolling fire to front and rear at the same time that but few of the eager horsemen ever came within spear's length of the British bayonets.

One of the most touching recollections of those times attracted our notice almost the last day we spent at Kirkee. An old chief, Jadowrow of Malagaom, had come to take leave of the departing Governor. He was head of one of the oldest Mahratta families, for his ancestors were famous as a very ancient royal house before the Mohammedans invaded the Deccan. The old man had borne arms as a youthful commander of horse when the great Duke was at Poona in 1802, just before the battle of Assaye, had been greatly distinguished for his gallantry in the battle of Kirkee, so fatal to his race, and had followed the fortunes of the Peishwa to the last. Disdaining to make separate terms for himself with the English conqueror, he remained one of the few thoroughly faithful to his sovereign—not from love, for he loved not Bajee Row, but "because he had eaten his salt"—and only after the Peishwa's surrender returned to his old castle near Poona. There for many years he lived, hunting and hawking over his diminished acres, and greatly respected as a model of a gallant and honorable old chief; but he could never be persuaded to revisit the capital of the Mahrattas after its occupation by the English. "He had no child," he said, "and his race would die with him." At last, as years rolled on, an only son was born to him; and then, touched by some unexpected act of liberality on the part of the British government which would secure his ancestral estate to this child of his old age, he resolved to go to Poona, and visited the Governor, whose temporary residence happened to overlook the battle-field of Kirkee. He gazed long and wistfully from the drawing-room windows and said, "This place is much changed since I was here last, fifty years ago. It was here the battle was fought, and it was from near this very spot that we charged down that slope on the English line as it formed beyond that brook. I never thought to have seen this place again."

Almost every hill, fort, and every large village round Poona, has some tradition, not only of the days of Alumgeer, Sivagee and of early Mahratta history, but of the campaigns of Wellesley in 1802 and of the last great struggle in 1817–18.

NOTE B.

ANNA'S remarks on the contrast between the present dearth and the "good old times" of cheap bread, when the rupee went so much further than it does now, are very characteristic. The complaint, too, is very universal, and is to be heard in the household of public functionaries, the highest as well as the lowest, in every grade of native society, and more or less in all parts of India.

The Narrator's notion, that "The English fixed the rupee at sixteen annas," is another specimen of a very widespread Indian popular delusion. The rupee always consisted of sixteen annas, for the anna means only the sixteenth part of anything, but to the poor the great matter for consideration in all questions of currency is the quantity of small change they can get for the coin in which their wages are paid. Formerly this used to fluctuate with the price of copper, and the quantity of copper change which a silver rupee would fetch varied as copper was cheap or dear, and was always greatest when the copper currency was most debased. The English introduced all over India a uniform currency of copper as well as of silver, and none of course were greater gainers in the long run by this uniformity than the very poor.

NOTE C.

I AM unable, at present, to give either the native words or music for this curious little Calicut song. The second part is probably of Portuguese origin, or it may have been derived from the Syrian Christians, who have been settled on that coast since the earliest ages.

The English translation of the words, as explained to me by Anna, is as follows:

PART I.

THE SONG FROM THE SHIP.

(*To be sung by one or more voices.*)

1. Very far went the ship, in the dark, up and down, up and down. There was very little sky; the sailors couldn't see anything; rain was coming.

2. Now darkness, lightning and very little rain; but big flashes, two yards long, that looked as if they fell into the sea.

3. On the third day the captain looks out for land, shading his eyes with his hand. There may be land. The sailors say to him, "What do you see?" He answers, "Far off is the jungle, and, swinging in a tree, is an old monkey, with two little monkeys in her arms. We must be nearing land."

4. Again the captain looks out; the sailors say to him, "What do you see?" He answers, "On the shore there walks a pretty little maiden, with a chattee on her head; she skips and runs, and dances as she goes. We must be nearing land."

5. The storm begins to rage again, and hides the land: at last it clears a little. The sailors say to the captain, "What do you see?" He answers, "I see a man ploughing; two bullocks draw the plough. We must be nearing land."

   It is all true; they have gained the shore.

PART II.

SONG FROM THE SHORE.

(*To be sung by one or more voices.*)

1. The ship's on the sea—
Which way is it coming?
Right home to land.
What cargo has it?
The ship brings the sacrament and praying beads.

2. The ship's on the sea—
Which way is it coming?
Right home to land.
What cargo has it?
The ship brings white paper and the Twelve Apostles.

3. The ship comes home to land—
What cargo does it bring?
Silver money, prophets and holy people.

4. The ship comes home to land—
What does it bring?
All the saints and holy people, and Jesus Christ of Nazareth.

5. The ship comes to our doors—
Who brings it home?
Our Saviour.
Our Saviour bless the ship, and bring it safely home.

The second song, "The Little Wife Watching for her Husband's Return," Anna had almost entirely forgotten.

It was, she said, very pretty, being the song of the little wife as she decks herself in her jewels to please her husband when he comes home. She lamentsits absence, fears he has forgotten her and bemoans her loneliness. M. F.

NOTES ON THE FAIRY LEGENDS.

PUNCHKIN.

PAGE 27.—The Rajah's seven daughters, taking it by turns to cook their father's dinner, would be nothing unusual in the household of a Rajah. To a chief or great man in India, it is still the most natural precaution he can take against poison to eat nothing but what has been prepared by his wife or daughter, or under their eye in his own zenana; and there are few accomplishments on which an Indian princess prides herself more than on her skill in cookery.

RAMA AND LUXMAN.

Page 107.—The little black and white owls, which fly out at dusk and sit always in pairs, chattering to each other in a singularly conversational version of owl language, are among the most widely-spread of Indian birds, and in every province where they are found are regarded as the most accomplished of soothsayers. Unlike other ominous creatures, they are anxious to do good to mankind, for they always tell each other what the traveler ought to do, and, if mankind were not so dull in understanding their language, would save the hearer from all risk of misfortune.

LITTLE SURYA BAI.

Page 118.—The sangfroid with which the first Ranee, here and in the story of Panch-Phul Ranee, page 164, receives the second and more favored wife to share her throne, however difficult to understand in the West, is very characteristic of Oriental life. In Indian households of the highest rank it would not be difficult to find examples of several wives living amicably together, as described in some of these stories; but the contrary result, as depicted in this story of Surya Bai and others, is far more common, for as a general rule human nature is too strong for custom, and under an external serenity bitter jealousies exist between the several wives of a royal Hindoo household, which are a constant source of misery and crime. Among the curious changes of opinion which are observable of late years in the Indian empire, none is more remarkable than the conviction, now frequently expressed by the warmest supporters of native governments at native courts, that the toleration of polygamy is one of their most serious dangers, the removal of which is of vital importance to the safety of any Indian dynasty, and indeed to the permanence of any Indian family of rank.

THE WANDERINGS OF VICRAM MAHARAJAH.

Page 131.—The Dipmal, or Tower of Lights, is an essential feature in every large Hindoo temple. It is often of great height, and furnished with niches or brackets, each of which holds a lamp on festivals, especially on that of the Dewali, the feast of lamps celebrated in the autumn in honor of the Hindoo goddess Bowani or Kali, who was formerly propitiated on that occasion by human sacrifices.

Page 132.—The story of Vicram's act of devotion is thoroughly Hindoo. It is difficult to understand the universal prevalence and strength of the conviction among Hindoos that the particular god of their adoration can be prevailed on, by importunity or self-devotion, to reveal to his worshiper some act, generally ascetic or sacrificial, the performance of which will insure to the devotee the realization of the object of his wishes. The act of devotion and the object of the devotee are both often very trivial; but occasionally we are startled by hearing of some deed of horror, a human sacrifice or deliberate act of self-immolation, which is quite unaccountable to those who are not aware that it is only a somewhat extreme manifestation of a belief which still influences the daily conduct of the great majority of the Hindoos.

And even those who have known the Hindoos long and intimately frequently fail to recognize the extent to which this belief influences the ethics of common life and action in India. To quote an instance from well-known history, there are few acts regarding which a European traveler would expect the verdict of all mankind to be more generally condemnatory than the murder of Afzul Khan, the general of the Imperial Delhi army, by Sivajee, the founder of the Mahratta empire. Sivajee, according to the well-known story, had invited his victim to an amicable conference, and there stabbed him with a wag nuck* as they embraced at their first meeting. It was a deed of such deliberate and cruel treachery that it could find few defenders in Europe, even among the wildest advocates of political assassination. A European is consequently little prepared to find it regarded by Mahrattas generally as a most commendable act of devotion. The Hindoo conscience condemns murder and treachery as emphatically as the European; but this act, as viewed by the old-fashioned Mahratta, was a sacrifice prescribed by direct revelation of the terrible goddess Bowani to her faithful devotee. It was therefore highly meritorious, and the beautiful Genoese blade which Sivajee always wore, and with which his victim was finally despatched, was, down to our own days, provided with a little temple of its own in the palace of his descendants, and annually worshiped by them and their household—not as a mere act of veneration for their ancestor's trusty sword, but because it was the chosen instrument of a great sacrifice, and "no doubt," as the attendant who watched it used to say, "some of the spirit of Bowani," whose name it bore, "must still reside in it."

An attentive observer will notice in the daily life of those around him in India constant instances of this belief in the efficacy of acts of devotion and sacrifice to alter even the decrees of Fate. It is one of the many incentives to the long pilgrimages which form such a universal feature in Hindoo life, and the records of the courts of justice and the Indian newspapers constantly afford traces of its prevalence

* An instrument so called from its similarity to a tiger's claw. It consists of sharp curved steel blades set on a bar, which fits by means of finger-rings to the inside of the hand, so as to be concealed when the hand is closed, while the blades project at right angles to the cross bar and palm when the hand is opened. It is struck as in slapping or tearing with the claws.

in cases of attempted suttee and other acts of self-immolation, or even of human sacrifice, such as are above alluded to. It must be remembered that Hindoo sacrifice has nothing but the name in common with the sacrifices which are a distinctive part of the religion of every Semitic race. Many a difficulty which besets the Hindoo inquirer after truth would be avoided if this essential distinction were always known or remembered.

Page 136.—This belief in the omnipotence of "Muntrs," or certain verbal formulas, properly pronounced by one to whom they have been authoritatively communicated, is closely allied to, and quite as universal as, the belief in the efficacy of sacrificial acts of devotion. In every nation throughout India, whatever may be the variations of creed or caste usage, it is a general article of belief, accepted by the vast majority of every class and caste of Hindoos, that there is a form of words (or Muntr) which, to be efficacious, can be only orally transmitted, but which, when so communicated by one of the "twice-born," has absolutely unlimited power over all things visible or invisible, extending even to compelling the obedience of the gods and of Fate itself. Of course it is rather dangerous, even for the wisest, to meddle with such potent influences, and the attempt is usually confined to the affairs of common life; but of the absolute omnipotence of "Muntrs" few ordinary un-Europeanized Hindoos entertain any doubt, and there is hardly any part of their belief which exercises such an all-pervading and potent influence in their daily life, though that influence is often but little understood by Europeans.

The classical reader will remember many allusions to a similar belief as a part of the creeds imported from the East, which were fashionable under the Empire at Rome. There is much curious information on the subject of the earliest-known Hindoo Muntrs in the *Aitareya Brahmana* of the learned Dr. Haug, the only European who ever witnessed the whole process of a Hindoo sacrifice. The reader who is curious on such matters will do well to consult the recently-published work of Professor Max Müller, which might, without exaggeration, be described as a storehouse of new facts connected with the religion and literature of the East, rather than by its modest title of *Chips from a German Workshop.*

HOW THE SUN, THE MOON AND THE WIND WENT OUT TO DINNER.

Page 194.—I have not ventured to alter the traditional mode of the Moon's conveyance of dinner to her mother the Star, though it must, I fear, seriously impair the value of the story as a moral lesson in the eyes of all instructors of youth. M. F.

SINGH RAJAH AND THE CUNNING LITTLE JACKALS.

Page 198.—This story is substantially the same as one well-known to readers of Pilpai's *Fables*. The chorus of the Jackals' song of triumph is an imitation of their nocturnal howl.

THE JACKAL, THE BARBER AND THE BRAHMIN.

Page 203.—The touch of the poor outcast Mahars would be pollution to a Hindoo of any but the lowest caste; hence their ready obedience to the Jackal's exhortation not to touch him.

The offerings of rice, flowers, a chicken, &c., and the pouring water over the idol, are parts of the regular daily observance in every village temple.

MUCHIE LAL.

Page 265.—The popular belief in stories of this kind, where the Cobra becomes the companion of human beings, is greatly strengthened by the instances which occasionally occur when particular persons, sometimes children or idiots, possess the power to handle the deadly reptiles without receiving any injury from them. How much is due merely to gentleness of touch and fearlessness, and how much to any personal peculiarity which pleases the senses of the snake, it is difficult to say, for the instances, though not few and perfectly well authenticated, are sufficiently rare to be popularly regarded as miraculous.

In one case, which occurred in the country west of Poona not long after our conquest of the Deccan, a Brahmin boy could, without the aid of music or anything but his own voice, attract to himself and handle with impunity all the snakes which might be within hearing in any thicket or dry stone wall, such as in that country is their favorite refuge. So great was the popular excitement regarding him, under the belief that he was an incarnation of some divinity, that the magistrate of Poona took note of his proceedings, and becoming uneasy as to the political turn the excitement regarding the boy might take, reported regularly to government the growth of the crowds who pressed to see the marvel and to offer gifts to the child and his parents! The poor boy, however, was at last bitten by one of the reptiles and died, and the wonder ceased.

CHUNDUN RAJAH.

Page 274.—There are innumerable popular superstitions regarding the powers which can be conveyed in a charmed necklace; and it is a common belief that good and bad fortune, and life itself, can be made to depend on its not being removed from the wearer's neck.

CHANDRA'S VENGEANCE.

Page 292.—The picture of the childless wife setting forth to seek Mahdeo, and resolving not to return till she has seen him, is one which would find a parallel in some of the persons composing almost every group of pilgrims who resort to the great shrines of Hindostan. Any one who has an opportunity of quietly questioning the members of such an assemblage will find that, besides the miscellaneous crowd of idlers, there are usually specimens of two classes of very earnest devotees. The one class is intent on the performance of some act of ascetic devotion, the object of which is to win the favor of the divinity, or to fulfill a vow for a favor already granted. The other class is seeking "to see the divinity," and expecting the revelation under one or other of the terrible forms of the Hindoo Pantheon. There are few things more pathetic than to hear one of this class recount the wanderings and sufferings of his past search, or the journeys he has before him, which are too often prolonged till death puts an end to the wanderer and his pilgrimage.

Page 294.—The "fire which does not burn" is everywhere in India one of the attributes of Mahdeo.

In many parts of the Deccan are to be found shrines consecrated to one of the local gods, who has been Brahminically recognized as a local manifestation of Mahdeo, where the annual festival of the divinity was, within the last few years, kept by lighting huge fires, through which devotees ran or jumped, attributing their escape from burning to the interposition of Mahdeo. Except in a few remote villages, this custom, which sometimes led to serious accidents, has in British territory been stopped by the police.

Page 298.—This story of the wonderful child who was found floating in a box on a river is to be heard, with more or less picturesque local variations, on the banks of every large river in India. Almost every old village in Sind has a local tradition of this kind.

Page 305.—Most households in Calcutta can furnish recollections of depredations by birds, at their nest-building season, similar to that of the Ranee's bangles by the Eagles in this story. But the object of the theft is generally more prosaic. I have known gold rings so taken, but the plunder is more frequently a lady's cuff or collar, or a piece of lace; and the plunderers are crows, and sometimes, but very rarely, a kite.

Page 313.—Purwaris, or outcasts, who are not suffered to live within the quarter inhabited by the higher castes, are very numerous in Southern India, and a legend similar to this one is a frequent popular explanation of their being in excess as compared with other classes of the population.

HOW THE THREE CLEVER MEN OUTWITTED THE DEMONS.

Page 314.—Old residents at Surat may remember an ancient local celebrity named Tom the Barber, among whose recollections of former days was a chronicle of a renowned duelist, who used to amuse himself by shooting with his pistol, somewhat after the fashion of the Pearl-shooter. The little tin can of hot water which Tom carried, slung from his forefinger as he went his morning rounds, was a favorite mark. So were the water-jars on the heads of the women as they passed the duelist's house coming from the well; and great was Tom's relief when an old woman, who could not be pacified by the usual douceur for the loss of her jar and the shock of finding the water stream down her back, appealed to the authorities and had the duelist bound over to abstain in future from his dangerous amusement.

So vivid were Tom's recollections of his own terrors that, after the lapse of half a century, he could ill conceal his sense of the poetical justice finally inflicted on his tormentor, who was killed in a duel to which he provoked a young officer who had never before fired a pistol.

P*